THE HOLISTIC HEALTH GUIDE

NATURAL CARE FOR THE WHOLE DOG

Doug Knueven, DVM

The Holistic Health Guide
Project Team
Editor: Heather Russell-Revesz
Copy Editor: Joann Woy
Indexer: Ann W. Truesdale
Design: Stephanie Krautheim
Series Design: Mada Design and Stephanie Krautheim
Series Originator: Dominique De Vito

T.F.H. Publications
President/CEO: Glen S. Axelrod
Executive Vice President: Mark E. Johnson
Publisher: Christopher T. Reggio
Production Manager: Kathy Bontz

T.F.H. Publications, Inc.
One TFH Plaza
Third and Union Avenues
Neptune City, NJ 07753

Library of Congress Cataloging-in-Publication Data
Knueven, Doug.
  The holistic health guide : natural care for the whole dog / Doug Knueven.
      p. cm.
  Includes index.
  ISBN 978-0-7938-3684-0 (alk. paper)
  1. Dogs--Health. 2. Dogs--Diseases--Alternative treatment. 3. Holistic veterinary medicine. I. Title.
  SF427.K49 2008
  636.7'0893--dc22
                        2007050827

The Leader In Responsible Animal Care For Over 50 Years!®
www.tfh.com

TABLE OF CONTENTS

Chapter 1

AN INTRODUCTION
to Holistic Medicine

For many reasons, more and more pet owners are seeking holistic care these days. You may have been drawn to this book because you have a sick pet who is not responding to conventional medical methods. Or, maybe a holistic treatment once helped you through a health crisis, and you want your dog to benefit from this same approach. Perhaps a friend's pet was helped by holistic therapies, and you are considering similar techniques for your canine friend. Or, you might be disillusioned with Western medicine altogether and are seeking an alternative. Regardless of why you are holding this book, you will not regret your choice in exploring alternative therapies.

This book will guide you through the sometimes confusing world of holistic care for dogs. Let's start with a look at holistic medicine in general, in order to demystify the subject.

WHAT'S IN A NAME? COMMON TERMS

Due to the recent popularity in the subject, the term *holistic* has become quite a buzz word. It is easy to become confused as to exactly what people mean when they call something holistic. (The other day a friend told me that her automobile repairman claimed to be a holistic mechanic—what, exactly, is he suggesting?) As we begin our exploration of the holistic care of dogs, let's look at some of the terminology we'll come across.

Allopathic Medicine

Allopathic medicine is a term you may run into as you study *holistic* medicine. It has come to mean Western medicine, but the word *allopathic* was originally coined by homeopaths to denote any medical procedure using a technique that does not cure by the "like cures like" method (see *Homeopathic Medicine*, page 7). So, technically acupuncture, traditional Chinese medicine, herbal medicine, and most other holistic treatments are allopathic, because they are not based on this method.

Alternative Medicine

Alternative medicine refers to any medical modality not taught in Western medical schools—human or veterinary. This term is technically not the same as *holistic* (see below) because it does not imply a specific philosophical mind set.

For example, cold lasers are a special laser technology. Unlike a surgical laser, which is used to cut, a cold laser can be directed at damaged tissue, helping it to heal. This treatment procedure is not taught in Western medical schools, so it is considered alternative. However, using a cold laser does not require looking at the patient as a whole, as a holistic treatment would. It can be used locally and symptomatically, so it is not necessarily holistic.

Even acupuncture, which was born out of a holistic world view, is currently being taught in some veterinary courses from a strictly neuromuscular standpoint. The entire condition of the patient is not addressed, and thus acupuncture practiced in this way warrants the *alternative* label but not the *holistic* one.

Complementary Medicine

Complementary medicine is a commonly used word. This friendly term emphasizes the fact that alternative methods can often be used in conjunction with Western techniques. This expression implies the primacy of Western medicine with the addition of holistic methods to augment the effect.

CAM is an abbreviation for *complementary and alternative medicine. CAVM* is the abbreviation for *complementary and alternative veterinary medicine*. This term was defined by the American Veterinary Medical Association (AVMA) in 2001 as "A heterogeneous group of preventive, diagnostic, and therapeutic philosophies and practices. The theoretical bases and techniques of CAVM may diverge from veterinary medicine routinely taught in North American veterinary medical schools or may differ from current scientific knowledge, or both."

Conventional, Traditional, and Western Medicine

Conventional, traditional, and *Western* are terms that describe the kind of medicine we have grown up with in North America. This type of medical practice utilizes surgery and drugs to help a patient fight disease. A fuller understanding of this approach to health and

Cold laser treatments are considered alternative medicine.

how it compares to holistic medicine will be made clear throughout this chapter.

Eastern Medicine

Eastern medicine generally refers to Traditional Chinese Medicine (TCM), a holistic approach to health developed in China thousands of years ago and still used today. It includes acupuncture, herbal medicine, meditation, exercise (tai chi), nutrition, massage, and lifestyle.

Holistic Medicine

Holistic medicine is a philosophical approach to healthcare. It encompasses many different techniques and practices, but they all share the common view that the entire patient—body, mind, and spirit—must be considered by the healthcare giver. The rest of this chapter is dedicated to providing a complete appreciation of this term.

Homeopathic Medicine

Homeopathic medicine is a term often confused with *holistic medicine*. In actuality, homeopathy is a very specific method of treatment within holistic medicine. As we will explore in Chapter 8, homeopathy is based on the idea that *like cures like*. In other words, a substance that causes a particular condition when taken by a healthy individual can be used to cure a patient suffering from that condition. Homeopathic medicine is holistic, but not all holistic treatments are homeopathic.

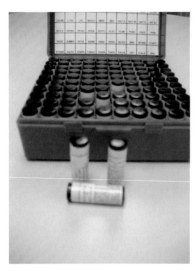

These homeopathic remedies are based on the theory that "like cures like."

Integrative Medicine

Integrative medicine is the practice of combining *holistic* and *conventional* therapies to take advantage of the strengths of each system. This more recent term implies an equal standing for holistic and Western procedures.

Natural Medicine

Natural medicine refers to the concept that *holistic* and *alternative* treatments usually work with the body's own natural, healing mechanisms. Many holistic therapies, such as herbs, are derived directly from nature. Unfortunately, the modern pet lifestyle—with its vaccines, drugs, processed diets, and indoor living—can be far from natural. Holistic medicine emphasizes working with nature rather than against it as much as possible.

As we strive toward this end, the question arises, "What is truly natural?" Looking closely at supplement ingredients reveals that more and more synthetic compounds are labeled as *natural* to cash in on the holistic market. In fact, many "natural" vitamins are chemical compounds manufactured by pharmaceutical companies. Today, the word *natural* has become almost meaningless. Let's face it—ultimately, everything comes from nature. Death, too, is a natural process but it's obviously not the goal of therapy.

DIFFERENCES BETWEEN HOLISTIC AND WESTERN MEDICINE

Now that we have the basics on terminology, let's take a closer look at what we mean by holistic care for dogs, based on how it differs from Western medicine.

Two main dichotomies exist between holistic and Western medical practices. First, Western medicine reduces the body's systems to their basic building blocks (reductionism), while holistic medicine addresses the entire being (holism). Second, Western medicine is based on the belief that all phenomena in the universe, including life itself, can be explained on a strictly physical basis (materialism), while holistic medicine is based on the belief that life is governed by a vital energy and cannot be fully appreciated on the basis of physics and chemistry alone (vitalism).

Holism Versus Reductionism

The term *holistic* means addressing the entire being—body, mind, and spirit. Using this outlook, the whole is considered greater than the sum of its parts. From the holistic point of view, what good is it to surgically remove a tumor if the health condition that allowed it to grow is not addressed? Can drugs effectively solve the problem of an animal's destructive separation anxiety if that pet's emotional needs are not met? How can Western medicine deal with the grief an animal experiences after the loss of a loved one? In my opinion, holistic thinking is essential for the health of any canine companion.

The concept of holism stands in direct opposition to the Western reductionist view. Modern Western medicine tends to break systems down into smaller and smaller pieces, reducing them to their basic building blocks in order to gain understanding. When living systems are broken down to their constituent parts, life itself slips away. The investigator is left looking at dead material.

My experience as a freshman in veterinary school illustrates the difference between the holistic and reductionistic approaches. The first class we budding animal doctors faced was anatomy lab. In this class, we dissected the bodies of canine cadavers down to the minutest detail to see just how the biological machine worked—like a mechanic taking apart a car engine in search of an oil leak. By the end of the semester, it was difficult to distinguish what species we had started with.

While this may be a harsh image for any animal lover to contemplate, I am thankful for the knowledge I gained from that experience. I recognize the importance of such study and how it taught me about the parts of the body. However, in the process, I lost an appreciation for the animal as a whole. I forgot what it would have been like to run with this pup or to snuggle up with him on a crisp, spring morning. This type of study just doesn't encourage considering the original, living dog. A being whose whole is greater than the sum of its parts.

Holism means addressing the entire being—body, mind, and spirit.

The holistic practitioner treats the entire patient. From my point of view, I have never treated cancer—I've treated animals with cancer. A tumor has never walked into my office, but multidimensional patients have. When helping a patient regain his health, every aspect must be taken into account.

Mind and Spirit

Psychoneuroimmunology

Psychoneuroimmunology—the concept that psychology and emotions have an effect on the physical well-being of the patient—has only recently been acknowledged by Western medicine.

In addition to looking at the body and disease process as a whole, true holism addresses the mind and spirit as well. For most veterinarians, the animal mind is considered to be a strictly stimulus–response mechanism—a realm left to dog trainers. Only when an animal does not respond appropriately to operant conditioning (a type of behavior modification) is it treated with psychoactive drugs to straighten out its brain chemistry. And, of course, the spiritual side of the patient is never acknowledged in conventional veterinary medicine.

In my experience, the Western veterinary medical education itself is structured in a way that diminishes a student's respect for the mind and spirit of each animal. As I think once again about anatomy lab, I realize that this class in particular was extremely effective at forcing veterinary students to numb our feelings for our patients. It was necessary for any rational, compassionate person to put these feelings on hold in order to make it through the course.

Unfortunately, the minds of most conventional medical practitioners have never left the anatomy lab. They view the body as an assembly of independent systems instead of an inseparable, spirit-filled whole. But just look at the long list of side effects on every drug label—it's impossible to cause changes in one body structure without influencing all the others. Still, many veterinarians rely strictly on drugs and surgery to fight disease when, in my opinion, more natural, gentler means are available for maintaining pet health.

Vitalism Versus Materialism

Another major point of departure between holistic and Western medical philosophies is a dispute that has raged in our culture for over 2,000 years—the conflict between materialism and vitalism, which began with the great Greek thinkers such as Democritus, Plato, and Aristotle. Materialists believe that all phenomena in the universe, including life itself, can be explained on a strictly physical basis. Vitalists, on the other hand, believe that, although living organisms are constructed of physical substance, life is governed by a vital energy and cannot be fully appreciated on the basis of physics and chemistry alone.

Western medicine is founded on the principles of materialism. For those working within our conventional healthcare system (both human and veterinary), life is the result of random molecular events that happened to come together synergistically. Therefore, the body is a biochemical–biomechanical piece of equipment, and when it is broken (diseased), it can only be fixed through physical manipulation (surgery) or with chemistry (pharmaceuticals). (By the way, I do not mean to imply that all modern healthcare providers are atheists—many Western medical personnel have sincere spiritual faith, but most check their personal beliefs at the door when they enter their secular, medical practice to treat patients.)

Holistic practitioners believe that vital life energy is the most important factor in the health of the patient. The acupuncturists call this life energy *qi* (pronounced *chee*), the homeopaths call it the *vital force*, and to chiropractors it is known as the *innate intelligence*. No matter the name, holistic medicine acknowledges that, while surgery and drugs can play a part in managing disease, if the role of life force energy is ignored, true healing will elude the patient. For the holistic practitioner, all disease starts as "dis-ease"—or an imbalance of energy—and the goal of therapy is to rebalance the life force to restore health.

From a scientific point of view, the idea of vitalism is seen as a superstition that arose from primitive peoples' ignorance of the laws of physics and chemistry that govern the universe. Modern doctors have no need for such a quaint notion because we now possess such vast scientific knowledge that the secret of life is no longer a mystery. This arrogant attitude reminds me of a quote from Mark Twain: *What gets us into trouble is not what we don't know, It's what we know for sure that just ain't so.*

Life Force Energy

Many ancient cultures have a word for life force energy:

- Native Polynesians called it *mana*
- Australian aborigines called it *maban*
- Egyptians called it the *ka*
- Ancient Greeks knew it as *pneuma*
- Romans called it *spiritus*
- In Hebrew, the word was *ruha* (the breath of life)
- Inuits call it *inua* or *sila*
- The Norse had the word *seid*
- In India, the Hindu word is *prana*

Because medical science has defined itself on a strictly physical basis, it is true that vitalism is unscientific. By definition, vitalism embraces a concept about a nonphysical force that can never be understood within the current scientific, medical paradigm. Of course, as modern physicists are discovering, many experimental findings cannot be accounted for by our modern biomedical scientific model.

A TALE OF TWO REALITIES: UNDERSTANDING HOLISM THROUGH PHYSICS

To understand the scientific underpinnings of holistic therapies we need to look at the world of physics. Physics is the study of how the universe works. The age of classical physics began in the seventeenth century with the work of scientists such as Sir Isaac Newton, a brilliant English mathematician and physicist whose work was the climax of the Scientific Revolution.

The basic laws Newton discovered allowed him to mathematically explain and predict natural phenomena, such as the effects of gravity and the motion of planets. To this day, classical physics continues to be predictive and helpful for understanding nature. In fact, the Western medical model is firmly grounded upon the laws of classical physics.

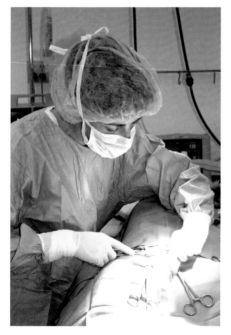

Surgery is an important part of Western medical practice.

Classical Physics

Classical physics itself is founded on certain seemingly obvious assumptions.

Materialism

Newton postulated that space is constant and uniform throughout the universe and that time marches on at a constant pace. He conjectured that the basic building blocks of the universe are material particles, and that matter can only interact by direct contact. In other words, classical physics is materialistic.

Determinism

A related assumption of classical physics is determinism. This is the belief that, in principle, the future can be exactly predicted if we know all of the starting conditions and fundamental relationships (such as velocity and direction of movement).

Reductionism

Like modern medicine, classical physics is reductionistic. It rests on the belief that the universe can best be understood by dissecting everything down to its most basic structure. This reductionism is what really got the classical physicists into trouble. It turns out that as scientists looked deeper and deeper into the fabric of reality, the principles of classical physics did not apply. This discrepancy led to the quantum revolution of the twentieth century, championed by Albert Einstein.

Quantum Physics

Quantum physics has a totally different view of reality than does classical physics. According to quantum physics, as particles are reduced to their basic structure, all that is left is energy (vitalism). Modern physicists also discovered a strange property of matter called *entanglement*—associated particles can communicate over vast distances faster than the speed of light. This concept of *action at a distance* is in total opposition to the classical belief in the exclusivity of action by direct contact.

The Heisenberg Uncertainty Principle of quantum physics is proof that it is not possible to know both the position and momentum of subatomic particles at the same time. Therefore, even in principle, it is impossible to predict the future with certainty, so the concept of determinism has been struck down. (This fact is made clear by checking the reliability of your local weather forecast.) Finally, Einstein demonstrated that space and time are not uniform. Space can be distorted by gravity, and time does not always proceed in the regular fashion that our watches would have us believe.

So, physics has presented us with two very different paradigms. On one hand, we have materialistic, classical physics; on the other, we have quantum physics with all its extraordinary effects. As strange as it seems, one by one, the foundations of classical physics have been dismantled and supplanted by the modern discoveries of quantum physics. Still, "modern" Western biomedical scientists continue to cling to the assumptions of classical physics. Holistic

Quantum Physics

We may therefore regard matter as being constituted by the regions of space in which the [quantum] field is extremely intense . . . there is no place in this new kind of physics for both the field and matter, for the field is the only reality.

—Albert Einstein

Dr. Doug and Einstein.

medicine, on the other hand, embraces quantum physics as the underpinning of its practices.

BIOLOGY AND HOLISM

Looking at recent developments in genetic research (DNA) can also highlight the difference between Western medicine and holistic medicine.

Dissecting Determinism With DNA

As previously mentioned, Newton's discoveries led him to adopt a deterministic view of the universe. He saw the universe as a great clock-like machine. Once it was set in motion, the outcome was absolutely predictable. In other words, it was conceivable that, if the position and velocity of every particle in the universe were known, then by calculating all the vast interactions, every future event could be determined. According to this view, the fate of the universe is fixed no matter what anyone does.

Genetic Determinism

The Newtonian idea of determinism is reflected in the concept of *genetic determinism* held by mainstream biomedical scientists. The conventional understanding is that DNA completely controls the physical traits, disease susceptibility, and even personality of every individual organism. In fact, the primacy of DNA is considered the *central dogma* of biology. This doctrine states that particular DNA genes code for specific strands of RNA, which in turn precisely produce individual proteins. In a system that does not acknowledge a life force, these proteins determine body structure and personal behavior. From this perspective, it appears that we and our pets are all hapless victims of our DNA. There is no place for free will in this philosophy.

Recent research throws a wrench into this clockwork theory of genetic determinism. The Human Genome Project was an incredible scientific accomplishment that mapped out the complete sequence of our human genetic code. Given the genetic determinism paradigm, biomedical scientists anticipated one gene for each protein in the human body: the human body contains over 100,000 proteins (each, it was assumed, with its corresponding gene), plus 20,000 regulatory genes (genes within the DNA that help direct cellular functions), for a total of 120,000 expected genes. Astonishingly, the Human Genome Project found only approximately 25,000 genes in the entire human genome. This is only about a thousand more genes than make up the genome of a simple microscopic worm called *Caenorhabditis*! How can this be?

It turns out that a single gene can code for more than one protein. The *central dogma* was proved incorrect. Genetic determinism is an outdated concept. In fact, cellular mechanisms can cut and splice genes back together in numerous ways to code for the many proteins of the body. So, there exist unanticipated cellular systems at work directing the use of an organism's genetic material. Additional research has elucidated the mechanics and implications of this discovery.

Newton's discoveries led him to adopt a deterministic view of the universe.

Who's in Charge Here? DNA and Environmental Signals

A Duke University study published in 2003 demonstrated that seemingly innocuous nutritional supplements, such as folic acid and vitamin B_{12}, fed to pregnant mice kept mutant, disease-causing genes from being expressed in their offspring. Furthermore, according to the researchers, the disease-preventing effect may well be passed to future generations.

This experiment is a demonstration of the effects of a new biological science called *epigenetics*. Epigenetics is the study of cellular factors that influence the expression of genes.

Holistic therapies can aid pets in ways that seem impossible to the Western mind.

These factors are passed from generation to generation by a means outside the DNA code. The concept of epigenetics totally befuddles conventionally minded biomedical scientists. How is it possible for nutritional supplements to change the way genetic material is read?

When you think about it, the DNA code is simply a blueprint for the formation of proteins. Just as a building's blueprint does not activate itself and build a house, neither does the DNA turn its genes on and off. Epigenetic mechanisms within the cell effectively control the reading of DNA segments. Signals from the cell's environment trigger receptors on the cellular membrane, which interact with the epigenetic machinery within the cell to activate or deactivate individual genes. This process allows the cells of the body to produce the right proteins and respond appropriately to their environment and the body's needs. So, instead of the DNA being in charge, it appears that environmental signals have the upper hand.

The process of epigenetic control involves the interaction of several million cell membrane receptors, of which there are several hundred types. Each different type of receptor responds to different signals. We mostly think of them as monitoring body chemistry by reacting to informational molecules such as hormones, glucose, ions, and other bodily substances. In such instances, the informational molecule binds to the receptor in a *lock-and-key* manner, causing the receptor to change shape. The movement of the receptor then triggers various cellular mechanisms—some of which are epigenetic.

This lock-and-key concept constitutes the current mechanistic, Western view of receptor–informational molecule relationships. However, research has shown that receptors can also read energy signals such as light, sound, and radio waves. Yes, energy can change a body's genetic expression. Score a point for vitalism. Perhaps mental energy in the form of consciousness, prayer, and intention can influence these receptors as well, changing the genetics of the organism. Imagine the possibilities.

SHEDDING LIGHT ON MEDICAL SCIENCE

So, where does this discussion of physics and biology leave us in our understanding of holistic medicine? There is no doubting the value of Western medicine. Conventional interventions such as drugs and surgery help countless animals every day. Yet, as we learn more about our universe and cellular biology, it becomes clear that conventional, biomedical science is based on outmoded concepts and does not hold all the answers.

Indeed, there are definite limits to our current medical model. A recent report in the *Journal of the American Medical Association* listed *iatrogenic* (adverse effects caused by medical treatment) as the third leading cause of human death in the United States. This includes 7,000 deaths per year from medication errors in hospitals; 20,000 from medical treatment errors in hospitals; 12,000 from unnecessary surgery; and 106,000 from adverse drug events. Obviously, something is amiss with the current system. The need for a different approach to health is clear.

Holistic therapies can aid pets in ways that seem impossible to the Western mind. Homeopathic remedies are often diluted to the point that no molecules of the original medicinal substance remain yet, unbelievably, they seem to adjust the energy system of the body. Acupuncture defies biomedical science by acting on channels of energy that are not acknowledged by Western medicine.

On one hand, we have a materialistic medical concept that is scientifically proven and accepted by our culture; on the other hand, we have an alternative system that defies what we understand about biology. Which approach is right?

Let There Be Light

Perhaps one way to look at the situation is by delving into one more mysterious physical phenomenon—light. With the invention of the light bulb, modern man has conquered darkness. We use light-based technologies for everyday things such as illuminating our cities and lighting up our refrigerators. We have even refined rays of light to produce powerful laser beams. In spite of the ubiquitous use of light, scientists are perplexed by its true nature.

Early experiments showed that light is a wave; later studies showed it to be a particle. Now, waves and particles are very different phenomena. For example, when two waves meet, they

Particles of light bounce off each other like billiard balls.

pass through one another, like ripples on the surface of a pond. Conversely, when two particles meet, they bounce off each other like billiard balls. How can light have such different characteristics at the same time?

Modern physicists have become relatively comfortable with the wave–particle duality of light. Light has properties of both waves and particles. Intriguingly, while working with this paradox, scientists have made even more profound discoveries. One such finding is that the behavior of light is influenced by the consciousness of the experimenter working with it. If the experiment is set up to prove light is a particle, then so it appears. If the study is meant to show that light is a wave, the rays oblige. If consciousness affects subatomic particles, then is it not likely that thoughts and attitudes affect biological systems as well?

In the final analysis, we may benefit from becoming comfortable with looking at health from both the Western and holistic perspectives. Healthcare does not have to be an either–or decision. We can keep the best of what conventional medicine has to offer while benefiting from the spiritually based holistic approach. This integrative concept of medicine is most valuable for the health of our dogs.

BASIC CONCEPTS OF HOLISTIC MEDICINE

Holistic medicine takes many forms, but there are common beliefs among these various techniques.

Dis-Ease

In holistic medicine, health is considered to be more than simply the absence of disease. It is a state of well-being expressed as a vitality that resists disease. Health is a dynamic balance of internal and external forces. From this point of view, a broad spectrum of physical conditions exist, ranging from perfect health to death.

Perfect Health ➡ Dis-ease ➡ Disease ➡ Death

Dis-ease begins as an imbalance that may go undetected by conventional means. If left untreated at this early stage, detectable disease and possibly death will eventually result.

Caregivers who are closely bonded to their dogs often notice when their pet is in the dis-eased state. They are able to tell that their dog is just not acting right. Unfortunately, when they take their four-legged friend to the veterinarian with such vague signs, the doctor is usually at a loss. Often, even extensive testing yields nothing, and the diagnosis is left open.

This frustrating situation is not the fault of the veterinarian. The problem is that Western medical testing often does not recognize a disturbance until it becomes serious. For example, blood tests cannot identify renal disease until 75 percent of kidney function is destroyed. Most holistic approaches have ways of detecting and treating a problem before it develops into disease.

So, optimal health is more than the absence of disease. Once detectable disease is present, the animal is often in serious shape. When an animal is truly healthy, it has a robust vitality that resists disease. That is the goal of holistic healthcare.

Wellness Is a Dynamic Balance

In holistic medicine, health is seen as a dynamic balance. Animals are affected by universal cycles and bodily phases. Universal cycles include the daily cycle of day and night, the monthly phases of the moon, and the yearly seasonal cycle. Bodily phases consist of the aging process from newborn to puppy to adolescent to adult to senior. For a dog to maintain health, these phases and cycles must be honored.

In holistic medicine, health is seen as a dynamic balance.

From a lifestyle perspective, the implication of this statement is common sense. For example, it is healthy to be active during the day and to rest at night. Overactivity on a hot summer day can lead to problems just as overexposure to the winter cold can cause disease. It is unhealthy to keep a puppy caged all the time, as he needs to exercise and explore and be socialized. It is equally inappropriate to expect an elderly dog to run and play as he did when he was young. Each circumstance calls for a unique response. This maintains a healthy balance.

Similarly, in holistic medicine, the universal cycles and bodily phases are considered when treating the patient. For instance, an acupuncturist applies shorter treatments for

Elsa's Story

At one year of age, Elsa was a bright, active Sheltie with a promising future in the show ring and agility course. However, all the big plans were put on hold when she came up lame and stiff in her hind quarter a month after her first birthday. Initially, her guardian, Lynn, thought she must have injured herself. Her veterinarian concurred and prescribed anti-inflammatory medication. The drug seemed to help temporarily but the symptoms soon recurred, and Lynn and her husband Tom became more troubled.

The couple was referred to an orthopedic expert who took X-rays of Elsa's back. An instability was found where the lower spine meets the sacrum. Cortisone was prescribed but, instead of improving, Elsa got worse. Two weeks later, the orthopedic veterinarian repeated the spinal X-rays and discovered that there was now an area of the sacrum where the bone was eaten away. It literally looked as if someone had drilled a hole into Elsa's sacrum.

Finally, six weeks after the initial symptoms, Tom and Lynn had their answer. Unfortunately, Elsa was diagnosed with discospondylitis—a serious, deep bone infection of the spine. This rather rare condition is caused when bacteria enter the bloodstream and lodge in a bone of the spine. In Elsa's case, it was surmised that the discospondylitis stemmed from a bladder infection she had as a puppy. The specialist gave a guarded prognosis and prescribed a long course of antibiotics for Elsa.

Lynn and Tom were upset and concerned by the whole ordeal. They truly love their pets as part of the family, and they wanted to do everything they could to help Elsa. The couple decided not to leave the fate of their beloved companion solely in the hands of conventional medicine. After researching alternatives and speaking with others in their Sheltie club, they brought Elsa to see me for holistic care.

An hour-long holistic exam was performed, involving a detailed analysis of Elsa's medical history, X-rays, and some holistic diagnostic techniques. Next, I had a discussion with her caregivers, and we decided to help the ailing pet by continuing the antibiotic therapy to kill the bacteria, plus adding acupuncture and chiropractic to the treatment plan. Acupuncture helps with pain but can also increase blood flow to the diseased bone, bringing the antibiotics where they are needed. Acupuncture also improves the immune system. Chiropractic is an excellent way to ease back pain and simultaneously it promotes the proper functioning of the spinal cord and nerves.

Both Tom and Lynn noticed an immediate improvement in Elsa's comfort and gait after the first treatment. The acupuncture and chiropractic treatments were continued on a weekly basis. Follow-up exams with the orthopedic veterinarian confirmed that the condition resolved quickly. Within one month, Elsa's X-rays showed her sacrum was back to normal. The specialist was surprised by how quickly she recovered. Elsa continues to have monthly chiropractic adjustments as part of her health maintenance routine.

Since the time that she was successfully treated for discospondylitis, Elsa has carried a large litter to full term, finished her breed championship in Canada, and earned six agility titles. According to Lynn, "Never in our wildest dreams did we think she'd recover to the point where she could carry a litter or compete in the conformation and performance rings. We don't believe that treating her solely with traditional medicine would have achieved the same result. The use of acupuncture, chiropractic care, and Chinese herbs in conjunction with traditional medicine made a visible difference in her level of recovery."

The integrative approach is not a cure-all, but it only makes sense to use every tool possible when faced with any health condition, especially a serious one like Elsa's. Plus, many holistic treatments can help head off impending health challenges as well as maintain a vibrant balance in healthy individuals.

Elsa being treated with chiropractic.

patients who are very young and for those who are old. Even in the same animal, certain foods and herbs are more suitable in the summer than in the winter. Disease conditions change with the seasons and with age, so the treatment must conform to the current needs of the patient.

As difficult as it is for our goal-oriented society to understand, there is no end point to wellness. You cannot cross the goal line of health, declare that you have made it, and then quit. Wellness requires a constant balancing act of applying the right remedy at the right time.

The Body's Pharmacy

Holistic therapies generally strengthen the body whereas conventional medicine fights disease. From the holistic point of view, the body contains its own pharmacy. Researchers are well aware of this fact as they deal with the *placebo effect*—a physiological glitch that predicts that 30 percent of subjects treated with a sugar pill (placebo) will improve no matter what their disease. Anxiety, hypertension, low blood pressure—any medical problem can be improved by mechanisms within the patient's body.

In humans, this medical anomaly is considered a case of mind over matter. No matter what the mechanism of action, the existence of the placebo effect proves that our bodies can heal themselves if conditions are right. Even though animals do not necessarily believe in the treatment, holistic therapies can produce the right conditions for pets to generate their own, internal pharmaceuticals.

Disease Prevention

The main thrust of the holistic approach is disease prevention. While Western medicine addresses disease prevention primarily with vaccinations, keeping the dog healthy in the holistic sense of the word requires a healthy lifestyle. As you will read in Chapter 3, nutrition plays a key role in this respect. You simply cannot maintain health without providing the proper building blocks for the body. Animals also thrive best in a healthy environment free of second-hand smoke, exposure to toxins such as flea medications, and chemicals in their food and water.

Of course, since holistic health deals with more than just the body, we must also be aware of the mental and spiritual well-being of our pets. Dogs are sentient beings and require mental

stimulation and intellectual challenges. If the canine mind is left to its own devices, it can come up with destructive outlets for its frustration. Mental frustration can also lead to internal medical problems.

When holistic medicine is done properly, it is not very exciting. Ideally, you start with a healthy puppy and you nourish him naturally. At the first sign of an imbalance, a gentle method is employed to regain harmony. The pet maintains health unless an unforeseen trauma occurs. Then more powerful holistic methods are used.

Holistic disease prevention requires the active participation of the dog owner. Do not expect that your only responsibility is to take your pet to a holistic practitioner to be fixed as needed. You are ultimately responsible for your pet's care, and no one else can do it for you.

Symptoms Are Our Friends

From the holistic point of view, symptoms are seen as the body's attempt to maintain balance or as an alert that a problem is present. Therefore, symptoms are not the enemy to be attacked. For example, when an animal has pain, it is a warning that something is wrong and needs to be addressed. In fact, pain keeps a pet from walking on an injured leg and thus helps protect the limb from further damage. Similarly, a fever is a very helpful body response. Many germs cannot survive for long in an overheated body, plus the raised temperature gears up the immune system to fight the trespasser.

Experiencing a symptom is similar to when the *check engine* light comes on in a car. Simply giving pain medication to a hurting pet or aspirin to one with a fever is akin to putting a piece of electrical tape over the warning light. It looks like the problem is solved but, if the real issue is not addressed, serious consequences could occur. Treating symptoms alone may actually hamper the body in its attempt to stabilize the situation.

This is not to say that treating symptoms is always wrong. There are times when an animal is experiencing pain, severe fever, or other symptoms that must be treated to give comfort while the underlying condition is addressed. However, too often in our society, symptoms are seen as the enemy to be conquered. Looking at disease holistically means looking beyond the symptoms to the true cause of the problem.

Moreover, what the conventional veterinarian sees as a disease, the holistic practitioner many times considers as simply a symptom of a deeper imbalance. For instance, ear infections are a common problem for dogs. Conventionally, an ear infection is regarded as a local problem involving an unwanted organism invading a particular part of the body. Treatment is then geared toward fighting that infection with topical ear medications and possibly systemic treatments meant to kill the intruder.

From a holistic perspective, that same ear infection is thought of as a symptom and a clue to the deeper disturbance. It is not considered an isolated event but rather as an indication of dysfunction within the whole patient. The holistic practitioner asks such questions as, "What predisposed this particular animal to get this infection?" and "What other abnormalities is this animal manifesting that point to the underlying cause?" Failure to follow this approach explains why some pets have recurrent problems— the underlying cause is never addressed.

At the risk of sounding like a car mechanic myself, here is another automobile analogy. A car with a flat tire must have it fixed. However, if poor driving habits caused the flat, then just patching the hole will not solve the problem for long. Holistic

From the holistic perspective, symptoms are an alert that a problem is present.

treatment of a patient is centered on discovering and treating the underlying condition that predisposes the patient to manifest sickness. Many animals have recurrent health issues because the entire body is not addressed and the deeper imbalance is not set right.

Constitutional Considerations

Every dog is born with his own unique characteristics. This constellation of physical, mental, and spiritual factors is called the pet's constitution and is of great importance to the holistic therapist. All animals have certain weaknesses

Dogs require mental stimulation and intellectual challenges.

in their systems. It is at the weak link that the chain will break.

Think about what happens when the flu makes its way around your workplace. Some people have vomiting, some have diarrhea, some get achy, and some do not get sick at all. The same germ can cause different symptoms in individuals, depending on their individual constitutions.

A similar symptom phenomenon is true for dogs. Just look at the complex condition regarding allergies. No matter what the allergy, some dogs get a rash on their tail base, some scratch their bellies, some get ear infections, and some scratch all over. Each animal is predisposed to certain patterns of disease.

Western medical practitioners group patients according to disease state and treat each condition uniformly. In this model, every dog with allergies receives the same medication. Holistic practitioners realize that, although each patient may be suffering from the same "disease," the unique way that disease manifests is an important clue to the best remedy for that individual. So, different dogs with the same disease might be treated differently. From a holistic perspective, it is more important to observe what kind of patient has a disease rather than what kind of disease a patient has.

The Healing Crisis

A concept commonly spoken of in holistic circles is the *healing crisis*. The idea is that for healing to occur, the disease situation must get worse before it gets better. Theoretically, symptoms worsen because disease-causing toxins are being liberated from the body and are temporarily fouling things up. For those who hold to this notion, it is actually a good sign if a patient appears worse after a particular treatment is applied because that means healing is on the way.

I find the common understanding of the healing crisis very troubling. In my experience, such occurrences are rare. Most of the time, if a pet seems worse after a treatment is applied, it is because the disease is progressing. I have seen holistically minded pet owners fooled into complacency thinking their loved one was getting better when indeed he was dying. It is important to be guided through your pet's healing process by a knowledgeable holistic practitioner.

Homeopathy is one holistic modality that commonly produces something akin to a healing crisis. As will be discussed in greater detail in Chapter 8, when homeopathy is properly applied, the pet will sometimes experience what the homeopath calls an *aggravation*. An aggravation occurs because the energy of the remedy closely matches that of the disease and the symptoms are temporarily exacerbated.

Two keys elements differentiate an aggravation from worsening of the disease. First of all, with an aggravation the symptoms are worse but overall, the pet is doing better. For example, a dog's skin rash may intensify, but his appetite and activity level improve. Second, an aggravation is a brief occurrence lasting one to two days tops. If an animal's overall condition is worse, and it lasts for more than a couple of days, then most likely the disease is truly progressing. Homeopathy takes great skill and experience to apply properly to animals, so if you choose this modality be sure to work with a well-trained veterinarian.

In holistic medicine, the healing process is often compared to the act of peeling an onion.

Healing Is Peeling

In holistic medicine, the healing process is often compared to the act of peeling an onion. According to this metaphor, disease often affects the body in layers—like the concentric peels of an onion. The dog starts off healthy. Eventually, he is affected by a relatively mild problem, such as recurrent ear infections. Later, he develops occasional vomiting. Next, the dog becomes epileptic.

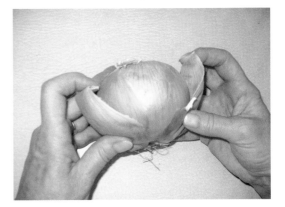

Finally, he is diagnosed with liver cancer. While the conventional veterinarian would conclude that this animal had a series of unrelated health conditions, a holistic veterinarian would consider that one process led to the next more serious condition. By the time the cancer rears its ugly head, there are layers of disease to deal with and a total cure of the patient is unlikely.

Just as the disease process developed in a stepwise fashion, so the course of healing proceeds in reverse order. In the above case, if healing were still possible then the cancer would need to be dealt with first. After the cancer was cured, the dog's seizures would likely get worse. Once that condition was handled then we would get back to the vomiting level. If that were cured, the dog would be likely to have more ear infections. When the true cause of the ear infections was eliminated, then the dog would once again be healthy. Thus, healing is like peeling an onion.

PSEUDOSCIENCE?

Because of the weird and wonderful nature of holistic medicine, skeptics in the medical community dispute its validity out of hand. These well-meaning professionals—many of them experts in their fields—simply refuse to acknowledge that alternative therapies have any basis in science. For them, holistic practitioners are frauds, and their patients are suckers. Is holistic medicine based on fake science? To answer this we must first understand the meaning of the word *science*.

Science has been defined as systemized knowledge derived from observation and study. Anyone who has researched holistic therapies in depth knows that they conform to this standard. However, in our modern, biomedical system, science has become synonymous with specific research standards involving what is termed *double-blind, placebo-controlled trials*. When properly applied, these medical studies can exclude the bias of the experimenter and the patient, thereby proving with certainty that a particular therapy really works.

Unfortunately, in practical application, medical studies may not be as pure as they appear. Consider the fact that, due to its extraordinary expense, most medical research is funded by drug companies. A study published in the medical journal *The Lancet* in 2000 determined that, "Reporting of pharmaceutical-industry–sponsored randomized clinical trials often result in biased findings

. . ." That explains why the latest and greatest wonder medication sometimes needs to be abruptly pulled from the market after being unleashed on the general public. It also elucidates why a 1991 study concluded that only 15 percent of medical interventions are supported by strong science.

Somehow, many medical practitioners seem to turn a blind eye to the shortcomings of Western medical research while poking holes in research supporting holistic modalities. This human tendency is actually such a common phenomenon that psychology has come up with a term for it. The expression *confirmation bias* refers to a situation in which evidence supporting one's beliefs tends to be perceived as plausible and evidence challenging one's beliefs tends to be perceived as implausible. So, by nature, biomedical scientists are apt to maintain the status quo regarding what they believe to be true.

Of course, confirmation bias only applies if the skeptic looks at the holistic research in the first place. Often, when I lecture to a group of veterinarians, I conduct a revealing experiment. I ask the audience to scan the room and pick out all the objects they see that are *red*. Then I have them close their eyes, and I ask them how many things they noticed that are *blue*. Although the surroundings contain many blue items, to date, no one has ever been able to recall any. This is because we only see what we are looking for.

Holistic practitioners might treat different dogs with the same disease differently.

Sasha's Story

Sasha was an energetic yet somewhat rotund yellow Labrador Retriever. She tended to have returning health problems. One week she would be suffering from an ear infection and her owner would bring her to me for treatment. Invariably, some topical medication would be prescribed and, with care and treatment, the problem would resolve. Then, often within a few weeks, Sasha would come down with a urinary tract infection. This would be treated with oral antibiotics to combat the bacteria. After the urinary tract infection was cleared up, the ear infection would once again appear.

This pattern continued to repeat. It seemed that an internal disturbance was present that was trying to thrust its way to the surface. When the condition was pushed down in one place, it popped up in the other and vice versa. I treated Sasha the best I could with conventional care as her owner requested. Holistic treatments could have been used to address the real problem and break the cycle of sickness.

No medical scientist who is skeptical about alternative medicine is likely to give research supporting holistic therapies a serious look. For him, it is as if the research does not exist.

Holistic medicine, like any new concept, will take time to be accepted by the mainstream medical community. This is not unlike the difficulty that fifteenth century Europeans had in comprehending that Columbus was not going to sail off the edge of a flat earth. Just because something is *common knowledge* does not mean it is true. The contrary often proves to be the case. Many medical facts of the past are today's myths. Mark my words— holistic medicine is the wave of the future.

Holistic medicine, like any new concept, will take time to be accepted by the mainstream medical community.

SAFETY

Having made the case for holistic medicine, I would like to inject a certain amount of caution. The opportunity for charlatanism certainly exists in the area of alternative medicine. A glance at many TV infomercials touting the value of various "natural" supplements is testimony to this fact. You will often hear testimonials from "successfully treated patients" (often paid actors) making outrageous claims. I can just hear the words my father always told me, "If it sounds too good to be true, it probably is." No remedy, whether natural or synthetic, is without possible side effects. The right remedy must be applied to the right condition, and it takes ample knowledge to do this properly.

Any reasonable holistic practitioner will speak realistically about the ability of his or her therapy to cure disease. The therapist can only direct the patient's body on the course toward health and provide the best conditions for recovery. Ultimately, healing itself is up to the patient and to the Higher Power. As with anything in medicine, the practitioner can do everything right and still have a negative outcome. There are no guarantees and if any therapist makes extreme, universal claims, he should be avoided.

It is important to have any problem your pet may be facing properly diagnosed by a veterinarian. It is equally important to have any holistic therapy administered by a practitioner who is trained in the use of such therapies *in animals*. Remember that anything that has the power to heal also has the power to harm if misapplied. I think that natural therapies are the treatment of choice for most conditions, but caution must be exercised, as appropriate application is important. When approaching holistic medicine, it is important to have an open mind, but your mind should not be so open that your brain falls out.

It is important to have any problem your pet may be facing properly diagnosed by a veterinarian.

Many holistic therapies are available for pets. It is best that any alternative treatment be administered by a properly trained veterinarian. Such a professional is not only thoroughly familiar with unique aspects of animal physiology and disease, but also an expert in how to apply the most appropriate holistic treatments to any given animal patient. No certification process exists for holistic veterinarians in general but many individual therapies—such as acupuncture, chiropractic, and homeopathy—do have certification courses. For more information on locating a holistic veterinarian, check out the resources in the back of this book.

Now that we have a firm understanding of the basics of holistic medical care for dogs, we are ready to look more closely at its practical application, as well as examine conventional veterinary medicine from an integrative perspective.

VACCINE *and* CONVENTIONAL
Medicine Integration

We've looked in detail at the fundamentals of holistic care for dogs and seen the philosophical and scientific differences between the holistic and conventional medical models. Now it is time to turn a critical eye to the medicine that we all grew up with. How can we integrate Western medicine with a holistic approach? In this chapter, we explore conventional care by starting with the controversial issue of vaccinations. Then we look at a potpourri of other topics (presented alphabetically).

VACCINES—A SHOT IN THE DARK?

Have you ever wondered why people get vaccinated only as children for most diseases, yet animals need to be revaccinated every year for life? Perhaps when you questioned your veterinarian, you were told that an animal's immune system is different or simply, "That's the way it is." Well for all you vaccine skeptics, I have great news.

The previously accepted approach to vaccinating pets is on its way out. For years, holistically minded veterinarians have voiced their objections to the idea of yearly vaccines. These pioneers have practiced what they preached, often going against the vaccine label recommendations and giving shots less frequently. Although some in the veterinary profession are still clinging to the outdated system of yearly vaccinations, a combination of common sense and research is causing the tide to turn. To get a handle on the current controversy, let's look at the history and science behind vaccines for pets.

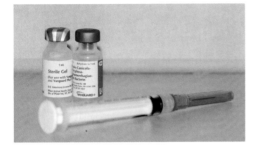

Many vaccines are available for pets, some of which protect against six or seven viruses in a single shot.

The Immune System

The practice of vaccinating pets began in the 1950s, when rabies and distemper viruses were common and devastating canine diseases. At that time, tests showed that the immunity imparted by the vaccines lasted about one year. Our understanding of the immune system and vaccine technology has come a long way since the 1950s, and the potency of these medications has improved. Today, many vaccines are available for dogs and cats, some of which protect against six or seven viruses in a single shot.

To understand the effect that all these vaccines can have on our companion animals we need to look at how the immune system works. The immune system is a complex network of organs, cells, and chemicals that are both affected by and incorporated into every organ and system of the body. Cells of the immune system learn to recognize certain proteins, called *antigens*, on the surface of invading organisms. After antigenic stimulation, some immune cells produce *antibodies*—proteins that attach to the antigen—that enter the bloodstream and aid the body in its fight against germs. At the same time, other immune cells are created to remember the antigens, so that the immune system can respond more quickly to future infections. Vaccines are an artificial way of delivering antigens into the body, so they stimulate both types of immune cells.

The Diseases

Vaccines are given to protect dogs from a variety

The Distemper/Parvo Combination Vaccine

When you take your dog to the veterinarian for a "distemper" vaccine, you are most likely getting more than you bargained for. You see, it is extremely rare for any veterinarian to give only distemper in a vaccine. The vast majority of distemper vaccines come with between four and seven different disease entities in one shot. The basic distemper vaccine includes distemper, parvovirus, adenovirus, and parainfluenza. The combo shot may also include two strains of leptospirosis and/or coronavirus. From the conventional point of view, this "supersizing" of the vaccine is considered a good thing—more bang for the buck. Holistic vets, however, have concerns about the effects such vaccines have on a dog's immune system.

of very dangerous diseases. Some of these pathogens, such as rabies, have been around for millennia while others, like parvovirus, have arrived on the scene more recently. It is helpful to review some of these diseases as we look into the practice of vaccination for dogs.

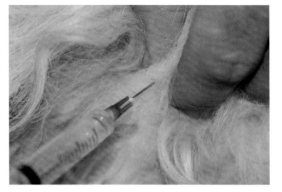

The basic distemper vaccine includes distemper, parvovirus, adenovirus, and parainfluenza.

Core Vaccines

The diseases canine adenovirus, canine distemper, canine parvovirus, and rabies cause infections that are both serious and widespread enough that, according to the American Animal Hospital Association (AAHA), every dog in the United States should be vaccinated against them. The AAHA considers these to be *core vaccines*.

Canine Adenovirus

Canine adenovirus, also known as *infectious canine hepatitis*, affects the liver, kidneys, and blood vessels. Symptoms include fever, inflammation of the nose or mouth, abdominal pain, diarrhea, loss of appetite, depression, and hemorrhage. Although this disease is rare, it is included in the distemper combination vaccine.

Canine Distemper

Canine distemper is a highly contagious viral infection that can affect the dog's nervous system, respiratory system, or gastrointestinal tract causing a range of symptoms including coughing, sneezing, nasal discharge, fever, loss of appetite, vomiting, diarrhea, and seizures. The disease is often fatal, even with aggressive treatment. It was a common killer of canines until use of the distemper vaccination became popular in the 1970s and 1980s. Although we rarely see this disease today, occasional outbreaks do occur and unvaccinated dogs are at risk. This is the best-known constituent of the distemper combination vaccine.

Canine Parvovirus

Canine parvovirus is a highly contagious and deadly viral infection that first appeared in the mid 1970s. This virus attacks the gastrointestinal tract and white blood cells. Common signs include loss of appetite, vomiting, and bloody diarrhea. Many dogs die despite treatment. This disease is still quite common in unvaccinated puppies. Protection against canine parvovirus is the most important component of the distemper combination vaccine.

Rabies

Rabies is a virus that invades the nervous system and is almost always fatal to humans and animals alike, unless treated early. It is spread through the saliva of an infected animal when it bites. Animals suffering from rabies often become vicious as a result of the infection's effect on the brain. They also tend to salivate excessively because of their inability to swallow due to paralysis of the throat muscles. Both of these behaviors exacerbate the spread of the disease. Although it is common for rabid animals to become aggressive, some infected animals simply become ill with nondescript nervous system signs. This can lead to unsuspected exposure for pet owners and veterinary staff.

Worldwide, it is estimated that up to 60,000 people die from rabies each year, and bites from domesticated dogs are the most common cause. Thanks to pet vaccinations, only a couple of fatal cases of rabies occur annually in the United States, and dogs are rarely the source of infection. It is hard to argue with the US requirement that dogs be vaccinated regularly for rabies.

Non-Core Vaccines

Non-core vaccines, such as bordetella, canine parainfluenza, leptospirosis, and Lyme disease, are only recommended if a particular pet is determined to have a significant risk of exposure to these diseases.

Bordetella

Bordetella is a bacterium which, like canine parainfluenza, is a member of the *kennel cough* family. Although we tend to think of kennel cough as a single disease, actually several different viruses and bacteria cause the condition. Bordetella causes the same symptoms as the canine parainfluenza virus (see below) and is usually more annoying than dangerous. Many kennels require this vaccine even though it is of limited usefulness. In fact, when a puppy daycare center near me recently had an outbreak of kennel cough, a higher percentage of dogs vaccinated for bordetella got sick than those who were not vaccinated.

Canine Parainfluenza

Canine parainfluenza is a highly contagious virus that is one of the causes of *kennel cough*. It is quickly spread among dogs in close quarters and causes a dry cough, depression, and runny eyes and nose. The infection is usually not life-threatening but can develop

---

Homeopathic Nosodes

Homeopathic nosodes are highly diluted disease factors administered orally in the attempt to create immunity in the pet. This concept is an offshoot of the homeopathic principles discussed in Chapter 8. There is no evidence that this intervention is effective, and I do not rely on nosodes to protect dogs from the deadly diseases mentioned in this chapter.

into pneumonia. This is another constituent of the distemper combination vaccine but is not considered a core disease by AAHA.

Leptospirosis

Leptospirosis is a contagious bacterial disease that can infect people as well as dogs. Wild animals (including rodents) and livestock act as a reservoir for the bacteria. It is often spread by urine, which can contaminate soil or standing water. This is a serious disease affecting the liver and kidneys and causing fever, vomiting, diarrhea, loss of appetite, and depression. The early signs of the disease can be difficult to detect, and it often goes undiagnosed until later stages.

Vaccines deliver antigens into the pet's body, thereby artificially stimulating the immune system to battle specific diseases.

Over 200 strains (called *serovars*) of leptospirosis exist, and the vaccine only protects against the four most common strains. In some areas of the United States, this infection is common; in others, it is hardly ever seen. Because of this intermittent distribution, leptospirosis is not considered a core vaccine. Only if you live in a "hot spot" should you even think about vaccinating your dog for this one. (Ask your local vet if the disease is common in your area.)

At the same time, if you do live in an area where many cases are reported, and your dog is often in the woods or on a farm, then you should give serious consideration to this vaccine due to the danger of this infection for both your dog and your family. Furthermore, the leptospirosis vaccine may not give a full year of protection, so I recommend that it be given in the spring so that the dog has the highest immunity during the seasons when he is most likely to be exposed. Leptospirosis is often included in the distemper combination vaccine and, in my experience, is the component most likely to cause an allergic reaction to the vaccine.

Lyme Disease

Lyme disease is a very serious bacterial infection that is spread by ticks. It can cause vague waxing and waning symptoms including fever, lameness, lethargy, loss of appetite, and depression. Lyme disease is difficult to diagnose and is common in the Northeastern and upper Midwestern United States. Dogs living in or traveling to those regions should be considered for vaccination.

Not Recommended—Canine Coronavirus

Canine coronavirus is a disease that has been linked to diarrhea in dogs because some dogs with diarrhea have the organism in their stool. Then again, some dogs with normal stool also shed this virus. I have heard canine coronavirus described as a vaccine looking for a disease. Even the AAHA has it on their list of vaccines that are *not recommended* for any dog. Unfortunately, some kennels still require the vaccine, and it is included in some distemper combination vaccines.

Types of Vaccines

Vaccines deliver antigens into the pet's body, thereby artificially stimulating the immune system to battle specific diseases. Vaccine technology is constantly developing, and more vaccines are being developed all the time; some are made to protect against different diseases and others are improvements on current vaccines. Several types of vaccines are available, each with its own pros and cons.

Modified-Live Vaccines

Modified-live vaccines contain live, disease-causing organisms that have been rendered unable to infect the pet. These vaccines do a great job of stimulating the immune system but carry the risk that some of the modified germs may revert back to an infectious form and therefore make the pet sick.

Killed Vaccines

Killed vaccines contain organisms that have been killed. Because they are dead, there is no chance that they will infect the pet. However, the immune system recognizes that the lifeless germs are not a threat and does not mount much of a response. To overcome this effect, *adjuvants* are added to the vaccines. Adjuvants are chemicals that cause inflammation and stimulate the immune system to respond more vigorously. Unfortunately, adjuvants have been linked to vaccine side effects, such as a specific form of malignant cancer in cats as well as dangerous systemic effects in both dogs and cats.

Subunit Vaccines

Related to the killed vaccines are the newly developed *subunit* vaccines. This technology utilizes genetic engineering to cause microbes to produce specific antigenic proteins. The vaccine is then made of these proteins in purified form. This creates a very

Let's Be Prudent

In addition to the diseases described here, vaccines against several other diseases are available, and more are being developed every year. Vaccines can be very important in the fight against infectious disease yet, at the same time, as you will read below, they are a double-edged sword. They have contributed to the control of such serious diseases as rabies, canine parvovirus, and canine distemper, yet their overuse is causing other deleterious medical conditions. In my view, prudent use of vaccines is beneficial for dogs.

safe vaccine. However, because this vaccine does not contain all of the germ's antigens, it may produce incomplete and short-lived immunity.

Recombinant Vaccines

Another recent development in vaccine technology are the *recombinant* vaccines. Through genetic engineering, antigen from disease-causing agents can be encoded into the DNA of harmless microbes. Because the organisms are alive, they stimulate the immune system without adjuvants. At the same time, since the germs are unable to cause disease, these vaccines cannot become infectious as modified-live vaccines can, but they do carry other risks, such as damage to the immune system.

Vaccine Concerns

No matter what type of vaccine is given, I have a number of concerns about vaccination in general.

One Size Fits All?

First of all, vaccines are the only medication I am aware of where one size fits all. That's right—a half-pound (.2 kg) Yorkie puppy gets the same dose as a 150-pound (68 kg) Great Dane. Something does not seem right about that. I also heard from an industry insider that the dose of antigen in a vaccine is determined for the average size dog—that quantity is then multiplied by ten to achieve the vaccine dose, just to be sure all the bases are covered. Now that dose for the puppy looks especially dangerous.

Subunit vaccines utilize genetic engineering to cause microbes to produce specific antigenic proteins.

Supersized Vaccines

Another major concern I have is that so many different disease antigens are injected at the same time. Our mentality of "supersizing" vaccines creates a highly artificial situation in which the immune system must respond to multiple diseases at the same time. When you add to this the common practice of vaccinating a pet whose immune system is currently fighting some sort of problem, such as an ear infection or skin allergy, it is easy

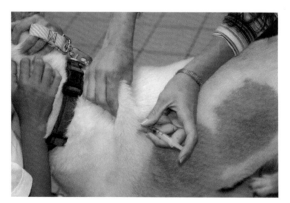

to see that we could be overstressing the immune system. Even the vaccine labels state that vaccines should only be administered to healthy pets.

Injection Site

Another problem with vaccines is the route of administration. The shots are given by injection under the skin. In contrast, most canine diseases are contracted when the microbes enter the nose or mouth. The naturally invading germs are first processed by the specialized cells in the tonsils and other immune tissue that is found in abundance in the back of the mouth and throat. This normal stimulation of the immune system is different from that produced by injecting the antigen.

Yearly Vaccines

The final blow to the immune system comes when we inject these overdosed, "supersized" vaccines into our pets year after year, even though ample evidence suggests that "yearly" vaccines instill immunity for at least four years. How much trauma do we expect our dogs' immune systems to take before they break down?

Ailing Immune Systems

Have you noticed the epidemic of immune system problems our pets seem to encounter these days? Allergies are a good example. An allergy is simply a misguided immune system in action. For example, if your dog is allergic to beef, it isn't the beef that's the problem—it's your dog's immune system reacting to an antigen that it should ignore. If you solve the problem by changing his food, your dog will soon begin reacting to the new food.

Have you noticed the devastating increase in cancer in our pets? The truth is that our pets produce at least one cancer cell every day. The reason all animals do not die of cancer is that the immune system detects and destroys these abnormal cells before they can take hold. Unfortunately, an unhealthy immune system may let a few of these cancer cells slip through. Although many other factors also affect the development of cancer, there is no doubt that a malfunctioning immune system plays a role.

Finally, let's look at the broad category of *autoimmune diseases*. An autoimmune disease occurs when a pet's immune system becomes sensitized to, and attacks, cells of its own body. A long

Vaccinosis

Practitioners of classical homeopathy have a very strong aversion to vaccinations. They coined the term *vaccinosis* to designate any medical problem caused by vaccines. The belief is that, on top of all the immune system concerns, vaccines have a strong negative effect on the body's vital force. This energetic disturbance can lead to a host of diseases from reverse sneezing to skin tumors. The homeopathic remedy *thuja* can be used after vaccination to mitigate the harmful energetic effects of the vaccine.

list of problems has been linked to autoimmune disease, including lupus, pemphigus, immune-mediated hemolytic anemia (IHA), immune-mediated thrombocytopenia (ITP), anterior cruciate ligament rupture, hypothyroidism, diabetes, and certain forms of arthritis.

Could the practice of overvaccination be contributing to the epidemic of chronic diseases our pets face? It is an undeniable fact that IHA and ITP in dogs and vaccine sarcoma (a form of cancer) in cats have been directly linked to vaccines. In fact, injection-site tumors that used to be seen only in cats have now been described in dogs as well.

Our mentality of "supersizing" vaccines creates a highly artificial situation in which the immune system must respond to multiple diseases at the same time.

The Vaccine Debate: Changing the Status Quo

In the past, vaccines were a no-brainer for veterinarians. Every animal came in every year, and we would hit them all up with as many shots as we could. Research showing that the vaccines imparted immunity for several years had been out since the 1980s, but most veterinarians thought it was better to be safe than sorry. Many had lived through devastating outbreaks of canine distemper and canine parvovirus. Plus, the vaccine reminders brought a dog in for his yearly exam, which is very important in maintaining an animal's health. Besides, many reasoned, we were not causing any harm. At the same time, there certainly was no financial incentive for veterinarians or vaccine producers to change the status quo.

Then, in the mid-1990s, cats began to develop malignant tumors between their shoulder blades. It didn't take a brain surgeon to figure out that the common denominator was vaccines. Suddenly, the medical imperative "first do no harm" came into play, and some veterinarians began to question the wisdom of administering so many vaccines. The charge was led by the feline practitioners.

In 1998, the American Association of Feline Practitioners Advisory Panel on Feline Vaccines recommended three-year boosters for the core feline vaccines. In 2001, after two years of study, the American Veterinary Medical Association Council on Biologic and Therapeutic Agents found that, as far as the core vaccines go, "…the one-year revaccination frequency recommendation found on many vaccine labels is based on historical precedent and USDA regulation, not on scientific data." So, according to the major conventional veterinary medical authority, since 2001, it has been pseudoscientific to vaccinate dogs yearly.

Then, in February of 2003, the American Animal Hospital Association Canine Vaccine Task Force released its recommendations for three-year distemper combination booster intervals, while they estimated that the immunity from these vaccines lasts at least seven years. More recently, a study published in the January, 2004 *Journal of the American Veterinary Medical Association* concluded, "In most dogs [98%], vaccination induced a response that lasted up to and beyond 48 months for all five antigens [found in the distemper combination vaccine]." Currently, many North American veterinary schools have adopted a three-year revaccination schedule for core vaccines in dogs and cats.

Sensible Vaccine Protocols

Unlike some holistic practitioners, I am not against vaccines for dogs. I worked at a humane society for five years and saw what often happens when animals do not get any vaccines. Canine parvovirus is a deadly disease that still infects unprotected dogs. Canine distemper is less common but just as deadly. In my twenty years as a veterinarian, I have not seen a properly vaccinated dog become ill from either of these diseases.

While I am not against vaccines, I am against *overvaccinating* our pets. Every dog does not need every vaccine, and they certainly do not need them every year. Experts agree that, after the initial series of vaccine boosters in puppies, they need a one-year booster, and then the core vaccines can be given every three years at most.

In my practice, I work the scheduling of vaccines so that the rabies vaccine and distemper combination vaccine alternate. That way, after the one-year booster, pets are never given all the vaccines in the same year. The pets get the distemper combination one year, the rabies the next year, and just the yearly exam the third year, and so on. Dogs get the non-core vaccines on an as needed basis.

Vaccine Titers

An excellent alternative to regular vaccines is having your dog's immune status to canine distemper and canine parvovirus checked by vaccine *titers*. Vaccine titers are a measure of the antibody level

Why Are Boosters Necessary?

Because of the way vaccines work, it is necessary to give at least one booster after the initial shot to adequately stimulate the immune system. A special case exists for boosters regarding puppies. It turns out that the immunity a puppy gets from his mother's colostrum interferes with the immunity instilled by vaccines. Because the pup's maternal immunity drops off at an indeterminate age—some time between six and sixteen weeks—boosters are necessary every three to four weeks during that period.

in the blood for specific diseases. According to experts, a high titer assures that your pet can adequately respond to the disease. These are simple blood tests that are performed by all the national veterinary labs.

There are a few drawbacks to doing vaccine titers. One is that the blood tests are more expensive than the vaccines. Maintaining good health sometimes costs extra. Another downside is that a small percentage of dogs are *non-responders* who do not produce antibodies even though they have immunity. This means that the titers may indicate a pet needs a vaccine when he really does not. This is a rare occurrence.

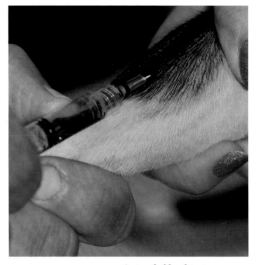

A simple blood test can determine your dog's antibody level for specific diseases.

A final problem with titers is that they are not predictors of future immunity. In other words, when a vaccine is given, immunity is imparted into the future. A titer, on the other hand, simply indicates that your pet is currently protected. His immunity could possibly drop in a month or two, and he could become susceptible to disease.

With vaccine titers, I feel that the pros outweigh the cons. I rarely find a low vaccine titer no matter how long it has been since the last vaccine, and the fewer vaccines administered the better for the health of the dog.

The Bottom Line on Vaccines

It is time for veterinarians, boarding kennels, groomers, and training organizations to follow the guidelines set by vaccine authorities. As a pet caretaker, you have the right and responsibility to refuse vaccines when that action is appropriate—get vaccine titers instead. Overvaccinating a pet can be just as dangerous as undervaccinating him. I urge all pet owners to be proactive and insist that the scientific vaccine recommendations be followed, for the health of our pets.

ANTIBIOTICS

Antibiotics are drugs used to help the body combat bacterial infections. They can be given orally, by injection, or applied topically. Some of these pharmaceuticals, such as penicillin, were originally derived from living organisms. However, these days, the vast majority of them are highly unnatural compounds. Some in the holistic community like to point out that the word *antibiotic* literally means "against life."

Side Effects

There is justification for being cautious of antibiotics. No medication is given without the risk of causing side effects. The most common negative consequence of antibiotic therapy is gastrointestinal upset, which manifests as diarrhea and/or vomiting. The reason for this problem is that antibiotics kill bacteria indiscriminately. It happens that there are "good" bacteria, called *probiotic bacteria*, which live in the canine intestinal tracts (and in ours, for that matter). These little guys have many important functions, and maintaining the right balance is vital for intestinal health. When antibiotics are given, the balance of gut bacteria is thrown off, resulting in problems.

Of course, every individual antibiotic also comes with a list of possible side effects. It is true that, in most cases, the chance of serious health consequences with the use of antibiotics is low. Even so, be sure to read the fine print on the label or the package insert before giving any medication to your dog, so that you are aware of possible problems. Then keep a close eye on your pet.

Overuse

Another serious issue regarding antibiotics is the fact that they are commonly overused. It has frequently been a tactic in veterinary medicine to prescribe antibiotics in order to give the caregiver something to do, even if the condition is likely to remedy itself. The reasoning is that people like to help their ailing pets and feel part of the healing process. Letting owners give something that is considered innocuous keeps them busy while the body mends. I understand from my M.D. friends that they have often done the same thing with their human patients. What's the harm?

Well, the problem is that any time antibiotics are given, there can be a few bacterial survivors. These germs stay alive because something in their genetic code makes them impervious to the medication. The defiant bacteria live to reproduce, creating generations of antibiotic-resistant strains of "super bugs." The more antibiotics used worldwide in people and animals, the more nasty germs there are for all of us to deal with. For this reason,

the unwarranted use of antibiotics in both human and veterinary medicine is on a decline.

Follow Your Vet's Advice

There are times when the use of antibiotics is important for your dog's health. Certain bacterial infections can be too much for a pet to handle without help. In such a case, listen closely to your veterinarian. Do not be afraid to ask if the animal really needs the medication. If he does, then follow the directions that are given. To some, it may seem safer to give a lower dose or to give the medicine for less time than prescribed. On the contrary, this tactic can lead to propagating resistant bacteria, leaving the pet in a far worse condition. If antibiotics are used, they must be used correctly to be effective.

Probiotics

One way of lessening the negative effect of antibiotic use is to give the pet a probiotic supplement while on the medication and for two weeks following the treatment. Probiotics are products that replace the good intestinal bacteria. Some holistic practitioners promote the use of yogurt to rebalance the gut, but it is not likely that a pet can get enough of the needed microbes from this source. Many pet probiotic products are available that work wonderfully.

If antibiotics are necessary, follow your vet's directions to the letter.

Support the Immune System

Another important consideration when a dog has an infection requiring antibiotics is the state of that animal's immune system. It is very possible that the reason the pet contracted the infection in the first place is because his immune system was not functioning up to par. In addition to that, it is a fact that antibiotics cannot successfully fight off an infection without the help of the dog's immune system. For both of these reasons it is helpful to support your pet's immune system with supplements while he is fighting an infection. Herbs such as echinacea, astragalus, garlic, ginseng, turmeric, and Oregon grape can improve an animal's immune function, as can the mushrooms reishi and shiitake (guidelines for dosing herbs and mushrooms can be found in Chapter 7), and vitamins

C (100 to 500 mg per day) and E (200 to 400 IU per day). Any of these supplements can be used along with antibiotics to help a pet fight an infection.

ANTI-INFLAMMATORY MEDICATIONS

Inflammation is a normal bodily process that allows an animal to clear up the debris from trauma and injuries as well as combat infectious invaders, thus laying the groundwork for repair and healing. It is a complicated process that involves the immune system, white blood cells, and a cascade of chemical reactions that are usually localized to the affected area. Inflammation in and of itself is not bad; it is only when the process gets out of control that things go awry. The cardinal signs of inflammation are redness, heat, swelling, and pain.

Because of the pain associated with inflammation, we are compelled to help our pets when they are suffering from a condition involving this reaction. It is never desirable for pets to experience pain. In fact, pain stresses the body and causes devastating effects on the immune system and the dog's overall well-being. In some cases, pain can propagate itself, which leads to a chronic pain cycle that can be very difficult to break.

Holistic remedies are often slow acting, so it is sometimes necessary to use medications for a short time, and then taper the dose when the natural therapies kick in. Sometimes the disease condition is such that alternative treatments alone cannot control the pain. When this is the case, the holistic thing to do is to use whatever form of medicine the pet needs. This integrative approach may include anti-inflammatory drugs.

Conventionally, anti-inflammatory medications are aimed at relieving the discomfort of inflammation. Unfortunately, it is impossible for any medication to influence only the area targeted. Anti-inflammatory medications are particularly notorious for causing side effects, especially when used long term. There are two major classes of anti-inflammatory pharmaceuticals: steroidal and nonsteroidal anti-inflammatory medications.

Steroids

A lot of confusion surrounds the use of steroids. Steroids comprise a group of hormones produced by the body. These

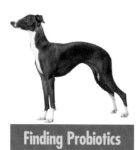

Finding Probiotics

Probiotics come in different forms—liquids, pills, capsules, and powders. This treatment has made it into the mainstream and now many conventional veterinarians carry probiotics. If your veterinarian cannot recommend a product for your dog, then you can find the human version at any health food store. Human probiotics are fine for dogs—just use the dosing calculation for herbs given in Chapter 7 (dog's weight divided by 150) to determine the fraction of the human dose to give your dog.

hormones have similar structures but can have very different effects on the body. *Anabolic steroids* are male hormones that cause the body to build muscle. Some athletes illegally take the synthetic form of these compounds to enhance physical performance. *Glucocorticoids* are stress hormones produced by the adrenal glands. These molecules have an anti-inflammatory effect.

Synthetic glucocorticoid medications include prednisone, prednisolone, and dexamethasone. These drugs are very potent for relieving inflammation and pain. They are commonly prescribed for many conditions including allergies, trauma, shock, brain injuries, inflammatory bowel disease, and back problems. They are even used as part of many chemotherapy protocols. Glucocorticoids are often used in a last ditch effort to help very sick animals. This sometimes-successful strategy has led to the medical axiom, "No animal should die without the benefit of steroids."

As helpful as glucocorticoids are, many side effects are associated with their use. In the short term they often cause the dog to urinate more, which results in an increased thirst. They also cause an increase in the appetite. More seriously, they suppress the immune system and can cause stomach ulcers. Long-term use of glucocorticoids can damage the liver and kidneys. The abrupt cessation of glucocorticoid use can cause a serious malfunction of the adrenal glands, so animals must be tapered off the drug.

There are often holistic alternatives to the use of anti-inflammatory medications.

Nonsteroidal Anti-Inflammatory Drugs

Nonsteroidal anti-inflammatory drugs (NSAIDs) suppress inflammation by a mechanism different from that of steroids. They are commonly prescribed to help pets deal with the pain and inflammation associated with arthritis, injuries, and surgery. They do not have a strong effect on the immune system, as steroids do, but they do have their own problems. Each NSAID has its unique chemical structure that dictates what organs it is likely to harm. The liver and

kidneys are the most common targets of NSAID damage. All NSAIDs have a negative effect on the stomach lining and can contribute to the development of ulcers. The risk of ulcers is worsened when they are used in conjunction with glucocorticoids.

Most NSAIDs are meant only for short-term use. Unfortunately, animals often suffer from conditions, such as arthritis, that cause chronic pain. When NSAIDs are used in such instances, the pet must be monitored with a physical exam and blood work on a regular basis—usually every six months—to minimize the risk of serious organ damage.

Alternatives for Anti-Inflammatory Medications

There are often holistic alternatives to the use of anti-inflammatory medications.

- **Fish oil** has an anti-inflammatory effect and has been proven to help alleviate the itching of skin allergies as well as the pain of arthritis.
- **Acupuncture** is an excellent method of easing chronic pain and can be used long-term without side effects.
- **Therapeutic laser treatments** can help alleviate pain.
- **Glucosamine** and **chondroitin** are nutritional supplements that have been shown to help pets with arthritis.
- **Boswellia**, **chamomile**, **licorice**, **turmeric**, and other herbs can be used to subdue inflammation.

Many alternative therapies are appropriate for various conditions involving inflammation. These treatments must be prescribed on a case-by-case basis as determined by the dog's unique condition.

DENTAL HEALTH

Oral hygiene is an often-overlooked area of canine health. Most people never lift up their dog's lip and look at the teeth way in the back. When they do, they are often surprised to see hard, brown material adhered to the surfaces of the molars and premolars. This dental tartar contains bacteria that can threaten a pet's health.

It is best to keep your dog's teeth clean from the start. When a dog eats a natural diet (as will be discussed in Chapter 3) his teeth stay naturally clean. I find that dry dog food does very little for pets' oral hygiene. In my opinion, chewing raw meat and bones is the way to go.

The Therapeutic Laser

We have all become familiar with lasers that are used for surgery. These high-intensity lasers actually burn through tissue in a precise manner. Another type of laser has a much different effect. The therapeutic laser (sometimes called a "cold" laser) utilizes a low-intensity beam that can promote healing. There is no consensus on the mechanism of action for this device, but I have seen its remarkable abilities. Therapeutic lasers are great for promoting the healing of skin wounds and burns. The laser beam can also penetrate into deeper tissues and help with joint injuries, arthritis, soft tissue injuries, and back problems.

Brushing your dog's teeth is another method for keeping the teeth clean. Can you imagine what your teeth would look like if you never brushed them? Even though we brush our teeth twice daily, we still need to go to the dentist for cleaning every 6 to 12 months. Is it any wonder that pets can have serious dental issues?

Pets may get dental tartar buildup from neglect or just because, like some people, certain dogs are prone to dental problems. Teeth cleaning is a commonly performed procedure at veterinary hospitals. The veterinarian cleans a dog's teeth the same way a human dentist does his human patients, using ultrasonic scaling and polishing. The only difference is that, to work on a dog's teeth, he must be put under anesthesia. The slight risk involved with anesthesia is the major drawback to this procedure.

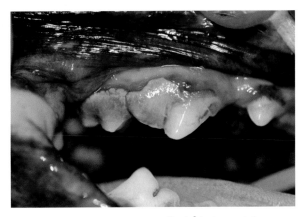

Dental tartar contains bacteria that can threaten a pet's health.

Many dog owners consider that it is not worth such a risk just to have a pet with clean teeth. If clean teeth were the only benefit, I would agree—but it is not. The tartar that builds up on a pet's teeth contains bacteria that can attack the tooth root causing pain, infection, and a tooth root abscess. The germs can also gain access to the dog's bloodstream, spreading infection to the heart, liver, kidneys, and other major organs. Besides, the minor risk that anesthesia poses can be minimized by having preanesthetic blood work done to check for hidden problems.

Maintaining your dog's dental health is a very important part of his overall wellness care. They say that daily flossing can add years to our lives, and it is equally valuable to keep our pet's teeth clean. It is sometimes necessary to have a dog's teeth professionally cleaned as part of his healthcare program.

EUTHANASIA

What could be more unnatural than intentionally ending a beloved pet's life? Many canine caregivers struggle with the choice of either humanely euthanizing a pet or watching him die a slow, agonizing, natural death. End-of-life issues are always difficult to deal with, and I in no way want to give the impression that I have all the answers, but let us examine the subject of euthanasia from a holistic perspective.

Euthanasia involves giving an injection intravenously to the patient. The drug used is an anesthetic, and the process is basically giving an anesthetic overdose. The drug renders the animal unconscious and then quickly stops the heart. The only pain involved is the sting of the needle entering the vein.

The greatest difficulty with the procedure is getting the needle into the vein. This problem is compounded if the animal is a debilitated older pet with collapsing veins or an active, painful animal. Every veterinarian has his own way of overcoming this difficulty. Many doctors give a tranquilizing shot in the muscle before the intravenous injection, to calm the animal and make the process go smoothly.

The Choice Is Personal

The choice of whether to euthanize a pet is very personal. It is extremely rare for a person to be given such power over the life or death of a loved one. There are those dog owners who feel it is wrong to take the life of a pet for any reason. While I respect this position, I personally feel it is an owner's duty as the animal's caregiver to ease his suffering and end the life of a pet when all hope for recovery is lost. Knowing when the time is right is the difficult decision.

This is one choice that cannot be taken back. Owners often

End of life decisions for a beloved pet are a personal choice.

ask me what I would do if it were my pet. Sometimes the answer comes easily but often I am compelled to tell the owner that, as bleak as the situation may look, sometimes animals surprise even me and recover against all odds.

Sometimes the issue of euthanasia brings to the forefront what it means to really be alive. Sure, the pet may be breathing and pumping blood, but what is its quality of life? Is an animal who has to be force fed and can barely stand enjoying life? Often pet owners grapple with the reason for keeping their pets alive. Are they doing it for the pet or for themselves?

In my opinion, when an animal has a terminal condition and stops eating on his own, it is his way of saying he wants to leave this life. When the decision is not as clear, it can help to ask the pet to give you a sign and then pay attention to the animal's behavior. It is important to give the pet your sincere permission to leave you. Many pets hold on beyond the point of reason because they want to please their caregiver. Let your companion know he has served you well, and he can go in peace.

From a Western medical standpoint, death means failure. People are sometimes kept "alive" with the use of machines because family members cannot deal with the pain of loss, and medical personnel cannot admit defeat. From a holistic point of view, death is simply a transition. I firmly believe that when animals leave this life, they move on to a better condition. In my view, euthanasia may be the last kind thing people can do for their pet.

PARASITE CONTROL

Parasites are creatures that live in or on another living thing at their host's expense. Our dogs are attacked by parasites of all kinds and from a variety of sources. There are internal parasites, such as intestinal worms and heartworms, and there are external parasites, such as fleas, ticks, and mites. Each parasite type and each individual pet situation necessitates a different control strategy.

Prevention is the key to any parasite-management plan. One overarching concept is that maintaining your pet's optimal health is very important to help him stave off parasites. These freeloaders most easily attack animals who are weak, sickly, and have impaired immune systems. Reducing vaccines and providing proper nutrition are important ways to keep your pet fit and his immune system healthy enough to combat parasitic attack.

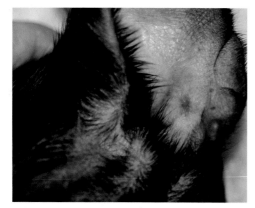

Be sure to have any ear problem that your pet may be experiencing checked by your veterinarian.

At the same time, to think that healthy pets can never be affected by parasites is a bit of an overstatement. Certainly, keeping your pet healthy is a very helpful aspect of parasite control; however, even healthy dogs pick up parasites. Besides, in my experience, very few truly healthy pets exist, due to poor breeding practices and unhealthy environments. Also, some parasites, such as certain intestinal worms, can be spread to humans. So, everyone needs a little help in this area now and then.

Pharmaceutical companies have put forth a great effort to develop medications to eradicate parasitic diseases in animals. While many of these products are very effective at killing parasites, common sense tells us that the fewer chemicals our dogs are exposed to the better. A balance must be struck between parasite control and drug toxicity. Let's look at common pest problems and their sensible solutions.

Ear Mites

Mites are microscopic parasites from the spider family. They live on the surface of animals, and a variety of mites affect dogs. Ear mites actually live deep down in the dog's ear canals, causing intense itching. They are spread from pet to pet by close contact. Ear mites are most commonly found in puppies raised in a poor environment. If an older dog has ear problems, it is probably due to a bacterial or yeast infection and not from ear mites. Be sure to have any ear problem that your pet may be experiencing checked by your veterinarian. An ear condition can result in a ruptured ear drum, which greatly affects the treatment approach.

Ear Cleaning

Ear mites create a large amount of debris in the ear canal. A first step in combating ear mites is to clean up the mess. When cleaning your dog's ears, it is important to realize that the canine ear canal is extremely long. It runs down the side of the head for one to three inches (2.5 to 7.6 cm), and then travels into the skull for another one half to one inch (1.2 to 2.5 cm). This makes it difficult to get debris out.

To clean the ears, use a strong chamomile tea solution. This solution makes a great flush and has the side effect of calming any inflammation that may be present.

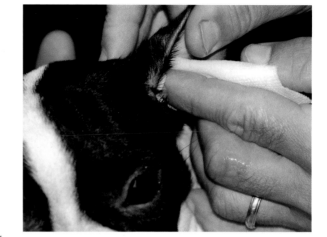

A strong chamomile tea solution can be used to clean out your dog's ears.

- Brew two bags of natural chamomile tea in a cup of boiling water and let it cool.
- Fill the ear canal with the cleansing liquid until you can see it at the top.
- Massage the ear at its base to break up the wax way down inside the ear canal—you should hear the fluid squishing.
- Let your dog shake his head, which flings the solution and wax to the surface. (You may want to do this outside, as the discharge may be thrown on the surrounding walls and carpet.)
- Use a cotton ball on the end of your finger to wipe out the debris—you can reach as far as you can with your finger without damaging the ear drum. (*Note: Using a cotton swab is not recommended as it could cause damage.*)
- Once the ear is cleaned, instill three to eight drops of olive oil into each ear to smother the mites.
- Massage the outsides of the ears to spread the oil inside the ears, so that the dog cannot shake it all out.

The cleaning and oil treatments usually need to be repeated every other day for two to three weeks to get rid of all the ear mites.

Fleas

Fleas are a very common external parasite in most parts of the United States. These tiny arthropods live on the surface of the body and feed off the dog's blood. Their bites irritate the skin and, in some dogs, trigger an allergic dermatitis. Fleas can also carry tapeworms to your dog.

Fleas spend the majority of their life cycles off the animal. For every flea on a dog there are 10 more in the environment.

Detecting Fleas on Your Dog

Fleas on your dog can be very difficult to detect. A very handy weapon in the fight against fleas is a flea comb. A flea comb has finely spaced teeth that can pull the fleas and loose fur off your pet. By combing your pet on a white sheet you may find the tell-tale, comma-shaped flea feces. Because this "flea dirt" is basically dried blood, you can tell it from other debris by soaking it in water. If it turns red, then it is flea dirt. Flea combing your dog can serve as an early detection method that allows you to really jump on a flea infestation before it gets out of hand, but I wouldn't rely on it as a sole means of flea control.

Check your dog for ticks and fleas after he's been outside.

If your flea-infested pet comes into the house, then you can bet the house is crawling with fleas too.

Each female flea lays hundreds of eggs every day. These eggs roll off the dog's skin and into the environment. If conditions are right—warm with at least some humidity—then the eggs hatch into minute larvae that look like miniature maggots. The larvae spin cocoons and eventually hatch into fleas.

Fleas are numerous year-round in warm, moist environments. In temperate climates, fleas overwinter on wild animals. During the warm months, flea eggs fall off squirrels, chipmunks, rabbits, and the like and, in time, fleas develop in the yard. From here the parasites end up jumping onto unsuspecting pets. By the time you notice fleas on your dog, the little pests have already gained a foothold. Prevention is the key with fleas.

Many prescription flea medications are now available that are either applied topically or given internally. All of them get into the dog's system. While they work well for preventing flea infestation, I worry about the effects these toxins may have on the dog's overall health. In some areas of the United States, such as the Southeast, these medications may be necessary to stave off the constant attack of fleas. In other parts of the country, natural means are available to help keep pets flea-free.

Natural Outdoor Control

Ultimately, our pets contact fleas from the out of doors, so this is an obvious place to begin flea control. Treating your yard for fleas does not mean you have to address the entire 50 acres that you may own or the whole neighborhood your pet visits. Even if your pet roams far and wide, setting up a buffer zone right around the house will help stop a problem. For yard treatment, I recommend the use of "friendly" *nematodes*.

Nematodes are microscopic worms that naturally live in the soil and feed on flea larvae and yard pests. They hunt for insects like no chemical can. They are totally harmless to people, animals, and insects that are not harmful to the lawn and garden. In addition to fleas, this natural, biological insecticide kills more than 230 types of soil and boring pests, including cutworms, gypsy moth larvae, Japanese beetles, and white grubs. Nematodes are so safe that they have been used to control pests on vegetation such as strawberries. They are the good guys of the microscopic world, and it is easy to see the value in boosting their population.

The thing I like most about nematodes is the irony of killing a parasite with a parasite. Isn't Mother Nature wonderful? To prevent a flea problem, nematodes must be applied to your yard at the very beginning of flea season. This natural flea control is safe and quite effective. Look for them at your local specialty garden center or holistic veterinarian.

Natural Indoor Control

The inside of your house is another environment that must be dealt with to prevent a flea foothold. Natural products are available for use inside that consist of very fine powders that dry out flea eggs and larvae in the carpet. In addition to these specialty products, you can sprinkle borax to have the same effect. This strategy can be effective at eliminating fleas in the house, which is often a major battleground.

Herbs

Some herbs have insect-repellant qualities. Pennyroyal, from the mint family, is one such herb. If ingested, it is toxic to dogs, but I have clients who have stuffed it into homemade pet beds or into cloth herbal flea collars. (If your dog is likely to chew up the bed, don't use it.) Certain essential oils such as cedar and citronella can be used in sprays, shampoos, and dips to help fend off fleas too. To make an insect repellant spray, add a teaspoonful of each of the oils to a quart (.9 l) of water and mist your dog every time he goes outside.

Diatomaceous Earth

Diatomaceous earth has been promoted as a natural indoor flea killer. Unfortunately, this powder can become airborne and lodge in the lungs, causing serious pulmonary problems. This is especially a concern for our pets who lay right on the carpet, and it could affect people as well

Lemon

Lemons are a source of natural flea-killing substances, such as D-limonene, plus other healing ingredients. Here is a simple and safe formula to make your own natural flea dip. Thinly slice one whole lemon, peel and all. Add it to 1 pint (.5 l) of near-boiling water and let steep overnight. The next day, strain out the lemon, sponge the solution onto your pet's skin, and let it dry. Be careful not to get the solution in your pet's eyes, and do not apply it to irritated skin. You can repeat the procedure daily for severe flea problems.

Garlic

Garlic in the diet seems to taint the dog's blood with a taste that fleas dislike. Feed fresh garlic at a dose of about one average-size clove per 50 pounds (22.6 kg). Most dogs enjoy the taste, and it can be mixed right into their food. In addition to keeping the fleas off, garlic benefits the immune system. Garlic is good for dogs (in appropriate doses) but should not be used in cats (see sidebar).

Topical Medications

As helpful as all these natural means are for preventing a flea infestation, I have to admit that nothing works as well as the topical prescription flea medications. I have found that over-the-counter topical flea medicines are not as safe as those prescribed by veterinarians. For dog owners facing an extreme flea infestation, it may be necessary to bite the bullet and use medications temporarily until the problem is brought under control.

Heartworms

As the name implies, heartworms are parasites that live in a dog's heart. Their microscopic larvae are transmitted from dog to dog by mosquitoes. Once injected into the body, it takes six months for the worms to mature in the heart. At that point, they have grown to be six to eight inches (15.2 to 20.3 cm) long. It is typical for an infested animal to house dozens of these parasites. This state of affairs is obviously very unhealthy for the dog.

The drugs used to kill adult heartworms are extremely harsh and must be used with care. Even when the drugs are successful, the dog is left with dozens of dead worms in his heart, which eventually flow into the lungs for the body to dissolve and absorb. The resulting inflammation can be deadly. It is clear that prevention is very important.

Prevention

There are no reliable, natural heartworm preventives that I am aware of. Therefore, I recommend the use of the monthly prescription heartworm medications for all dogs in areas where heartworm disease is prevalent. Because of the six-month lag time between infection and detection, and because no medication is 100 percent effective, I advocate periodic testing of dogs for the disease—even if they are on preventive medication year round. For those who choose not to put their dogs on heartworm prevention, yearly testing is important because treatment is much more successful if the disease is caught early. This is definitely one of those diseases for which the conventional approach is best.

Intestinal Worms

Several types of worms can invade the canine gastrointestinal tract. They can be detected by fecal examination done by a veterinarian. This test is not foolproof, though. The fecal exam is a way of checking the stool for worm eggs. It is possible that worms in the intestine may not have laid eggs in the particular sample submitted. So, a positive stool test tells you the dog has worms, but a negative test does not rule them out.

Roundworms and Hookworms

Roundworms look like spaghetti and are often responsible for the potbellied look of infested puppies; they feed off the nutrition in the host's intestine. Hookworms have small, string-like bodies and latch on to the intestinal lining. They actually suck blood and can cause life-threatening anemia in puppies.

Roundworms can be transmitted from a female dog to her puppies before birth and during nursing.

Both roundworms and hookworms can be transmitted from a female dog to her puppies before birth and during nursing. Once inside, these worms travel into the body and form cysts in the muscles of the host. The cysts are impervious to worming medications so, once an animal in infested, they have worms for life. Some of the worms come out of the cysts and go into the bloodstream any time the host is stressed. Pregnancy stresses the dog, which releases the worms into her system, and thus passes the worms to the next generation. Of course, they can also be picked up from the stool of infested animals.

Both of these parasites can be transmitted to humans. Their microscopic larvae, which hatch from eggs in the stool, can actually penetrate the skin to access our bodies. These larvae are ubiquitous in public, outdoor settings such as playgrounds. Just one more reason to keep your children's shoes on while outside.

Tapeworms

Tapeworms hook onto the lining of the small intestine and feed off the pet's food. They consist of segments that form a long, flat body. As the segments farthest from the head mature, they break off as sacks of eggs, pass in the stool, and sometimes appear as what looks like grains of rice around the pet's anus. Tapeworms can be transmitted by ingesting fleas or by the consumption of rodents.

Whipworms

Whipworms are tiny, threadlike worms that live in the dog's colon. They often cause periodic diarrhea that may contain blood or mucous. Their eggs stay viable in the environment for years, so it is common for dogs to get reinfested once they have contracted the worms.

Tapeworms hook onto the lining of the small intestine and feed off the pet's food.

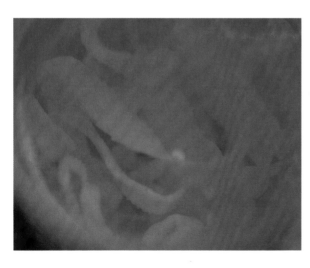

Treatment

Herbal worm medications, such as black walnut, can have a high risk of toxicity. Some over-the-counter wormers are neither safe nor effective. I find the modern worm medications sold by veterinarians to be very mild and effective, so I recommend using them when worming is needed.

Because of the life cycles mentioned above, all puppies should be wormed for hookworms and roundworms at least twice, at two-week intervals, starting at two weeks of age. Each different type of worm requires a different medication, so be sure to have the problem properly diagnosed and treated.

Mange

Skin mites cause the condition commonly called mange. Several distinct types of mites cause the various kinds of mange that bother our pets. We will discus the two most common forms.

Your dog's immune system must be healthy to help fight demodectic mange.

Demodectic Mange

The first type of mite is called *Demodex* and is responsible for *demodectic mange*. These tiny bugs can be found in the hair follicles of normal animals. In fact, if you plucked one of your eyebrows and looked at follicle under the microscope, you might find a demodectic mite. Normal animals with a healthy immune system keep the number of these mites under control. In some other animals, however, these mites can reproduce uncontrollably and cause mange.

Demodectic mange usually appears as areas of hair loss without much redness or itching. Of course, there are always exceptions. Some pets with demodectic mange do itch. Demodex is not contagious from animal to animal, nor from pets to people. This disease can affect small patches of skin or, occasionally, it can affect the entire surface of the body. The latter condition is called *generalized demodectic mange*, and it is much more serious. Animals with this situation have a major problem with their immune systems and are often in overall poor health.

Treatments

Conventional treatments for generalized Demodex involve dips or other medications to kill the mites. These treatments are somewhat toxic and often fail. This result is not surprising since the mites are not the problem—the animal's immune system is the problem. Medications may be needed to bring the mites under control, but at the same time the animal must be made healthier through proper nutrition and supplements. In addition to a natural, whole-foods diet, extra vitamin E, vitamin C, chelated zinc, and essential fatty acids boost skin immunity.

Sarcoptic Mange

The second type of skin mite is the *sarcoptic* mite, which causes *sarcoptic mange*. This mite causes an intensely itchy, red rash and is often first seen on the edges of the earflaps, elbows, ankles, and underside. It often quickly spreads over the entire body.

Sarcoptic mange is highly contagious from animal to animal. Direct contact is not needed for the spread of this disease. Your pet can simply walk where an affected animal has been and pick up some mites. They can even live on human skin for a short period, where they cause an itchy rash.

Treatments

Sarcoptic mange is usually treated with special insecticidal dips or topical prescription medications. Although it is not ideal to expose your dog to these chemicals, they are very effective. Due to the intense discomfort caused by sarcoptic mange and the chance of human infestation, I would recommend the conventional course of treatment. It is also important to clean up the environment to avoid recontamination. Of course the same nutritional recommendations as for demodectic mange apply here as well.

Ticks

Ticks are bloodsucking parasites that come in a range of sizes. Some are as small as the head of a pin and others are as large as a pencil eraser. They all start out flat, but swell like balloons as they fill with blood. They can spread diseases such as Rocky Mountain spotted fever and Lyme disease.

Ticks like to be on animals, but they can live for long periods on their own and can even hibernate through the winter. While off the host, they infest areas covered with small bushes and shrubs found at the edges of woodlands. They require a relatively moist environment. Ticks hang out on the tips of plants and latch onto animals as they brush against the weeds.

Because ticks live on high weeds and underbrush, one prevention tip is to eliminate these areas from your

Ticks live on high weeds and underbrush.

yard and keep your dog away from such spots during tick season. Insect-repelling herbs and essential oils, as well as feeding garlic (as mentioned above in the flea section) are helpful. Another key is to check your dog frequently for ticks and remove them as soon as possible. The less time a tick is attached to the pet, the less likely it is to spread disease.

In my experience, ticks are more difficult to deter than fleas. If your pet lives in a tick-infested area where Lyme disease is common, you may need to resort to prescription products and the Lyme disease vaccine.

Removing a Tick

Ticks insert their mouth parts deep into their host's skin and actually glue them in place, making it difficult to pull them off. Their heads and bodies always stay on the outside of the animal. To remove a tick, simply grasp it with a tweezers as close to the skin as possible and gently pull.

Be sure it is a tick you are removing. Certain skin growths resemble these creatures, and you don't want to rip a wart off your dog. Look for the tick's legs to tell the difference. If in doubt, see your veterinarian.

SPAY/NEUTER

Sterilization surgery is the most common operation that most veterinarians perform. For male animals, this involves removing the testicles and for females it entails removing the uterus and ovaries. This surgery leaves the animal in a very unnatural state, devoid of important, hormone-secreting glands. And yet, as a holistic veterinarian, I strongly recommend this procedure for dogs intended as pets.

Population Problem

One huge reason to spay or neuter your dog is the pet population problem. Euthanasia of unwanted animals is the *number one* cause of death for pets in the United States. It is estimated that three to four million animals are killed at shelters every year. In just six years, a female dog and her unsterilized offspring can produce as many as 67 thousand puppies. There just are not enough homes for all of them.

"Just One Litter"

I have met dog owners who consider letting their dog have just one litter so the family can experience the miracle of birth. Other people buy a female, purebred dog at the pet store for hundreds of dollars and start seeing dollar signs in their heads as they multiply that price times the number of puppies the dog might have. Most pet store dogs are sold as *pet quality*. These dogs do not meet breed standards, and their puppies have little value due to poor genetics. People come up with many reasons for breeding a pet. However, even if a person has homes lined up for all the puppies their dog will have, they must realize that every home accepting one of their puppies is one less home for a puppy at the shelter.

Sterilization Issues

While it is definitely best for dogs to be spayed or neutered, there are some issues to be aware of. These surgeries do require general anesthesia, which carries a low possibility of complications. Be sure that your animal is thoroughly examined before any surgery. It is even advisable to have presurgical blood work done to detect underlying organ system problems that might influence the pet's processing of anesthesia.

The concept that sterilizing dogs makes them fat is untrue. Consuming more calories than are burned off makes an animal fat. Many spayed and neutered dogs maintain an ideal weight. On the other hand, spaying and neutering often has the effect of slowing the metabolism. This can cause an animal to think he needs more food than he actually does. Ultimately, your dog's exercise routine and food intake—and thus his weight—are in your hands.

Spayed female dogs do have a higher incidence of urinary incontinence than unspayed dogs. This rare surgical side effect is exacerbated if the dog is spayed before six months of age. It is best to have your dog spayed when she is six to eight months of age, and before her first heat.

Although it is unnatural for dogs to be sterilized, it is also unnatural for them to have unfulfilled hormonal drives. There is always a downside to any medical intervention, but in the case

There are many health benefits to spaying and neutering.

of spaying and neutering pets, sterilization is always better than the alternative. Besides the larger social reasons for spaying and neutering dogs, there are health benefits as well.

Why Neuter Male Dogs?

Neutering male dogs can benefit their health and the pet owner's sanity.

- The procedure diminishes male hormones, reducing the pet's urge to reproduce.
- Neutered male dogs show less aggression, anxiety, and roaming, thus lessening the chance of being hit by cars, getting into dog fights, or becoming lost.
- Neutered males dogs do less urine marking.
- Neutering eliminates the risk of testicular cancer and reduces other cancers fed by hormones.
- Neutering helps the prostate gland stay healthier.

Considering that a male dog can smell a female in heat from several miles away, you are not doing your dog any favors by keeping him intact.

Why Spay Female Dogs?

There are many benefits to spaying a female dog.

- When a female dog is spayed, she no longer comes into heat, thus eliminating the associated messy discharge.
- Spaying means no visits from unrelenting, unwanted suitors. (Considering the olfactory range of male dogs, it takes only a few minutes of unchaperoned outdoor activity to result in your unspayed female dog becoming pregnant.)
- As with males, a spayed female is less prone to certain hormone-related cancers, such as malignant mammary tumors.
- For a spayed pet, ovarian and uterine cancers are not a concern since these organs have been removed.
- Another health benefit of spaying is that it prevents uterine infections called *pyometras*. These life-threatening afflictions are difficult to diagnose and not at all uncommon in older, unspayed females.

For the sake of the pet population problem, a responsible dog owner has his pet spayed or neutered. Sterilized pets make better companions and are healthier.

WESTERN MEDICAL DIAGNOSTICS

Dogs have a natural instinct to hide their pain, and they can be quite adept at concealing medical problems. This tendency is due to the fact that, in the wild, an animal who is seen to be weak, sick, or injured is fair game for predators. The weaklings are also moved down on the pecking order by more dominant pack members. Our pets can be so good at keeping their problems to themselves that even observant pet owners can miss early signs of disease. For this reason, it is important that dogs have regular physical exams.

Regular Exams

During a physical exam, your veterinarian uses her knowledge, skill, and special instruments to look for latent signs of medical problems. A thorough exam starts by asking the caregiver about any changes in the pet's behavior. Then the animal's body is inspected from head to tail including looking at the eyes and ears with special scopes, checking the teeth and other mouth structures, listening to the heart and lungs with a stethescope, palpating the abdomen, feeling for lumps on the body, checking the lymph nodes, examining the skin and hair coat, and taking the animal's temperature and weight.

Normal healthy dogs should be examined at least once a year. This is extremely important because dogs age more quickly than we do, and yearly exams for them are equivalent to a person being seen by his doctor every five or six years. Dogs in their senior years, those dealing with medical problems, and those on long-term medications need to be checked at least every six months.

Think Before You Breed

Anyone considering the idea of breeding their female dog should be sure to think it through. Professional breeders know that a lot of things can go wrong. It may seem that giving birth and raising young ones should come naturally to dogs, but this is not always true. Sometimes there is trouble with the delivery and an expensive c-section surgery is needed. Also, some females are poor mothers, and the owner ends up bottle-feeding the entire litter every two hours for a couple of months.

Dr. Doug checks over a patient; it is important that dogs have regular physical exams.

Testing

Often, diagnostic testing is needed to determine the nature of a pet's problem. These special assessments are sometimes essential, because we are trying to help animals who cannot communicate how they feel or where they hurt. Western medicine excels at the ability to find hidden problems. The use of blood work, X-rays, ultrasound, and other diagnostics are invaluable, even from a holistic perspective. As a holistic practitioner, I want to be confident of the Western diagnosis even though I may look at the problem differently and choose alternative therapies.

We have just examined a full range of conventional medical interventions and how they fit into the scheme of the holistic paradigm. As you have seen, the integrative approach to healthcare that I promote often seeks alternatives to Western ways, but sometimes embraces conventional care while using holistic therapies to ease the unwanted side effects.

NATURAL NUTRITION
for Dogs

We've all heard the old adage, "You are what you eat." It certainly is true that the body can only build tissues (muscle, bone, brain, etc.) and maintain function based on the raw materials with which it is provided. This same concept is just as true for our canine companions. Sometimes even the slightest deficiency in a key nutrient can have devastating results. It behooves us to provide our pets with the best possible nutrition.

So, you should look to your veterinarian for dietary advice, right? Not so fast. According to a survey published in the *Journal of the American Veterinary Medical Association*, nutrition training in veterinary schools is inadequate and the quality of continuing education on nutrition is inferior. Unfortunately, most veterinarians are too busy treating sick animals and keeping informed on the latest drugs and surgical procedures to give much thought to nutrition. Besides, in veterinary school we were basically told that the food companies know what they are doing—"Just recommend a quality pet food," we were told. After a time in practice, I began to ask the questions, "Do the pet food companies really have it all figured out?" and "What is the best diet for my canine patients?"

This chapter is my answer to those vital questions. We will start with a thorough assessment of commercial foods from a holistic perspective. From my experience, I can tell you that there is no greater obstacle to canine health than the poor diets we are told to feed our dogs. You will see that, from the ingredients to the additives to the processing, instead of creating health, we are creating problems. We then will look at how we can best mimic the natural canine diet. Next, we will explore the whole-food philosophy and how it applies to supplements for dogs. We will conclude with a discussion of what I consider to be the five supplements every dog needs.

Throughout this chapter, I would like you to reflect on the question, "Who knows better, Mother Nature or us?"

COMMERCIAL DOG FOODS: "COMPLETE AND BALANCED"?

I admit, I am not a fan of processed, commercial pet foods. Just imagine for a moment that you are sitting in your medical doctor's office after your yearly exam, and the doctor pulls out a 40-pound (18 kg) bag of kibble and plops it in front of you. Your eyes are immediately drawn to the beautiful images of vibrant people eating handfuls of dry nuggets. And then you see the label: *People Chow*.

Then your doctor tells you that you can go home and get rid of your refrigerator and stove, and when you go to the grocery store you can bypass the fruits, vegetables, and meats, and head straight to the *People Chow* aisle. He informs you that this new "complete and balanced" product is the only food you should eat for every meal, day in and day out, for the rest of your life.

Hopefully, you would refuse such medical advice. Eating only processed food does not make sense. How could this food company be so arrogant to think they could create balanced nutrition in a bag? Besides, if you were not killed by malnutrition, you would likely die of boredom. So, how is it that we have bought into this idea for our pets? No wonder our dogs eat garbage when they get the chance!

A poor diet is the biggest obstacle to achieving canine health.

Nutritional Testing

A "complete and balanced" guarantee is made right on the package of commercial pet foods. That should be comforting to pet parents, right? Well, let's explore this misguided concept.

The Association of American Feed Control Officials (AAFCO), a private advisory board whose members are representatives from state, federal, and foreign government agencies, regulate animal feeds in the US. AAFCO's mission is to develop uniform definitions for pet food ingredients and their proper labeling. Any pet food labeled "100% complete and balanced" is following AAFCO guidelines. There are two methods AAFCO uses to make this determination.

The first and preferred nutritional test is called a *food trial*. A food trial consists of feeding the food to as few as eight animals for 26 weeks and monitoring their condition before, during, and after the test. Based on this meager data, AAFCO can certify that a dog food is appropriate to feed a pet—every meal—for life. Even veterinary nutritionists agree that this process can miss chronic nutritional deficiencies or excesses.

Feeding the same food over and over can create food allergies.

The second AAFCO nutritional test is called a *food analysis,* in which a chemical analysis of the food is required to contain the 36 nutrients that AAFCO considers to be essential. Never mind that hundreds of known nutrients exist, with more discovered every year. Plus, this testing does not prove that the nutrients contained in the food can actually be absorbed by the body.

Problems With Testing Methods

Both of the testing methods are based on average, healthy animals. For dogs who are stressed by performance, disease, or surgery, this AAFCO-sanctioned nutrition may not be adequate.

Another factor to consider is that the nutrients are linked to the calorie content of the food. In other words, if you need to feed less of the food than the label recommends in order to maintain a healthy weight for your pet, then your dog may not be getting the required vitamins and minerals.

Plus, the claim that a pet food is "100 percent complete and balanced" has led many veterinarians to recommend owners find a food that works for their pet and feed it for the life of the animal. However, according to experts, animals often become sensitive to the foods they eat most often. Feeding the same food over and over is a great way to create food allergies.

For a pet food company to make the statement that its food is "100 percent complete and balanced," it must assume that it has

What the Experts Say

What do nutrition experts have to say about the AAFCO profiles?

- According to Dr. David A. Dzanis, the veterinarian in the Food and Drug Administration's (FDA) Center for Veterinary Medicine, "The formulation method does not account for . . . the availability of nutrients. Yet the feeding trial can miss some chronic deficiencies or toxicities."

- Dr. Quinton Rogers, professor of Physiological Chemistry at the University of California, Davis adds, "Although the AAFCO profiles are better than nothing, they provide a false sense of security."

- Dr. Tony Buffington, the nutritionist at the Ohio State Veterinary College had this to say, "The recommendation to feed one food for the life of an animal gives nutritionists more credit than we deserve."

These comments are not very reassuring for the pet-owning public.

100 percent complete knowledge of nutrition and biology. Now that is a bold assertion. Even veterinary nutritionists realize that they are not smarter than Mother Nature—they currently recommend pet foods be rotated to avoid the deficiencies and excesses that any one food may cause.

Nutritional Deficits: Two Cases

You do not have to look far to see that experts do not have 100 percent knowledge of nutrition.

Taurine Deficiencies

When I was in veterinary school in the 1980s, we saw many feline patients dying of a heart disease called *dilated cardiomyopathy* (DCM). This malady involves a weakening of the heart muscle causing the heart to pump ineffectively and therefore to balloon with blood. At the time, veterinarians assumed this problem was caused by some sort of infectious or toxic injury to the heart. We knew it could not be a dietary deficiency because the cats' diet of commercial foods was "100 percent complete and balanced."

Then, in 1987, it was discovered that DCM was actually caused by a lack of the amino acid taurine in commercial feline diets. Researchers found that even though cat food in the raw form had plenty of taurine, ingredient processing decreased it to a deadly level. One researcher even commented that the cats who didn't become ill were those going outside and catching mice. Cat food manufacturers scrambled to supplement their foods with taurine, and now DCM is seldom seen in cats. So, who knows better, Mother Nature or us?

DHA

After the taurine debacle, surely today we are smarter than we were back then; dietary deficiencies *must* be a thing of the past.

Both cats and dogs have suffered from dietary deficiencies found in commercial foods.

I only wish it were true. Recent research indicates problems still exist with conventional pet diets. Let's look at a study involving docosahexaenoic acid (DHA).

DHA is a very important omega-3 fatty acid. It is naturally found in fish oil, organ meat, wild game meat, and brain tissue. In fact, 5 percent of the brain is made of DHA. Obviously, DHA is an important nutrient for proper brain function (imagine flying in a jet that is missing 5 percent of its engine parts). Studies on laboratory animals have shown that increasing dietary levels of DHA causes an increase in cognitive ability.

In 2004, a national commercial pet food company decided to do a test. They looked at two groups of pregnant dogs and their resultant puppies. The control group was fed the national brand-name commercial dog food, and the experimental group was fed the same diet plus fish oil, which is high in DHA.

At nine weeks of age, the puppies began a strict, thirty-day program of training and evaluation. At the end of this process, the training performance index (a measure of canine intelligence) for the puppies in the high-DHA group was more than double that of those in the low-DHA group. One of the researchers concluded, "When you consider that the number one killer of dogs is euthanasia due to behavior problems, we should be recommending high-DHA diets."

While this study demonstrates the importance of DHA, it also raises questions about current nutritional standards. Remember the control group—the less intelligent puppies? They were fed the national brand of dog food which, according to the label, is "100 percent complete and balanced." Are we to believe that dogs are inherently dim-witted, but this "new" nutrient can make them smart enough to keep alive? Or, is it more likely that we have created, and continue to create, behavior problems in our dogs due to our uninformed attitude about nutrition. What other insidious mental and physical health conditions are we someday going to learn are due to nutritional deficiencies?

WHAT'S IN COMMERCIAL DOG FOODS?

Let's take a look at typical ingredients found in commercial diets, and why they may be harmful to your dog.

Additives

Commercial pet foods often contain artificial flavors, colors, and preservatives. Unfortunately, pet food additives are not actively regulated due to lack of governmental resources. Furthermore, government regulators require proof that a given ingredient is unsafe as opposed to the opposite. So, a lack of scientific evidence regarding additives can allow potentially unsafe ingredients to be included in pet foods.

The labeling situation for dog foods can be deceiving.

Artificial Flavors and Colors

The flavor-enhancing chemicals are needed to entice unsuspecting canines to eat substances they were never meant to eat. As for the colors, do you think that a dog cares if his food looks red and meaty? I assure you that he does not. The color additives in pet foods are there for the human pet food purchaser, not for the dog. As to problems associated with these chemicals, a recent study in England links artificial food colorings and benzoate preservatives to hyperactivity in preschool children. It is likely that this correlation holds for dogs as well.

Preservatives

As you look farther down the dog food ingredient list, you will likely run into words that you cannot pronounce, such as *butylated hydroxyanisole* (BHA), *butylated hydroxytoluene* (BHT), *propyl gallate, propylene glycol,* and *ethoxyquin.* These chemicals have been linked to a variety of diseases, and there is little documentation about their safety when consumed long-term. Believe it or not, the average 25-pound (11 kg) dog eating a commercial pet food takes in between 6 and 9 pounds (3 and 4 kg) of preservatives each year. This surely is not a healthy situation.

Furthermore, just because you do not see a particular preservative on the label does not mean it's not in the food. If a dog food manufacturer adds the preservative during food production, it is listed; but if they purchase material that is already chemically preserved, the ingredient does not make it on the label.

Lying Labels

The labeling situation for dog foods can be deceiving. Here are just a few examples of how hard it can be to trust pet food labels:

Preprinted Packages: If a dog food company changes the ingredients in its food, those changes are made on the package. However, if the company has preprinted packages with the old ingredient list, they are allowed to use up those labels for the new food formulation — even though the label does not match what is actually in the food. In other words, there's no telling what really is in commercial dog foods.

Protein Analysis: Pet food labels are required to list and are analyzed for "crude protein." However, this ingredient is actually measured by the nitrogen level of the substance, since protein is high in nitrogen. So, an unscrupulous supplier of wheat gluten (a common source of pet food protein) could adulterate its raw ingredient with some other compound that is high in nitrogen — such as melamine — making the gluten look especially nutritious while in reality it is more toxic.

"Whole" Meat: You would think that seeing a whole meat such as "whole chicken" on the ingredient list of a dry dog food would be a good thing. It certainly sounds more wholesome than "chicken meal." You just fell into another pet food label trap. Whole chicken is 70 percent water. This water is removed during food processing, thus reducing whole chicken to chicken meal. It takes about three pounds (1.3 kg) of whole chicken to make one pound (.4 kg) of chicken meal. The ingredients as listed on the label are in order of preprocessed weight. So, having "chicken meal" as the first ingredient is three times more impressive than having "whole chicken" listed first. A whole-meat ingredient is just another ploy to make it appear that there is more meat in the product.

Carbohydrate Cons

What are some effects of a high-carbohydrate diet?

- A study involving sled dogs showed that dogs fed a high-protein diet performed much better than those on a high-carbohydrate diet.
- Ample research links high-carbohydrate diets to obesity. This is one possible explanation why a 70-pound (32 kg) Labrador Retriever can gain weight eating a cup and a half of food per day.
- Carbohydrates in the diet aggravate diabetes.
- Cancer cells preferentially feed off carbohydrates, as opposed to fat and protein, so high-carbohydrate foods predispose dogs to cancer.

Carbohydrates in the canine diet are not only unnecessary, they are unhealthy.

Grains

As you peruse any commercial kibble label, you will see a preponderance of various grains (rice, wheat, corn, soy, etc.) consisting mostly of carbohydrates. Many food companies try to hide the amount of grain in clever ways, such as fractioning the grain. For example, wheat flour and ground wheat can be listed as two different ingredients, even though the only difference between the two is the size of the ground particle. The only logical reason to do this would be to make the label look as if the food contains less grain—because if the amount of grain is split in this way, then it falls lower on the ingredient list. Another ploy is to include several grains, so that, proportionately, the food has more meat than any one grain. Both of these techniques allow the meat component to be brought to the top of the ingredient list, making the food *look* more healthful. The lesson here is to look at the first four or five ingredients on a pet food label to get a better idea of the amount of grain in the diet.

Some dry dog foods can be composed of as much as 90 percent grain, even though canines have no dietary requirements for carbohydrates.

Some dry dog foods can be composed of as much as 90 percent grain. Yet, according to veterinary nutritionists, the canine diet has no dietary requirement for carbohydrates. You do not see wolves—our dogs' wild counterparts—out grazing in corn fields. In the wild, carbohydrates constitute between 2 and 14 percent of the canine diet. So, the question is, "Why is there so much grain in dog foods?"

It's for two reasons. First, the carbohydrates in grains are an inexpensive way to increase the calories and energy in the food. Second, in the case of dry dog food, it is impossible to make kibble without some source of carbohydrates to glue it together. Notice that neither of these reasons has anything to do with the health of the dog. It is all about cost and convenience.

Problems With Grain Contamination

Grain can easily become contaminated with molds, some of which produce deadly toxins called *aflatoxins*. These poisons can cause anemia, kidney failure, immune system failure, and cancer. Over the years, aflatoxins from commercial diets have been responsible for hundreds of canine deaths in the United States. Disease-causing molds tend to contaminate lower-quality grain allocations—the very grain that ends up in pet foods. In addition, since mold spores are common indoor air pollutants, the open 40-pound (18 kg) bag of dog food in the pantry could easily become contaminated with toxin-producing molds in the privacy of your own home.

Problems With Allergens

A recent study showed that many dogs with allergy problems may be reacting to allergens from grain-storage mites. These allergens are not destroyed by processing. So, the grains contained in pet foods contribute to the widespread problem of canine allergies.

Problems With Soy

Soy is a common grain used in dog foods. A lot of controversy surrounds this food. In some ways, soy protein appears healthier than meat protein. However, soy is a source of phytoestrogens, which are plant compounds that mimic the hormone estrogen. While providing estrogen in this way can be good for menopausal women, it can also predispose dogs to problems such as mammary cancer. Astonishingly, research shows that certain commercial dog foods contain phytoestrogens in amounts that could have biological effects when ingested long-term.

Problems With Alternate Carbohydrate Sources

Some "natural" dry foods try to avoid problems caused by grains by using other sources of carbohydrates, such as potatoes or even tapioca. While this is a step in the right direction, all of

FDA Reports

For the full report on pentobarbital in pet foods, go to www.fda.gov/cvm/FOI/DFreport.htm.

For the statement on mad cow disease, go to www.fda.gov/bbs/topics/NEWS/2003/NEW00910.html.

these carbohydrates are quickly broken down into sugars by the body. No matter what the source of the carbohydrates, that can be a problem.

Meat

Somewhere high on the dog food label ingredient list you should find a meat, such as chicken, beef, or lamb. Unfortunately, it is impossible to tell the quality of that protein source from looking at the label. In fact, the meat making up commercial pet foods can be inappropriate and unhealthy.

"Four Ds"

Sometimes, livestock deemed unfit for human consumption can end up in pet foods. These are termed "four Ds meat," which means meat that comes from animals that are dead, dying, diseased, or disabled when they reach the meat packing plant.

Rendering Plants

"Food products" from rendering plants can also end up in pet foods. The rendering process begins with raw animal material consisting of slaughterhouse waste, livestock and poultry carcasses, and supermarket meat rejects. Even more troubling is that euthanized pets are sometimes added to the mix. This material is cooked at 280°F (138°C) for one hour and then further dehydrated into a powder used for—among other things—pet foods. The dog food ingredient "meat and bone meal" designates material from rendering plants. Indeed, the FDA has found traces of pentobarbital (the drug used to euthanize animals) in pet foods.

You might think that pet food officials would be concerned about this situation. Well, think again. In a 1997 TV interview, when asked about the presence of dogs and cats in rendered food products ending up in pet foods, the then AAFCO president, Hersch Pendell, said: "If the ingredient says meat or bone meal, you don't know if it is cattle, or sheep, or horse . . . or Fluffy." It truly is a dog-eat-dog world.

Mad Cow Disease

Another FDA report from 2003 is equally disturbing. It turns out that the carcass of the Canadian cow that tested positive for mad cow disease (bovine spongiform encephalopathy) in 2003 may have been used to manufacture pet food, some of which was reportedly shipped to the United States.

Processing

Raw-ingredient processing is a major feature of pet food manufacturing. Processing involves cooking the unrefined components at high heat and pressure to sterilize the mixture and make the grains more palatable. Unfortunately, this procedure destroys most nutrients including vitamins, enzymes, and amino acids. High-temperature cooking also converts some meat and carbohydrates into carcinogens. Studies have shown that health problems often develop in epidemic proportions when human populations switch from their natural, native diets to processed Western foods. The same may be true for dogs.

Raw Meats to Avoid

I discourage the use of pork in a raw meat diet due to the risk of parasites. Also, some deer hunters feed raw deer meat to their dogs, but this meat can be contaminated by disease-causing organisms, so I am against this practice as well.

NATURAL CANINE DIETS

It seems to me that, conventionally, we are going at canine nutrition from a totally wrong direction. We start with ingredients that carnivores were never meant to eat, then we strip out all the nutrients with our processing, and finally we sprinkle in some synthetic vitamins and supplements to try to balance obvious deficiencies. A more intelligent approach would be to start with a look at what canines have evolved eating over the past five million years. Evolution is a slow process, and dogs have certainly not adapted to processed foods during the past 70 years that these foods have been available. (Maybe veterinary nutritionists need to include more DHA in their own diets.)

The wolf is the closest wild relative of our pet dogs. In the wild, wolves have a varied diet that depends on seasonal availability.

What's Commercial Packaging Doing to Food?

Just when we think it is impossible to mess up our pets' diets to a higher degree, another study proves us wrong. Research published in the *Journal of the American Veterinary Medical Association* in 2004 showed a link between canned cat food and feline hyperthyroidism (overactive thyroid). Feline hyperthyroidism was very uncommon just 20 years ago, and veterinarians have started to wonder why we diagnose it so much more frequently these days.

Researchers found that cats eating canned food—specifically the pull-top variety—had an increased risk of the disease. When they questioned the difference between regular cans and pull-top cans, they found that a special inner can coating is used. Further investigation revealed that chemicals from this varnish had leached into the cat food. Even though this specific disease only affects cats, there are potential correlations to canine diets. It is certainly plausible that canned dog foods are suffering similar contamination that is leading to chronic canine health problems.

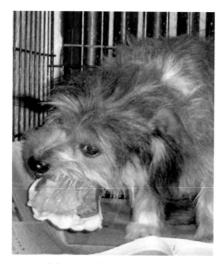

A natural diet should consist of raw meat, bones, shredded fruits and vegetables, and organ meat.

They prey on the weak members of big-game herds such as elk and moose. They also eat small game, earthworms, grasshoppers, fruits, berries, and other vegetation. When the first wolves became domesticated dogs, about 100,000 years ago, this new species became more reliant on human food scraps. This diet consisted of unused portions of butchered animals as well as "table" scraps.

Raw Food Diet

If we learn anything from this natural diet, it's that the starting point for formulating a food for dogs should consist of raw meat, bones, shredded fruits and vegetables, and organ meat.

Some controversy exists among natural diet advocates as to the best way to combine these ingredients. Some feed raw chicken—bones and all—to their dogs, believing that the chewing gets the digestive process started and the bones clean the dog's teeth. This type of raw food diet is often called BARF, which stands for *Bones and Raw Food* or *Biologically Appropriate Raw Food*. Other natural food advocates grinding the bones to avoid the potential choking hazard posed by feeding whole bones. Some cook the food to kill bacteria (often called home-cooked diets) and still others include some grains with the above-mentioned natural diet ingredients.

Let's take a closer look at the components for a raw diet.

Meat

The most common lean meat sources used in natural diets include chicken, turkey, beef, and lamb. Keep in mind that, just as we benefit from variety in our diets, the same is true for our pets. It is helpful to change meat sources and other food ingredients in the natural diet from time to time.

Ideally, homemade pet food should use organic sources for the meat and other ingredients. Unfortunately, this directive is both impractical and prohibitively expensive for many people. The conventionally grown foods we ourselves usually eat are of much higher quality than the raw ingredients used in most commercial pet foods.

The same common-sense rules that govern safe meat handling for our meal preparation apply equally when making homemade dog food. Raw meat should not be left on the counter to thaw, as this encourages the growth of bacteria. Always thaw the meat in the refrigerator. Using the microwave to thaw the food can destroy some of the nutrients. If unforeseen circumstances necessitate quickly thawing meat, then I recommend immersing the container of meat in hot water for 20 to 30 minutes.

Once thawed, raw meat should only be kept refrigerated for up to three days before discarding it. Raw meat should never be refrozen once it has been thawed, as this allows for the growth of bacteria. Raw meat should never be left in the dog's food bowl for more than 10 to 20 minutes. If your dog does not eat the food immediately, it should be discarded or re-refrigerated for later use.

The chef's hands should be washed thoroughly after handling raw meat. Everything that contacted the meat, including knives, bowls, counters, cutting boards, and other surfaces, should be disinfected.

Bones

Bones are an important component of the canine diet because they provide calcium and minerals in the form that nature intended. Also, the joint cartilage on the ends of bones supplies nutrients needed for healthy joints.

Raw bones are much different from cooked bones. I would never suggest that someone feed a pet cooked bones of any kind because they are hard, brittle, and likely to splinter into dangerously sharp fragments. I have seen many problems caused by dogs eating cooked bones, including life-threatening intestinal blockage and perforation. However, raw bones are softer and much easier for dogs to consume and digest. Chicken necks and backs in particular are made of small bones that do not splinter into harmful pieces. Having said this, there is a risk of choking when feeding even raw bones to a dog. Ground raw bones are a safe alternative to letting the animal eat them whole.

If you choose not to feed bones to your dog, it is important that the diet contain some other form of calcium. Meat is high in phosphorous, which must be balanced by calcium to avoid health issues.

Fruit contains sugar, so they should only make up a small proportion of your dog's diet.

Fresh, locally grown, organic produce is the best source for vegetables—but any kind is better than none at all.

Vegetarian Dogs?

Although some people thrive on a vegetarian diet, the same is not true for dogs. Dogs need meat as the major part of their diet—it is the food source they have evolved to eat. It is possible to create a balanced vegetarian diet for dogs, but I do not recommend it because of the difficulty and risk of nutritional imbalance. I prefer to stick as close as possible to the dog diet Mother Nature intended.

Food-quality bone meal is the best source, and you should provide about one tablespoon per pound of meat.

Fruits and Vegetables

Most vegetables can and should be part of a dog's diet. A recent study showed that simply adding veggies three times a week to the diets of Scottish Terriers (a breed prone to bladder cancer) reduced the risk of bladder cancer by 70 to 90 percent! Green leafy vegetables such as spinach, kale, mustard greens, and Swiss chard are especially nutritious (iceberg lettuce has very little nutritional value). Carrots, cauliflower, broccoli, beans, and beets should be included as well. Sweet potatoes and yams are chock full of nutrients and can be included in the diet; white potatoes contain mostly carbohydrates and should be left out. Garlic can be added sparingly—up to one clove per fifty pounds (22.7 kg) of body weight per day. This ingredient can aid the dog's immune system and help to stave off fleas. Onions can be toxic in large quantities and should not be fed to your dog.

A variety of fruits, such as apples, pears, plums, and bananas, should make up a small proportion of a dog's diet. Grapes and raisins can cause kidney failure in some dogs, so these should not be included. Apple seeds contain cyanide, a poisonous substance, although a dog would have to consume many apples to be at risk. Cherry, peach, and apricot pits contain another toxin called amygdalin, and these seeds do pose a threat if fed to dogs. Because all fruits are high in sugar, they should only be a small part of the canine diet.

Fresh, locally grown, organic produce is the best source for these ingredients but any kind of fruits and vegetables are better than none at all. The most effective way to provide our canines the needed nutrients from fruits and vegetables is to be sure the food is shredded. A carnivore's digestive tract is shorter than that of an herbivore. Dogs simply cannot completely digest chunks of vegetables. Anyone who has fed their dog a piece of carrot will tell you that most of it passes out the other end of the animal virtually unchanged.

Organ Meats

A final important ingredient in a dog's natural diet is organ tissue, such as liver, kidneys, and heart. Different tissues of the body concentrate different nutrients. Organ tissue provides essential vitamins and minerals to balance the canine diet.

Potential Concerns With Raw Diets

Raw meat harbors potentially dangerous bacteria, such as *Escherichia coli* and *Salmonella*. In my experience, this is rarely a problem for dogs. They can handle the bacteria, as their ancestors have for millennia. In fact, I have watched my own dog take a raw chicken back and bury it in the woods in the middle of the summer, only to dig it up and eat it several days later, with no deleterious effects. The concern about bacteria is more for the humans in the house. A dog's consumption of raw meat may expose humans to harmful germs from the animal's mouth or stool. For this reason, I do not recommend raw feeding for any animal in a household with someone who has a weakened immune system (such as a person who is receiving chemotherapy).

Another complication when trying to mimic Mother Nature's canine diet is that we simply do not have access to all its natural elements. For example, when animals are slaughtered at our packing plants, the blood is drained and used for other products. So, the raw meat we have available to feed our dogs may be deficient in vital minerals such as iron. Also, most of the meat we buy comes from grain-fed animals, whereas the wild animals that wolves eat graze on grasses. The meat of grain-fed food animals is high in omega-six fatty acids, while that of grass-fed wild animals is high in omega-three fatty acids. Add to this the fact that wolves eat the DHA-containing brains of the wild game they catch, and you can see that raw food diets are short on omega-three fatty acids. That's why supplementation is important.

For some, a drawback to the raw diet is the lack of convenience. Not every pet parent has the time to prepare daily meals for her dog. Luckily, several national pet food companies currently produce high-quality raw dog foods. This is not only convenient, but may be the best way to assure proper nutrition for your dog. Unfortunately, commercial raw food products are more expensive than processed pet foods, just as healthy food for us is usually more costly than fast food. It's a tradeoff between time and money:

What About Grains?

Although corn and other grains are technically vegetables, they are usually considered as a separate food group. As mentioned earlier, grains were not part of the dog's ancestral diet, and they are associated with several health concerns. In general, I do not recommend that grains be part of the canine diet. There are possible exceptions to this advice. For example, a dog suffering from renal failure may benefit from a low-protein diet that often must include grain to make up for the calories lost by reducing the meat content. Also, some individual dogs just seem to do better when some grains are fed.

The resources section of this book contains a list of books and websites to help get you started feeding your dog a raw diet.

making your own pet food can be time-consuming, but the cost may be comparable to processed food. Many people find that, although sacrifices must be made to feed their dog a healthy diet, those costs are more than recouped by the improved health of their pet, who then requires fewer veterinary visits.

Home-Cooked Diet

I am fully aware that as healthy as it may be, raw feeding may not be for everyone. If the idea of feeding your dog raw meat scares you, be assured that you can make a cooked homemade diet that is more nutritious than commercial foods. You do not have to be a nutritionist to make a diet for your dog. You were most likely not raised by a nutritionist, and your current diet is probably not formulated by an expert. Why then would it be necessary for your dog's diet to be professionally formulated?

When making a home-cooked diet, it is important to start with trustworthy recipes and follow them closely. Variety is the key to balance. Each different meat and selection of fruits and vegetables provides varying nutrients. As with our diets, every meal may not be perfectly balanced, but over time the needed nutrients are provided. You should also keep in mind the supplements mentioned below.

If you are making a cooked homemade diet, a week's worth of food can be prepared all at once and some of it can be frozen and thawed as needed. Any supplements should be added just before feeding to assure full activity of the nutrients.

NO DIET DOGMA

No one diet is right for all dogs. Every animal differs in his nutritional needs and tolerances. Most dogs do best on raw food diets, but some do not. Many canines require very little (if any) grain in their diets, while others thrive on higher levels. Some

Bacteria and Commercial Food

Yes, bacteria in raw food are a concern. However, a recent study published in the *Journal of the American Veterinary Medical Association* found that 33 percent of dry dog food samples tested were contaminated with *E. coli*, and one canned dog food contained cryptosporidium (another disease-causing organism). So, conventional diets are not as safe as we're led to believe.

disease conditions mandate that the food be cooked or be low in protein. Some diet plans base the foods given to particular breeds on the fare available in their country of origin. And the Chinese have a system for choosing ingredients based on the energetic imbalance of the patient—a system that does seem to translate to our canine companions. With the help of a holistic veterinarian and a little trial and error, you can find the diet that best matches your dog's individual needs.

When making a home-cooked diet, it is important to start with trustworthy recipes and follow them closely.

Nutrition Strategies: Improving Conventional Diets

As bleak a picture as I have painted for commercial pet foods, I have to admit that there are dogs who live long, happy lives eating nothing but these diets. I truly believe that animals stand a much better chance of maintaining their health if they are fed a more natural diet, but I realize that feeding raw or homemade dog food may not appeal to every pet owner for various reasons. If you choose to feed a conventional dog food, you can still improve the level of nutrition your companion receives.

Choosing a Conventional Dog Food

At a recent nutrition conference I attended, veterinary nutritionists agreed that it was impossible to gauge the quality of a dog food based on the food label, ads, brochures, and website information. They advised veterinarians in the audience to make food recommendations based on their clinical experience with patients, to note what brand of food every patient was eating, assess each patient's health, and evaluate any patterns that might appear.

So, how is the typical pet owner supposed to know what commercial food to feed?

Here are some ways to help evaluate a dog food.

- **Cost.** It is impossible to make a high-quality food with cheap ingredients. Inexpensive foods with a preponderance of cheap ingredients, such as corn gluten, wheat, and soy, should be avoided.

- **Meat sources**. Look for foods with as many meat sources as possible in the first three ingredients.
- **Go organic.** Organic ingredients are a plus.
- **Natural preservatives.** Look for natural preservatives such as vitamin C, vitamin E, citric acid, and rosemary.

Rotating Food

Rotating foods can help your dog nutritionally because it mitigates imbalances inherent in any individual diet. Most dogs can tolerate changing foods periodically as long as they are tapered from one diet to the other over the course of a week or so. Each time you go to the store for dog food, simply buy a different brand. If you run into a food that your pet does not tolerate, then avoid that one in the future. Try to find three or four foods to rotate into your dog's diet.

Water

A simple way to improve on commercial dry dog food is to add water. It is true that this will take some of the crunch out of the kibble, but the idea that chewing hard food cleans a dog's teeth is a fallacy. Think about it—chewing on corn chips all day does not prevent plaque buildup on your teeth. Watering down dry food helps bring it to the moisture level of a dog's natural diet. It also keeps the food from expanding after it is swallowed—a process that

Adding water makes dry dog food healthier.

can cause an uncomfortable stretching of the stomach or even bloat (a life-threatening condition).

Healthy Additions

Make your dog's commercial food healthier by supplementing it with real food—food from your table. Yes, I know this concept sounds dangerously close to the forbidden feeding of "table scraps," but that's not exactly what I mean. Table scraps are typically unhealthy for two reasons. First, most of us do not eat healthy foods—feeding your canine companion pizza crusts is definitely not a good idea. Second, the meat odds and ends we discard tend to have a very high fat content, which can touch off digestive upset and contribute to obesity.

Instead of table scraps, I suggest you prepare a healthy meal for yourself, and cook a little extra for your dog. Lean cuts of meat and cooked vegetables can add nutrition and variety to your pet's diet. When you supplement the diet in this way, be sure the real food does not constitute more than 20 percent of the total ration, so the balance of the commercial food is not destroyed. Likewise, be certain to feed proportionately less commercial food so as not to increase your dog's calorie intake.

If you are brave enough, feed your dog's meat serving raw or rare. If you have time, shred his veggies and feed them raw instead of cooked. Raw foods retain more natural nutrients than the same foods in cooked form.

WEIGHTY ISSUES

Whatever feeding strategies you adopt, every dog can benefit from one very important concept: *Keep your dog slim!* A recent study compared two groups of Labrador Retrievers. Group one was allowed to eat as much food as they wanted, while those in group two were fed 25 percent less than the first group. Not surprisingly, the dogs in group one were overweight. Meanwhile, the slender dogs in group two lived on average 1.8 years longer than their chubby counterparts. The group-two dogs also had a 2.8 year delay in onset of symptoms of arthritis and other chronic diseases. Keeping your dog slim can add years to his life and life to his years.

Is My Dog Overweight?

To find out if your dog is at an ideal weight and body condition, using firm pressure, stroke along your dog's sides, behind the shoulders, along the rib cage. You should be able to feel the ribs, like rubbing a washboard. The ribs should be felt easily, but if you can see them, then your dog is too thin. Looking at your dog from the side, you should see an indentation underneath, behind the ribcage. Looking from the top, there should be indentations on either side behind the ribs and in front of the pelvis. It's called a *waist*, and every dog should have one.

The amount of food you feed your dog should be based on his body condition, not arbitrary guidelines. Pet food label feeding recommendations are an estimate. To keep your dog in good shape,

Starting a New Diet

Whenever a dog is switched to a new diet, it is best not to do it "cold turkey" (pardon the pun). A quick change in food causes some dogs to develop gastrointestinal problems. Gradually add in the new food while decreasing the old food by an equal amount. Over the course of a week, the transition can be made smoothly. If your dog has a history of not tolerating any change in his diet, the problem can often be lessened by giving probiotics during the changeover.

Obesity causes many health problems.

start by measuring how much he eats. Once the portions are under control, weigh your dog every two weeks. If he is gaining weight beyond his ideal body condition, then either cut back on his regular diet or switch to a weight-loss formula. If your dog is losing too much weight, then either increase the amount fed or switch to a high-performance diet. Remember that if inclement weather or aging leads to reduced activity for your dog, then his calorie intake should reflect that change.

SUPPLEMENTS

No matter what type of diet you choose to feed your dog, you must add nutrients in the form of supplements. Remember that supplements are so named because they are meant to be given *in addition* to a healthy diet. All the supplements in the world will not make up for poor nutrition.

Synthetic Versus Whole

In general, the best source of nutritional supplements is whole foods, not the synthetic type. Supplements derived from whole foods are made by concentrating the nutrients from food through the removal of water and fiber. These supplements contain the natural vitamin forms and nutrient proportions, plus currently unknown cofactors (see sidebar).

Synthetic supplements come from pharmaceutical companies. They consist of synthetic chemicals made to look like natural compounds. But an animal's body is not easily fooled. Research

The Nutrition Spectrum

From my perspective, a range of preferences exists in canine diets. At the lowest, least desirable level are generic commercial diets. Just up from that are low-quality store brands. At the next level are typical national brands. Better yet are high-end, high-quality "premium" pet foods. Just above this on the list are commercial, processed, natural (if possible, organic) dog foods. Preferable to these would be a well-balanced home-cooked diet. Superior to this is a balanced, raw-food diet—either homemade or commercial—made with conventionally grown ingredients. And the best diet for dogs that I can conceive of is a balanced, raw-food diet made with all organic ingredients.

shows that the body is better able to absorb and utilize vitamins derived from whole foods as opposed to synthetic forms. One study that tested the ability of beta-carotene and vitamin A to prevent cancer in smokers was stopped 21 months early because the synthetic vitamins actually increased the occurrence of cancer.

Do we really know better than Mother Nature? To produce most synthetic supplements, one key ingredient in a particular food is isolated, mimicked in a chemistry lab, and produced in tablet form. Modern nutritional wisdom suggests taking such tablets is basically equivalent to eating the real food. But is taking a vitamin C tablet as good as eating an orange, with all its hundreds of other nutrients? Science is discovering that the body does not recognize synthetic vitamins as food and works hard to get rid of this "foreign material." This process can actually stress the liver and kidneys. Plus, adding a synthetic vitamin supplement to a commercial diet that already contains synthetic vitamins can actually lead to a vitamin overdose. Synthetic vitamins can cause more harm than good.

The whole-food philosophy is based on the idea that, by breaking nutrients apart, the food's synergistic, nutritional nature is lost. Essential cofactors are left behind, leaving the vitamin unable to fully accomplish its mission in the body. From the holistic point of view, food is like a mechanical watch. If you take a watch apart and then try to re-form it using just the hour hand, the spring, and a gear, it will not work well. Similarly, in nutrition, the whole is greater than the sum of its parts. When you add to this the fact that scientists are incapable of exactly duplicating nutrients, then you can see the problems with conventional, synthetic supplements.

Unknown Cofactors

Yes—it is hard to believe—but we do not know everything there is to know about nutrition. New nutrients are being discovered all the time. Ten years ago, we knew nothing about the beneficial phenolic antioxidants in red wine or the health-promoting flavonoids in dark chocolate. It seems that every day new nutrients and phytochemicals are brought to light. Whole-food supplements contain both known and yet-to-be-discovered nutrients.

Supplement Pitfalls

Canine nutritional needs are complicated, and dogs can benefit from the right supplements. But finding the right source of supplements is a challenge. The major issue is reliability. Because there is little federal oversight of nutritional supplements, you cannot be sure that you're getting what the label says.

For example, a study published in June 2000 showed that only six out of twenty-four store-bought glucosamine supplements met label claims—some contained as little as 25 percent of what the label listed. The same study showed that 26 out of 32 health-food store chondroitin supplements had less than 90 percent of label

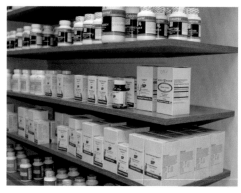

You should add nutrients to your dog's diet in the form of supplements.

Mega Dosing

I am not a fan of mega-dosing vitamins. For example, some dog owners give extra vitamin C to their pets for its well-known antioxidant effect. However, dogs were never meant to consume hundreds of milligrams of vitamin C every day. A recent human study demonstrated that as little as 500 milligrams of vitamin C daily can have a detrimental effect on the immune system. Also, mega-dosing vitamins C and E can interfere with chemotherapy in cancer patients.

claims and 14 of them had less than 10 percent. Standards for supplements are not as rigorous at those for medications, and therefore you cannot trust the labels. If you buy bargain-brand supplements, you are probably wasting your money. So, who or what can you trust? Experience!

This is where your holistically-minded veterinarian comes in handy. Over the years, I've discovered through trial and error certain brands of supplements and particular products that I know I can trust. I am not saying that all other supplements are inferior; only that I know that these work. Your local veterinarian is just as sure to have his own favorites.

Another tip for selecting a trustworthy supplement is to check if the producer is a member of the National Animal Supplement Council (NASC). Seventy-five percent of all animal supplement companies are members of the NASC. These businesses are committed to stringent quality-control standards. The NASC also tracks product safety using a unique adverse-event reporting system. While some good companies are not members of this organization, the NASC seal is a helpful indicator of a reliable animal supplement.

THE FIVE SUPPLEMENTS EVERY DOG NEEDS

In my experience, no matter what kind of diet is being fed, every dog can benefit from the following supplements. Although all of these are helpful for a dog's health, I have listed these supplements in order of importance.

Products range in potency. Also, the ideal dosage depends on the health condition of your pet. For these reasons, I recommend following the package recommendations and the advice of your veterinarian when deciding how much of a supplement to give

#1: A Balanced Multivitamin/Mineral

Vitamins and minerals are nutrients the body needs to function properly and cannot manufacture on its own. Nutritional deficiencies can be found in both commercial and raw food diets. In addition, stresses such as surgery or illness and athletic performance, may require extra nutrition. Also, dogs whose rations have been reduced due to weight issues often need supplements. Multivitamin supplements should be derived from whole-food sources.

#2: Fish Oil

Fish oil is an incredibly important nutrient for all dogs. Both raw food and conventional diets lack the fatty acids supplied by this oil. I have seen almost miraculous responses when fish oil is added to the diets of health-challenged pets. To date, over 2,000 scientific studies tout the many benefits of this supplement, and more studies are being published every year. The importance of fish oil for dogs becomes obvious as we explore the chemistry and biology of fats.

Fat, grease, and oils are made of fatty acids, just as meat is made mostly of proteins. Fatty acids are categorized by their chemical structures, which dictate their effects on the body. Broadly speaking, all fatty acids are either saturated or unsaturated to various degrees. The saturation of a fat has to do with the number of hydrogen atoms attached to the main molecule—the more hydrogen atoms, the more saturation.

Multivitamin supplements should be derived from whole-food sources.

Essential fatty acids (EFAs) are unsaturated fatty acids that the body needs for health but cannot make on its own. EFAs must be obtained from foods. The body needs EFAs to make and repair cell membranes. EFAs are involved with producing energy from food substances and moving that energy throughout the body. They govern growth, vitality, mental state, oxygen transfer, and hemoglobin production, and they control the movement of nutrients through cell membranes. In short, EFAs play a part in almost every function of the body—and two important types are omega-6s and omega-3s.

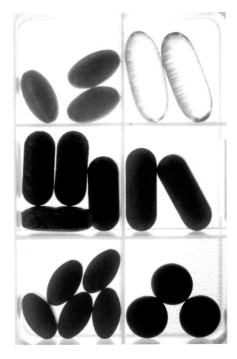

Omega-6 fatty acids are naturally found in grains, plants, and animal-based fat sources such as poultry fat. The conventional commercial canine diet is rich in these oils.

The most important omega-3 fatty acids for dogs are DHA and eicosapentaenoic acid (EPA),

Adding fish oil to the diet can reduce stiffness, pain, and inflammation.

which can be found in fish oils and flaxseed oil. Unlike humans, dogs lack the enzymes necessary to obtain DHA and EPA from flaxseed oil, so fish oil is the preferred supplement for obtaining omega-3 fatty acids. Omega-3 fatty acids are sorely lacking in the vast majority of commercial pet foods.

A balance of omega-6 to omega-3 fatty acids is vital for health. Although the exact healthy ratio has not been conclusively determined, researchers believe that a two-to-one omega-6 to omega-3 ratio is optimal. Alarmingly, many commercial pet foods may contain ratios of up to and above 50-to-1! This dietary imbalance leads to many chronic health disturbances for our canine friends.

Fish Oil and Inflammation

The bodies of animals (people included) are set up with competing mechanisms that, in the normal, healthy state, keep the body in balance. These systems of *homeostasis* can be thought of as a scale weighted equally on each side. As the stresses of life shift body chemistry, a gentle counterbalance can bring the levels back to normal.

One such balance system involves inflammation. Within the body, complicated chemical pathways lead to inflammation (proinflammatory) and counterbalancing pathways suppress inflammation (anti-inflammatory). In a healthy dog, these mechanisms work together in harmony, providing inflammation when needed (when trauma requires the cleanup up of destroyed tissue) and then turning the process off (when the clean up is complete).

EFAs play a key role in both the proinflammatory and anti-inflammatory pathways. Omega-6 fatty acids weight the scale toward inflammation while omega-3s are anti-inflammatory. Now the significance of a dietary imbalance of omega-6 to omega-3 fatty acids becomes apparent. The typical commercial dog food promotes inflammation throughout the body, because of the overabundance of omega-6. Research indicates two specific areas of importance for the proinflammatory effects of pet foods.

The first area is the skin. The skin is the largest organ of the body and, in dogs, the usual place where allergies manifest. Allergies are simply a manifestation of inflammation and are promoted by an unbalanced inflammatory system. Pets are plagued with allergies these days, and I have little doubt that this problem is diet related. Recent research has shown that 45 percent of dogs with inhalant allergies had a good to excellent response to simply raising the omega-3 fatty acid level in their diets to achieve a ratio of 5-to-1 (omega-6 to omega-3).

Joints are second area of the body influenced by the dietary imbalance of EFAs. Many of our dogs suffer from arthritis, and this problem seems to be affecting younger and younger canines. Arthritis is merely an inflammation of the joints. This condition can be predisposed by many factors such as conformation (as with hip dysplasia) or trauma. But research indicates that the lack of dietary omega-3 fatty acids plays a role as well. Studies have shown that adding fish oil to the diet can reduce the stiffness, pain, and inflammation associated with this debilitating disease. Considering what we know about the proinflammatory effects of unbalanced pet foods, it follows that supplementing with fish oil can prevent or reduce the development of arthritis in the first place.

Supplementing your older pet with fish oil may help his cognitive function.

Fish Oil and Cancer

Cancer is the leading cause of death in older cats and dogs. One of the most important areas of research involving the fatty acids found in fish oil (DHA and EPA) is how their supplementation can aid in controlling cancer. According to recent research, adding fish oil to the diet increases the survival time of cancer patients by 30 to 50 percent. It also causes longer periods of remission for cancer patients undergoing chemotherapy, and it counteracts the metabolic changes that cancer can cause, such as characteristic wasting. The study concludes that *the omega-3 fatty acids found in fish oil are probably the most important nutrients to consider for dogs with cancer.*

A closer look at cancer shows that pets produce

cancer cells every day. The reason all of our pets do not die from cancer is because those with a healthy immune system eliminate the abnormal cells before they get out of control. It makes sense that we should do all we can to balance the scales in favor of eradicating cancer cells. Providing fish oil in the diets of healthy pets can help to achieve this goal and prevent cancer.

Fish Oil and Cognitive Function

Earlier, I summarized a study showing that supplementing fish oil in the diets of pregnant females and their offspring doubled the learning ability of those puppies. It's easy to understand when you realize that 5 percent of the brain is made of DHA. If we do not provide the building materials, then the body cannot construct a normally functioning brain.

Research in people, which I believe translates to pets, shows that high dietary intake of fish oil can help with depression and Alzheimer's disease, and can reduce the risk of strokes caused by blood clots. Omega-3s have even been shown to improve schizophrenia and attention deficit/hyperactivity disorders, so it may not be too late for your neurotic Border Collie.

EFA Supplementation

Supplementing the diet with fish oil is preferable to supplementing it with flax seed oil.

Because of the recent research on EFAs, some pet food companies are supplementing certain select diets with fish oil. This is a step in the right direction. However, the effectiveness of this new development is questionable. Due to their chemical structure, EFAs are inherently unstable and reactive—they easily oxidize and become rancid. In fact, EFAs are rendered useless by exposure to heat, light, and air. So, even if plenty of EFAs are present in the food to begin with—and they withstand processing and sitting around on the store shelf—as soon as you open the bag and expose the food to air, the EFAs begin to deactivate. For this reason, I prefer that my patients be supplemented with fish oil that can be properly stored and applied to the food, fresh with each meal.

It is important to carefully research any fish oil supplement to see how it is harvested, packaged, preserved, and tested. To maintain the integrity of the EFAs, the oil must be processed with as little exposure to heat, air, and light as possible. Also, because fish can be a source of mercury and other toxins, it is imperative that the fish used come from unpolluted waters and that testing is done on the oil to ensure purity.

Two rare problems are associated with supplementing fish oil, especially at higher doses. If your pet is prone to pancreatitis (a disease that causes the pancreas to over-respond to dietary fat), then adding fish oil to the diet could aggravate the condition. The other problem that occasionally happens is that the extra oils in the diet can cause diarrhea. If your pet has a tendency toward GI troubles, minimize these issues by starting at a low dose and gradually working your dog up to the desired level.

Cod Liver Oil

I have a caution regarding cod liver oil. Although cod liver oil is a rich source of the same omega-3 EFAs as found in fish oil, it also can contain high levels of vitamin D, depending on the brand. Vitamin D is provided adequately in commercial pet foods, and it is possible to create toxicity by oversupplementing this nutrient. For this reason, I prefer to stick with fish oil.

#3: Digestive Enzymes

Digestive enzymes are chemicals made by the pancreas and excreted into the intestine to further break down food particles so that they can be absorbed into the bloodstream. Ample enzymes are essential for the body to absorb all the nutrients from food. Even healthy animals need extra digestive enzymes.

A closer look at enzymes reveals that every living cell contains enzymes that help it function. When an organism dies, the cell enzymes are released and begin a self-digestion action called *autolysis*. So food, whether plant or animal, begins the digestion process on its own. Unfortunately, heat destroys the cellular enzymes, so cooked and processed foods require extra digestive enzymes for the animal eating these foods to properly process them.

Animals are able to produce fewer and fewer digestive enzymes as they age. This can be a major cause of the wasting seen in elderly pets. Extra enzymes increase the absorption of many nutrients. In fact, essential fatty acids, like those in fish oil, have a 71 percent increase in assimilation when digestive enzymes are taken concurrently. Animals simply thrive when their diet is supplemented with digestive enzymes.

#4: Glucosamine/Chondroitin

The nutrients glucosamine and chondroitin are components of healthy joints. They help joint cartilage maintain its 65 to 80 percent water content that gives the joint its shock-absorbing quality (much like a wet sponge). Joint cartilage lacking these substances becomes like a dry sponge and develops arthritis.

Throughout an animal's life, two competing processes are at work on joint cartilage. On the one hand, some cells continuously break down joint tissue. At the same time, other cells rebuild the tissue. This is how the body refurbishes itself. If the raw ingredients for rebuilding, such as glucosamine and chondroitin, are deficient, then the rebuilding process cannot keep up with the destructive process and the joint degenerates.

Glucosamine and chondroitin not only aid existing arthritis, studies show they help prevent arthritis from developing in the first place. All dogs can benefit from these nutrients—especially performance dogs whose joints take a lot of wear and tear.

Anti-Inflammatory Drugs

Conventional medicine uses drugs to help treat arthritis. The nonsteroidal anti-inflammatory drugs (NSAIDs) used for arthritis decrease inflammation and pain, but also inhibit the cartilage reconstruction process. This worsens the condition they are used to treat.

#5: Probiotics

The canine intestine is teaming with bacteria. In fact, there are many more bacteria in the intestine than there are cells in the body. Some intestinal microbes can cause disease. Others, called *probiotic* bacteria, are actually beneficial because they keep disease-causing germs under control, help to release more nutrients from what's left of the food, and even help strengthen the immune system. An imbalance in the intestinal flora can lead to diarrhea and nutritional deficiencies.

The good bacteria in the intestine can be thrown off by medications (especially antibiotics), dietary irregularities, and stress. If your pet gets diarrhea while on antibiotics, it is usually because of this effect. In the wild, wolves commonly eat their own stool to rebalance their gut bacteria, and this is sometimes the reason our pets resort to *coprophagia* (eating feces).

Probiotics are supplements that help to replenish the good bacteria in the intestine. Most pets do not need to be kept on probiotic supplements continuously, but all dogs need a balancing dose three or four times a year. It is a good practice to give probiotics at the change of seasons as well as during and after treating a pet with any medication.

Louie's Story

Louie, a 90-pound (41 kg) Newfoundland mix breed, was a mess when I first met him. He came to me with an uncertain history. He had been adopted from a veterinary clinic that got him from a kennel that was closed down. He was a young adult, but it was difficult to tell his age—in part because of his disfiguring skin condition.

His coat was sparse, and his skin was leathery and flaky. His body reeked of a nasty, rancid fat smell that characterizes severe skin cases. He had been diagnosed with generalized *demodectic mange*. As mentioned in Chapter 2, demodectic mange is not contagious, and normal animals have a few of these parasites populating their hair follicles.

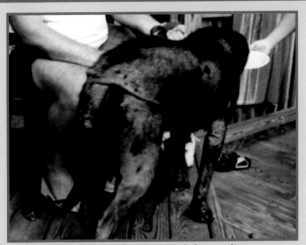

Louie had been treated the conventional way with dips and medications to kill the mites. The trouble with this plan (which often fails) is that the mites are not the problem. Louie did not "catch" these mites. The real problem is that his immune system was incapable of controlling the mites that were a normal part of his skin flora. Louie's immune system needed a boost, and all the drugs used to kill the mites were pointless.

Louie had generalized demodectic mange, which means his immune system had major problems.

I immediately changed Louie from his commercial food to an all raw food diet. I also added a few whole-food supplements, including fish oil. I did nothing to kill the mites except strengthen Louie's system naturally. It took patience, but within a year he had a thick, sleek, healthy hair coat. It was obvious that Louie was made healthier, inside and out, simply by providing his body with the needed nutrients.

Louie after his immune system recovered.

The importance of proper nutrition for dogs cannot be overstated. It is impossible to have a healthy organism without providing the raw materials that Mother Nature intended. I have seen numerous animals overcome troubling conditions simply by making dietary changes. Not every disease can be cured with nutrition, but all conditions can be aided through this natural approach. Healthy nutrition is the foundation for every dog's well-being, which may be further augmented by various holistic therapies.

4

ACUPUNCTURE

A lthough acupuncture is a strange, new therapy for many American pet owners, its origins date back about 8,000 years. The word *acupuncture* comes from two Latin root words: *Acus* meaning *needle* and *pungare* meaning *to pierce*. In the simplest sense, the word acupuncture means to stick someone with a needle. But of course, the treatment is much more complicated than that.

WHAT IS ACUPUNCTURE?

In 1996, the American Veterinary Medical Association (AVMA) defined acupuncture this way: "Veterinary acupuncture and acutherapy involve the examination and stimulation of specific points on the body of non-human animals by the use of acupuncture needles, moxibustion, injections, low-level lasers, magnets, and a variety of other techniques for the diagnosis and treatment of numerous conditions in animals."

Don't worry; I will explain more of this definition throughout this chapter. But as a working definition, let's say that acupuncture involves the use of very fine needles to stimulate special points on the body to induce a curative response.

It is interesting to note that, according to the AVMA, acupuncture is a means of diagnosis as well as treatment. This is because the acupuncturist can detect imbalances in a dog's system by carefully feeling certain acupuncture points. Palpation of the points is part of a thorough acupuncture examination.

Another important point to note is that acupuncture is considered *veterinary medicine*, which means that nonprofessionals are banned from using this modality on animals. It would be considered practicing veterinary medicine without a license for a lay person to use acupuncture on animals. In some states, an exception is made for licensed human acupuncturists.

ACUPUNCTURE BENEFITS

What can acupuncture be used for? Because all disease can be reduced to an imbalance of energy, acupuncture can aid in the treatment of any canine health problem. It is most effective at treating painful conditions such as arthritis, back problems, and injuries. Acupuncture is also very beneficial for those suffering from such neurological conditions as paralysis and stroke. I have had success treating internal medical problems, including kidney failure, liver failure, thyroid disease, asthma, vomiting, diarrhea, and reproductive problems. It can be used as an adjunct treatment for seizures, and can even improve the quality of life for cancer patients.

When applied properly, acupuncture does not cause side effects (as drugs often do), and it can be used alone or in conjunction with conventional therapies.

ACUPUNCTURE HISTORY

According to an ancient Chinese legend, acupuncture was discovered when a warrior rode a lame horse into battle and the horse became sound after being pierced by arrows at key points. More realistically, the roots of acupuncture can be traced back to at least 2000 BCE. At that time, Taoist monks in China spent much of their time in deep meditation, which helped them become aware of the subtle energies in their bodies. Their contemplative lifestyles kept them very close to the natural world, and they developed a unique philosophy of life and medicine. The earliest artifacts of acupuncture are stone implements called *bian,* which were used to stimulate points on the body. (Ouch!)

By 1500 to 1000 BCE, Chinese acupuncturists developed bronze needles. Some time between 1122 and 770 BCE, certain acupuncturists branched into treating only animals and became the world's first documented veterinarians. In 1929, the Chinese government outlawed acupuncture in an attempt to modernize medical care. The practice became somewhat clandestine until it was restored to a prominent place by the communist government when it took power in the 1940s.

The spread of acupuncture to the West was facilitated by Jesuit missionaries who established contact between Europe and China in the 1600s. The use of acupuncture by Western veterinarians was first documented by the British Veterinary Association in 1828.

Acupuncture and Allergies

In my experience, skin allergies represent the area of least effectiveness for acupuncture. Luckily, nutritional supplements, herbs, and a healthy lifestyle can help in this area.

Although acupuncture was introduced into the United States in the nineteenth century, it did not catch on until the early 1970s, when President Nixon took his historic trip to China. During that trip, a reporter traveling with Nixon became ill and was treated with acupuncture. The resulting media coverage led to widespread interest in acupuncture in America.

In 1975, the International Veterinary Acupuncture Society (IVAS) was formed in the United States. This group's courses for veterinarians became more and more popular throughout the 1980s and 1990s. Today, besides the IVAS course, several other organizations instruct veterinarians in the practice of acupuncture, and some courses are taught as postgraduate-level classes at veterinary colleges.

HOW DOES ACUPUNCTURE WORK?

This is almost always the first question I'm asked by people who are contemplating the use of acupuncture. First, let's take a look at how acupuncture functions as a part of Traditional Chinese Medicine (TCM), then we'll discuss Western scientific theories of acupuncture.

Acupuncture involves the use of very fine needles to stimulate special points on the body.

Traditional Chinese Medicine

To understand acupuncture, it is necessary to recognize that the ancient Chinese had a much different way of looking at the body than we currently do in the West. Early Chinese doctors did not have blood work, X-rays, or other sophisticated diagnostic tests. These ancient physicians were armed only with their five senses, astounding reasoning powers, experience, and intuition. They were so in touch with their bodies and with nature that they were able to develop an intricate medical model that has withstood the test of time. This medical system developed into what today we call TCM.

In the West, we credit the discovery of blood circulation to William Harvey, in 1628; in fact, the Chinese documented this information in 200 BCE. We believe that diabetes was first understood by Thomas Wills in 1600. However, the Chinese were

The Ice Man

In 1991, the body of a man dating back to 3200 BCE was found in the Italian Alps. The **Ice Man**, as he came to be known, was a unique, ancient human specimen. Because the body was frozen, the skin was well preserved. As scientists examined his skin, they were immediately drawn to various tattoos on his body. It is well documented that ancient cultures often decorated their skin with such markings. The unusual thing about the Ice Man's tattoos was that many were found under his clothing—not where you would expect adornments.

A closer look at the tattoos revealed that many of them demarcated acupuncture points. When an acupuncturist was consulted and asked why he might use these particular points, he responded that the points would typically be used for a person with back problems. Incredibly, body imaging of the **Ice Man** revealed that he did indeed have arthritis of his spine. How can it be that a non-Asian man in Italy received acupuncture treatment in 3200 BCE? Apparently, even the history of acupuncture is quite a mystery.

The roots of acupuncture can be traced back to China, 4000 years ago.

treating it 1,000 years earlier. The use of inoculations to prevent disease outbreaks began in the West in 1714, but this technology was originated by the Chinese, who first developed the practice around 900 CE. We began using thyroid hormone medicinally in 1890, but the Chinese were using it as early as 600 CE. In the late 1800s, as many Europeans made the long journey from the Old World to America, we became aware of the importance of nutritional deficiencies. The Chinese had this understanding in 400 BCE, and effectively used foods as part of medical therapy. We thought we were so cool in the 1960s when we discovered biorhythms—but the Chinese were using information about biorhythms in 200 BCE.

So, maybe we have more to learn from the Chinese than we would like to believe. Although their terminology and medical understanding is very foreign to our way of thinking, I believe there is true value in making the effort to understand Chinese medicine. For the ancient Chinese, healthcare was a way of life. Diet, exercise, massage, meditation, sleep patterns, work patterns, herbs, and acupuncture were all integrated to maintain balance within the body. At the heart of TCM is the concept of *Qi* (sometimes spelled *Chi*).

Qi

Qi is life force energy. It is the vital energy that animates a living creature. Consider the difference between a live dog and a dead dog. They both have a brain, they both have a heart, and they both have blood. What then differentiates the living from the dead? According to the Chinese, the answer is *Qi*. The live dog has it, and the dead dog does not.

Qi has both structural and functional qualities. It is that substance from which all physical form is composed. It is also the energy that flows in a cyclic, orderly course throughout the channels of the body, allowing for the normal functioning of organs and tissues. *Qi* is matter on the verge of becoming energy, and energy on the verge of materializing. This sounds very strange to us until we consider the implications of Albert Einstein's famous equation: $E = mc^2$. This simple formula states that energy (E) and matter or mass (m) are essentially two different forms of the same substance. That substance is *Qi*.

The medical implications of *Qi* are straightforward. Health is the state of harmonious flow of *Qi* in the channels, organs, and

In TCM, diet, exercise, massage, meditation, sleep patterns, work patterns, herbs, and acupuncture are all integrated to maintain balance within the body.

Five Basic Functions of *Qi*

1. **Qi** is the source of all harmonious transformation in the body, such as the transformation of food into energy.

2. **Qi** is the source of, and accompanies all movement in the body, including the movement of the blood throughout the body, the contraction of muscles, and even the movement of molecules into and out of cells.

3. **Qi** warms the body, so it is responsible for metabolism.

4. **Qi** protects the body as part of the immune system.

5. **Qi** governs the retention of the organs and substances of the body—it keeps everything in its place.

tissues of the body. Disease is caused by an interruption in the flow of *Qi*. Any time an organ is not functioning properly—as in kidney failure, or a limb not moving freely because of arthritis—we can say a disturbance of *Qi* is present.

Yin and Yang

Yin and *yang* comprise another important TCM medical concept. The idea of yin and yang came from ancient times in China, and was suggested by the way a mountain looks. A mountain has a sunny side, referred to as *yang*, and a shaded side, referred to as *yin*. So, one mountain has these two opposite yet complementary aspects.

The Chinese believed that everything in existence has both a yin and yang nature as seen in the list below:

Yin	Yang
Darkness	Light
Night	Day
Female	Male
Rest	Activity
Heavy	Light
Solid	Gas
Matter	Energy
Cold	Hot
Damp	Dry
Weak	Strong
Inhibition	Excitement
Structure	Function

You can see how this can apply to current medical terms:

Yin	Yang
Chronic	Acute
Nonvirulent	Virulent
Hypothermia	Fever
Hypofunction	Hyperfunction

Yin and yang represent relative opposites. For example, the room you are in may be considered yin with respect to light compared to the sunlit outside, and yet it may be yang compared to a dark closet. Thus, yin and yang can exist simultaneously. Therefore, no absolute yin or complete yang exists.

All diagnosis and treatment in TCM may be reduced to the concept of yin and yang. Health is simply a state of harmonious balance between yin and yang; disease is a condition of imbalance between yin and yang.

Chinese Organ Systems

Chinese organ systems use the same names that Western medicine gives to the major organs, but they believe these same

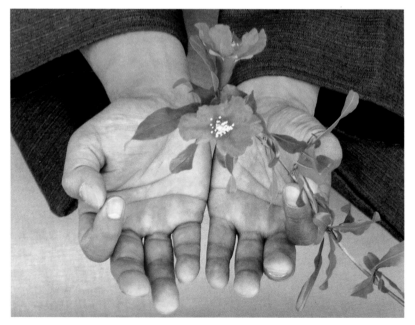

Qi is life force energy.

Tai Chi

The Chinese captured the concept of yin and yang in the symbol known as the **Tai Chi**, pictured here.

In this diagram, the black areas denote yin and the white spaces are yang. Notice how the figure demonstrates the dynamic nature of yin and yang. In addition, note that in the area of maximum darkness a point of light exists, just as the stars and moon light up the midnight sky. A spot of dark is also found in the widest area of light, as the shade of a tree offers refuge from the midday sun.

organs have very different functions. In TCM, the organs are more a collection of functions rather than physical structures. (To differentiate the Chinese organs from the Western understanding of them, we will capitalize the name for the Chinese organs.) For example, the Chinese Liver is responsible for the smooth flow of *Qi* throughout the body and the Chinese Spleen is responsible for digesting food.

All organs are classified as either yin or yang and are placed in functional pairs. The following is a list of the major Chinese organs.

Yin	Yang
Heart	Small Intestine
Pericardium	Triple Heater
Lung	Large Intestine
Spleen	Stomach
Liver	Gallbladder
Kidney	Bladder

After looking at this list, the first question likely to come to mind is, "What the heck is a Triple Heater?" Again, the Chinese looked at organs as a group of functions. The Triple Heater involves hormone balance and fluid transport in the body. Although you will never dissect a body and find a Triple Heater, that "organ" is an important part of the Chinese system.

Further study of this list reveals that the Chinese seemed to have overlooked the brain as a major organ. The reason for this apparent blunder is that the Chinese consider that each organ has consciousness. For example, the Liver is a source of anger (you may have heard of someone having a bilious personality), the emotion for the lungs is grief (when you grieve you often sob), and the Kidneys house fear (when you are really frightened you might wet your pants). As strange as this notion sounds to us, recent research adds credence to this concept.

Dr. Candace Pert, who in 1972 discovered the opiate receptor on brain cells, has done significant research in the area of neurochemistry. She discovered that our emotions are mediated by messenger molecules called *neuropeptides*. Biologists have commonly considered that communication in the brain happens like the wiring of a computer—from neuron to neuron through the nerve cell connections called *synapses*. To the contrary, Dr. Pert discovered that only 2 percent of the brain's communication happens this way. Amazingly, 98 percent of brain communication is accomplished using neuropeptides. Furthermore, every organ in the body has receptors for these molecules of emotion. Not only that, every organ of the body produces neuropeptides. This proves that the mind is not confined to the brain. Apparently, the Chinese were not too far off in their beliefs. Remember that the next time you have a *gut feeling*.

Meridians are the pathways that demark the flow of Qi.

Meridians

Meridians are the pathways that demark the flow of *Qi*. Actually, the word meridian is a mistranslation of the Chinese term. A meridian is considered an imaginary line, such as the meridian lines on the globe. The Chinese never thought of these as imaginary lines. For the Chinese, the meridians are truly channels of energy that flow on the inside as well as the outside of the body. They therefore link the exterior of the body with the internal organs. *Qi* flows through the channels in a particular direction, and it flows from one channel to another via connecting pathways. Along these channels lie most of the acupuncture points.

There are fourteen main acupuncture meridians. Each channel is named for the TCM organ to which it is most strongly associated. The channels are also paired in the same yin-yang relationship as the organs. Every acupuncture meridian is mirrored on both sides of the body. So, just as there is a Large Intestine Meridian that starts on the right index finger and ends at the nose, there is a Large Intestine Meridian that goes from the left index finger to the nose.

Along with the fourteen paired meridians, two unpaired channels exist. One travels up the front midline of the body and is called the Conception Vessel Meridian. The other courses up the back midline of the body and is called the Governing Vessel Meridian.

Acupuncture points are discrete spots on the surface of the body.

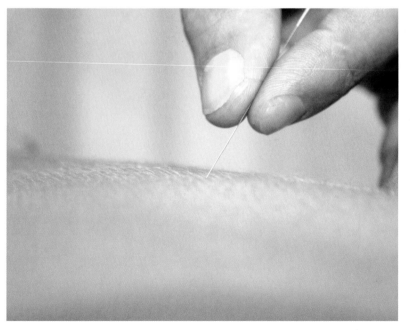

Acupuncture Points

Acupuncture points are very special, discrete spots on the surface of the body. The diameter of each point is in the range of 1/8 to 1/4 inch (3 to 6 mm) for most dogs. The points allow access to the energy channels of the body. Each point is like a dam along a river. Needling an acupuncture point can increase or decrease the energy flow at that spot in the channel, which can help to balance the overall *Qi* of the body.

Over 360 acupuncture points are present on the meridians. The Chinese named each point to either indicate its special function or to denote its location. For example, *he gu* means *adjoining valleys* and refers to the point's location in the web of the hand, between the thumb and forefinger. *Zu san li* is located just below the knee and means *foot three miles*. It is a strong, energizing point on the body. Legend has it that this name was given because Chinese messengers were treated with acupuncture at this point every three miles along their journey to keep them going.

The modernized acupuncture system has abandoned the naming of the points in favor of numbering them. Today, each point is denoted by the meridian on which it lies and the sequential point number along the flow of that channel. For example, *he gu* is known as Large Intestine 4 (LI 4) because it is the fourth point on the Large Intestine meridian. *Zu san li* has become Stomach 36 (ST 36) because it is the thirty-sixth point on the Stomach meridian. The new scheme is very functional and easier to remember—but it is not as poetic as the ancient Chinese intended.

Scientific Theories on Acupuncture

Now that we've looked at how acupuncture works by

Acupuncture as Anesthesia

Acupuncture cannot be used for anesthesia. Acupuncture causes pain relief, not unconsciousness. It is true that the analgesic effects of acupuncture are adequate for surgeons to perform operations on people. However, this does not translate well to pets. A person having surgery under acupuncture analgesia can understand the importance of lying still, while an animal cannot. Also, although the patient feels no pain, he does feel pulling and other strange sensations. For these reasons, acupuncture is not used as the sole means of restraint for canine surgical patients.

understanding the basics of TCM, let's study some of the Western theories on how acupuncture works, using a scientific point of view. (I personally believe that acupuncture utilizes a unique system incorporating aspects of all the given theories. The following theories require advanced degrees in anatomy, neurology, and physiology to truly comprehend, so I'll try to simplify things to make it all readily understandable.)

The Gate Theory

The *gate theory* was one of the first explanations of how the pain-relieving properties of acupuncture work. It holds that acupuncture causes *analgesia* (pain relief) through stimulation of inhibitory *interneurons* (nerve fibers that intercept pain signals before they reach the brain).

Manipulating the Body's Pharmacy

Acupuncture raises the levels of endorphins, serotonin, reproducitve hormones, and cortisol.

Anyone who has had a serious injury has likely experienced an inhibitory interneuron in action. Many times, immediately after severe trauma, the affected area is numb for a brief period. This phenomenon has an evolutionary benefit. Imagine a caveman getting bitten by a saber-toothed tiger. If the unfortunate victim were immobilized with pain, he would become dinner. The inhibitory interneuron effect allowed the Neanderthal to escape certain death.

So, according to the gate theory of acupuncture, the acupuncture needle stimulates an inhibitory interneuron that turns off the pain signal to the brain, numbing any soreness.

The Humoral Theory

The *humoral theory* (where *humor* refers to bodily fluid) attempts to explain how acupuncture changes the chemistry of the bloodstream by delivering various messenger molecules throughout the body.

Early on in Western acupuncture research, it was evident that this therapy had a relaxing effect on the entire body. In an attempt to understand this process, scientists joined the bloodstreams of two rabbits and then performed acupuncture on one of them. To their amazement, both bunnies relaxed. It was evident that acupuncture did not just affect the nervous system, but also caused the release of something into the blood. Later, researchers discovered that the relaxation effect is caused by *endorphins*—the body's internal tranquilizers.

Acupuncture not only manipulates the level of endorphins in the system but also has the potential to adjust the levels of serotonin, reproductive hormones, cortisol, and many other internal messenger molecules. In other words, according to the humoral theory, acupuncture allows the practitioner to access and manipulate the body's own pharmacy.

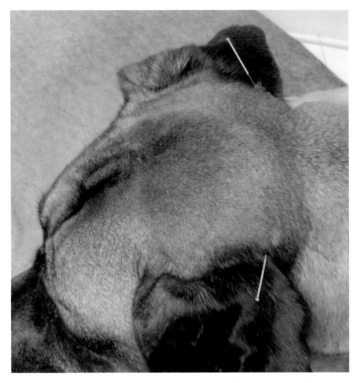

Needling points on the body has biological effects on the surrounding tissue.

The Autonomic Theory

The *autonomic theory* explains that acupuncture utilizes certain reflexes within the nervous system. The autonomic nervous system is the division of the nervous system that responds automatically—without conscious thought. It is responsible for keeping the heart beating at an appropriate rate, moving food through the digestive system, constricting blood vessels, and other vital functions.

The body's nerve pathways contain *viscerosomatic reflexes*. These responses are evidence of neurological communication between the internal organs (viscera) and the outer body (soma). An example of a viscerosomatic reflex is the pain radiating down the inside of the arm that heart attack victims experience. (Incidentally, the Chinese Heart Meridian happens to run down the inside of the arm.) In this case, an event inside the body (heart attack) is affecting the outside of the body (arm pain).

The viscerosomatic reflex responds in both directions. In other words, just as events inside the body can affect the outside, so stimulating the outside of the body with needles can cause changes inside. The autonomic theory explains many of the incredible healing effects of acupuncture.

The Local Effects Theory

The *local effects theory* of acupuncture simply explains the fact that needling points on the body has biological effects on the surrounding tissue. One such effect is that the needle causes *microtrauma*. It damages a very small amount of tissue. Tissue damage causes inflammation and that leads to a healing response by the body. Of course, we are talking about a microscopic amount of damage. However, because acupuncture points have a unique concentration of nerves, blood vessels, and inflammatory cells (as discussed below), the needling effects are augmented.

A second local effect of acupuncture involves the fact that many acupuncture points are at the motor point of muscles. Stimulating these points can relieve muscle spasms. This effect is especially helpful around the spine. The muscle spasms caused by back problems often exacerbate the situation. By relaxing the muscles, acupuncture can help the spine return to normal function more quickly.

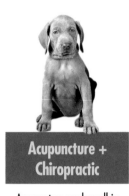

Acupuncture + Chiropractic

Acupuncture works well in conjunction with chiropractic care for the treatment of back and neurological conditions.

The Bioelectric Theory

The *bioelectric theory* is based on the fact that an electrical field surrounds the body. Some scientists theorize that this field acts as a template for the body's physical structure. Think about it—we know that DNA codes for the development of all the organs in the body, but how does it know *where* to put the various organs? How does the liver know to form in the abdomen and the brain in the head? Our current understanding of genetics cannot answer these questions. According to the bioelectric theory, the electrical field around the body guides not only the development of the organism but also its healing and repair. An interesting experiment

demonstrates the implications of this idea.

Orthopedic surgeon Dr. Robert O. Becker studied the body's electrical field. He became interested in the difference between salamanders and frogs. A salamander is considered a *regenerator* because, if a limb is amputated, it will grow back. A frog is a *non-regenerator* because if a limb is amputated it will not grow back. Both animals are amphibians, but salamanders have this very intriguing ability to regenerate body parts. What could possibly account for this healing capacity?

Dr. Becker found that the electrical field at the amputation site of the salamander is different from that of the frog. When the researcher mimicked the frog's electrical field at the amputation stump of the salamander, its limb did not grow back. When he replicated the salamander's electrical field on the frog's amputation site, significant regrowth of the limb occurred. Dr. Becker actually repeated this experiment with some success in laboratory rats as well. From this research, we can see the significance of manipulating the body's electrical field.

It is known that needling the body causes a change in the electrical charge of the tissue. This adjustment of tissue charge changes the surrounding electrical field. The bioelectric theory of acupuncture considers that this ability to manipulate the body's electrical field accounts for the healing effect of acupuncture. This

During treatment, acupuncture needles are placed at acupuncture points on your dog's body.

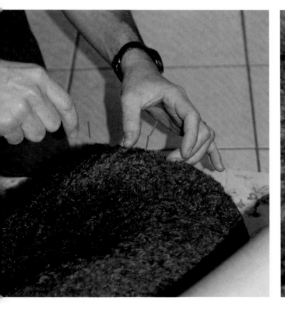

may also explain the importance of the difference in electrical resistance at acupuncture points versus other areas of skin (as discussed in the following section).

DOES ACUPUNCTURE WORK?

With an understanding of the theories behind acupuncture under our belts, it's time to look at its efficacy—in other words, does this modality actually work?

Acupuncture is the most researched therapy within holistic medicine. Many studies have proven its efficacy at relieving pain. In fact, pain relief is probably the most common reason people seek an acupuncturist. However, research has shown many other neurological effects of acupuncture, including hastened recovery from strokes and improved nerve regeneration.

Research has shown that acupuncture has healing effects on other systems of the body as well. It can help aid with the pain and time involved with the birthing process, improve bladder problems, and reduce urinary incontinence. Acupuncture can be used to reduce blood pressure, improve heart function, and increase exercise performance. It is well known for reducing nausea and can decrease gastric acid secretion. Acupuncture has also proven effective as a treatment for asthma. There is almost no condition that cannot be improved with the use of acupuncture.

Do Meridians and Points Exist?

Research validates the existence of the Chinese concept of acupuncture meridians and points. The electrical resistance of the skin is lower at acupuncture points than at nonacupuncture points. Thus, electricity flows more readily at acupuncture points than at other areas of the skin.

Biopsies of acupuncture points reveal that each point is centered on a bundle of microscopic nerves and blood vessels. A higher than normal number of *mast cells* also occur at acupuncture points. Mast cells play a key role in the inflammatory response of the body.

Three-quarters of all acupuncture points are located at the motor points of muscles. The motor point of a muscle is the place where the least amount of stimulation causes the maximum amount of relaxation for that muscle. Many acupuncture points are also over superficial nerves or groups of nerves.

From this research, we can see that acupuncture points are

Willie's Story

Willie, a rugged, lovable Rottweiler, first came to me in March of 2004, but his problems began a year earlier. In the spring of 2003, at the age of 11, his rear legs became progressively weaker and uncoordinated, causing him to have difficulty managing steps and getting into the car. Conventional veterinary care did not help, and Willie's condition continued to worsen. His caregivers, Mary Catherine and Jeff, were heartbroken when they were told that he had arthritis and that they should expect this deterioration in an "old dog."

Mary Catherine, Willie's self-proclaimed "mom," was especially devastated. She and Willie had spent eight years on the show circuit together. Willie thoroughly enjoyed the rides to the events—he was one of the special dogs who was allowed to sit on the seat while the others were confined to kennels in the back of the van. The outstanding canine athlete had a long and varied career. He was an American Kennel Club (AKC) champion and multiple "Best of Breed" winner. He also held an AKC sheepherding title and was a registered therapy dog. Finally, as a blood donor for the University of Pennsylvania, he helped to save other pets in dire need. It was difficult for Mary Catherine to watch her dear friend slowly slip away. The once wild Willie was reduced to a sluggish shadow of his former self.

Jeff and Mary Catherine had resigned themselves to Willie's hopeless prognosis until they saw the incredible recovery of Zeus, a friend's ailing seven-year-old Rottweiler. Zeus had been crippled by a herniated neck disc for over a year. His condition quickly improved with acupuncture, so Mary Catherine tagged along for one of Zeus's treatments to check it out. As unorthodox as the therapy appeared, it was hard to argue with success. Mary Catherine decided to give it a try—maybe there was hope for Willie after all.

Willie's mom and dad noticed improvement after the first treatment. As the weekly acupuncture continued, he regained his strength and had less trouble navigating steps. Soon, he no longer fell over when bumped by one of the other dogs in the household. He had even re-established his dominant position among the seven Rottweilers in the family pack.

Mary Catherine was especially pleased and saw more recovery than she anticipated. For some time, Willie was able to truly enjoy life. Mary Catherine was deeply moved when Willie was able to get up on the passenger seat and ride next to her on one of their subsequent drives, just like old times. She was delighted to have her old friend back for another six months before he finally passed away.

Willie during an acupuncture treatment.

Acupuncture needles come to a tapered point that pierces the tissue and causes little discomfort.

indeed unique. The fact that they have unusual electrical features must play a roll in how they work. Also, these points seem to allow special access to the blood vascular and nervous systems. Finally, needling many of the points can have a relaxing effect on the underlying muscles.

Tracing the Meridians

In an attempt to further understand acupuncture, scientists have injected mildly radioactive material at acupuncture points so that they could trace any flow of fluid. They found that the material did not follow the course of blood vessels, nerves, or lymphatics but instead traced the course of the meridians. When they injected the fluid into nonacupuncture points, the material stayed where it was injected.

Pilomotor Reaction

A *pilomotor reaction* is the phenomenon of the hairs standing on end (as when a person has an extremely frightful or spooky feeling). Occasionally, a pilomotor reaction occurs along the Bladder Meridian in horses when several points along the Bladder Meridian are needled. Amazingly, and on rare occasions, the hairs at acupuncture points all along the Bladder Meridian stand erect. There is no scientific explanation for this spontaneous occurrence, other than the fact that acupuncture points and meridians do exist.

ACUPUNCTURE METHODS: WAYS OF STIMULATING THE POINTS

Many methods are used to stimulate acupuncture points and achieve a healing effect.

Needles

Of course, the use of the traditional acupuncture needle is the most common method—but even acupuncture needles come in a multitude of varieties. Traditional needles have a copper wire handle coiled around the blunt end, and a stainless steel shaft. It is believed that this configuration enhances the electrical effect of needling.

Newer needles have been designed to allow them to slide into the tissue in a smooth, painless fashion. Some have plastic handles and are coated with silicone to ease needle insertion. I have found that, although these are more comfortable, the easier a needle slides in, the easier it will fall out, which can be a problem with an active canine patient.

Acupuncture needles differ from the hypodermic needles used for injections. Hypodermic needles have a beveled edge that cuts through tissue, causing trauma and pain. Acupuncture needles come to a tapered point that pierces the tissue and causes little discomfort.

Aquapuncture

In addition to needles, aquapuncture is another way to stimulate the body's points. This procedure involves the injection of a small amount of fluid into the acupuncture point. Most

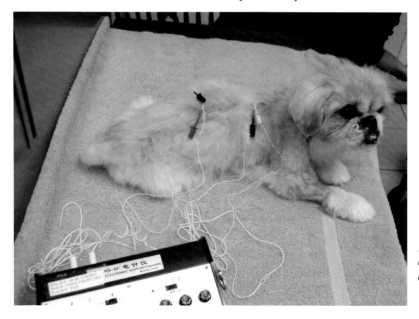

Electrical instruments can be used to stimulate acupuncture points.

The Chinese herb moxa can be used to stimulate acupuncture points.

commonly, vitamin B$_{12}$ is used for the injection. The advantage of aquapuncture is that it is quicker and does not require the animal to lie still. I use this option if the patient is unruly or unable to be calm in the veterinary setting.

Cold Laser

A cold laser can also be used to stimulate acupuncture points. This technology involves the use of a pen-like probe that pinpoints the laser beam into the acupuncture point. Absolutely no discomfort is involved with this procedure, so it works well for the pain-intolerant patient.

Electrical Instruments

Electrical instruments can be used to stimulate acupuncture points. In one type, a probe that delivers a slight electrical shock is touched to the points. The skin is not pierced, but some pets do not appreciate the mild shock sensation. Another electrical technique involves attaching electrodes to inserted needles. A low-intensity electrical current is then run through the tissue from one set of points to another. This allows for greater nerve stimulation and muscle relaxation than with the use of needles alone.

Moxa

Sometimes the Chinese herb *moxa* is used to stimulate acupuncture points. The ground, dried plant material (from the herb mugwort or *Artemisia vulgaris*) is compressed to form either cigar-like sticks or small wads called *punks*. The sticks are lit, and then the smoldering stick is either held over the point or touched to a needle placed in the point. Burning punks of moxa can be attached directly to the handle of an inserted needle. The smell of burning moxa is said to resemble that of marijuana—a fact that has led to more than one interesting situation in my office.

Moxa is used when the energy imbalance calls for warming the meridians, such as the arthritis patient whose condition is made worse by cold weather. The practitioner must be very careful using moxa on dogs due to the sensitivity of their skin to heat and the flammability of their fur.

TREATING WITH ACUPUNCTURE: WHAT TO EXPECT

Because acupuncture developed over thousands of years and over a vast area, many systems are used. In general, the Chinese believe that, to be successful, the patient must feel a strong sensation when the needle is inserted. The Japanese use a gentler approach. In France, acupuncturists practice an entirely unique system of using only points in the ear to affect the body. Every veterinary acupuncturist has his own technique for treating animals. There is no right or wrong way to do it.

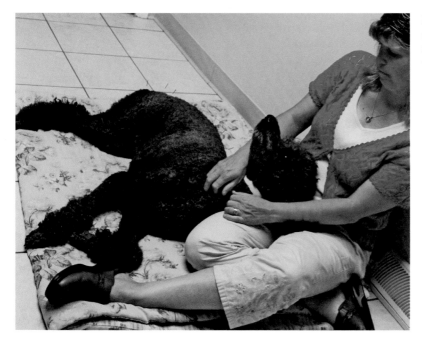

During treatment, your pet can lie on a blanket or baby mattress with you sitting with them.

Frequency

The initial frequency of the treatments ranges from every few days to once a week. That timing is continued until the improvement plateaus. At that point, the time between sessions is gradually increased to the maximum time span that will maintain the dog's health. Acute injuries often do not require maintenance treatments, while most chronic conditions must be treated every four to twelve weeks for life.

Response Time

Although some patients respond quickly, it may take up to eight treatments to start to see a response from acupuncture. The initial improvements usually consist of vague signs of brightened attitude and enhanced well-being. Acute injuries tend to respond faster than chronic conditions.

During Treatment

At my office, during the treatment itself, I usually have the pet lie on a blanket or baby mattress with their owner sitting with them, although some dogs are more comfortable standing. After a brief evaluation of the animal's progress, I insert the needles and leave the room while relaxing music plays softly in the background. After the allotted time, I return to the room and remove the needles. Often the animal is then turned to lie on the opposite side so other points can be accessed.

Concerns

Pain

The biggest concern that most people have about acupuncture is that the needles will cause pain. In my experience, the patient rarely feels the prick of the needles. As a matter of fact, some animals fall asleep during the treatment, which may last from five to forty-five minutes depending on the problem being addressed.

Dogs are often apprehensive for their first treatment or two; after all, I'm asking them to lie down and relax in a vet's office (nothing fun ever happens there!). Amazingly, after a few sessions, most dogs come to enjoy their therapy and actually pull their owners back to the treatment room. They enjoy the endorphin high that needling gives them. Some of my long-term patients are so

Stoney's Story

Stoney was fourteen years old when he was carried into my office by his owners. His rear legs had been paralyzed for seven weeks, and conventional treatments had not helped. X-rays revealed severe arthritis of his spine, but that alone did not explain his condition. Possible causes for his neurological deficit included a spinal tumor, a ruptured disc, or even a blood clot to the spinal cord. A diagnosis could only be made with an MRI or myelogram, but his owners did not think it was in his best interest to put Stoney through those tests. Acupuncture was his last chance.

An aged pet with longstanding rear-leg paralysis does not warrant a rosy outlook, and I was not optimistic about the ability of acupuncture to help him. Even after hearing about the acupuncture process and the poor prognosis, Stoney's owners decided that they wanted to give him every chance they could, and we proceeded with the treatment with hope in our hearts.

Stoney came to my office for weekly treatments, always right on schedule. When his owners carried him in for his eighth session, I told them that I was seeing no improvement and suggested it was time to admit defeat. But his owners were encouraged by the fact that he had begun to wag his tail, so the treatments continued. You could have picked my jaw off the floor when Stoney walked into my office two treatments later!

We were able to taper his treatments to every three to four weeks and maintain Stoney's mobility. He enjoyed another three years with his owners until his body finally gave out at the age of seventeen.

Stoney relaxing during acupuncture.

accustomed to the procedure that if I'm a few minutes late getting into the room, I find them lying on the blanket with a dazed look in their eyes and a puddle of drool under their mouths. They have obviously started without me—I often wonder if I even need to put the needles in!

As accepting as most dogs are to acupuncture needling, a few pain-intolerant canines never get used to the sensation. For them, laser treatments are more appropriate.

The Needles

The biggest concern I have is the remote possibility that a pet may decide to remove a needle with his mouth and then swallow it. I always caution the owner to keep an eye on her dog during the treatment.

The biggest obstacle to an acupuncture treatment is keeping the pet still while the needles work their magic. If the animal fidgets just a little, then some of the needles may fall out. Although this is not a harmful situation, it is not very helpful. It is important for both the dog and his human companion to rest in a comfortable position for the treatment.

Does It Always Work?

Acupuncture is not a panacea. Even in China, it is only *part* of the medical system. If after eight to ten treatments there is no improvement in the patient, then acupuncture is probably not going to help.

FINDING A VETERINARY ACUPUNCTURIST

Thankfully, acupuncture is becoming more accepted within the veterinary community every day. It is by far the most familiar holistic therapy used by veterinarians. Currently, four different institutions offer certification courses for veterinarians in the United States, including two at veterinary colleges. Certification in veterinary acupuncture involves 150 hours of class work plus testing, a preceptorship, and continuing education.

To locate a certified veterinary acupuncturist near you, check out the resources at the back of this book.

HOME CARE: ACUPRESSURE

Acupressure is simply using touch to activate acupuncture points to help balance the body's energy system. All the points, meridians, and treatment strategies are the same as those used in acupuncture. Anyone can learn to do acupressure, and this technique can be practiced at home.

Acupressure can help with many conditions involving pain, arthritis, organ failure—basically any condition that can be helped by acupuncture. Applying acupressure to your pet can also help to extend the time between acupuncture appointments or ward off problems before they become serious. However, acupressure is not a substitute for proper veterinary care. If your pet is seriously ill, be sure to see your veterinarian.

Too Tired?

Do not do acupressure on an animal who is exhausted from a workout, because the pet's energy level is too low to be properly manipulated.

Getting Started

Several important principles are involved in stimulating the acupressure points.

Get Relaxed

It is optimal if both the giver and receiver of the therapy are relaxed and at ease. Be sure you and your pet are in a comfortable position. Allow at least a half-hour of uninterrupted time for the session. Take a few deep, relaxing breaths to blow off the day's stress. Remember that your pet can pick up on your emotions. If you find that you just cannot unwind, then don't do the acupressure session.

Food

Acupressure should not be performed on a pet who has a full stomach. Just after eating, the body's *Qi* energy is busy transforming and transporting the energy from the food. Also, a hungry animal will likely be distracted and therefore does not make an ideal subject. Acupressure is best applied to a pet an hour or so before or after meals.

Using Your Fingers

Any blunt object can be used to apply the pressure. You can use a knuckle or even a pencil eraser, but I find that the fingertips work best. Due to their sensitivity, your fingertips make great point detectors. Your fingertips also can sense the right amount of pressure to use. Finally, fingertips are the end points of some of your channels, a fact that makes them especially well adapted for manipulating *Qi* energy.

Hitting the Target

Acupressure points are like targets. The closer to the bull's eye you are, the stronger the effect. But, as long as you are close, you are likely to do some good. If you happen to be way off target, don't worry—you can't do any harm by pressing on a nonacupressure point. If you mistakenly stimulate the wrong point, remember that this system is designed to rebalance the body, and energy is not likely to flow where it is not needed. However, prolonged or repeated inappropriate use of the system could possibly worsen a condition.

Applying Acupressure

Your attitude and intention are by far the most important part of the healing process. Your intention carries energy. Be sure to hold the intention of doing the best possible good for your pet throughout the acupressure session. Focus this intention on your fingertip and into your pet.

To apply acupressure:

1. Start with your dog lying down (although this can be done standing up as well, since relaxation is part of the prep work, lying down is the usual and preferred position).

Cautions to Consider

- Apply pressure gradually. If oversensitivity occurs at any point, do not use it.
- Do not use acupressure on a pregnant animal. Some points can induce labor.
- Acupressure must be used cautiously when dealing with cancer. It is possible to actually add energy to the cancer, thus worsening the situation.
- Do not work directly on a wound or injury.
- Do not work directly on a recently formed scar. Allow at least one month for healing before working near an incision.
- If your pet has a serious condition, seek veterinary attention.

2. Place your free hand on your pet. This helps to complete the electrical circuit plus can help you detect any muscle twitches or other reactions to the acupressure.

3. Apply finger pressure for about one minute directly on the point, perpendicular to the surface of the skin.

4. Start off by lightly touching the point, then use gradual, steady, penetrating pressure.

5. Move your awareness to the tip of your finger. Feel the energy.

6. Slowly apply the pressure and, at the end of the allotted time, slowly release the pressure. This allows the tissues time to respond and promotes healing.

7. At the end of each session, record the points that you used and any immediate reactions that you noticed.

8. Before your next session, make note of any changes you have seen in your pet since the last treatment. The changes are likely to be subtle, so pay close attention. Keeping track of these things will help you plot your pet's progress and change your choice of points if necessary.

Some points may be sensitive. If your pet is slightly resistant to your touch, use light pressure and very gradually press harder. If there is extreme sensitivity at a particular point, it is best not to use it.

For best results, use pet acupressure on a daily basis—unless your pet is also receiving acupuncture. In this special case, consult your veterinary acupuncturist about optimal frequency of acupressure.

Be patient. Acupressure is a gentle technique that is not likely to produce profound, instantaneous results. Persistence is required to harmonize the energy system. Many times, we are dealing with conditions that have been developing for years. Even diseases that seem to suddenly appear have their roots firmly established. Although it is possible to see immediate changes in such cases, it is more likely that it will take several weeks before you notice any improvement.

ACUPRESSURE POINTS

The following are just a few acupressure points that may help your pet when dealing with certain health conditions.

Large Intestine 4 (LI 4)

Location: On the front foot, in the web between the dewclaw and the second toe.

Uses: The Chinese considered this point the master point for the face. It can help with any condition affecting the face, including problems of the eyes, ears, or nose. Also, because the Large Intestine meridian travels from the foot, up the leg and neck, and ends on the face, LI 4 can help alleviate pain in the foot, front leg, and throat. It can also help a dog deal with diarrhea and can even help a pregnant dog deliver her pups.

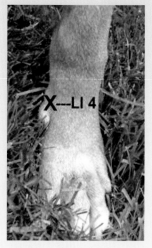

Large Intestine 4 (LI 4) acupressure point.

Large Intestine 11 (LI 11)

Location: With elbow flexed, at the outside end of the crease of the elbow.

Uses: It can be used for pain in or paralysis of the elbow and forelimb, abdominal pain, vomiting, diarrhea, sore throat, or fever.

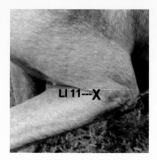

Large Intestine 11 (LI 11) acupressure point.

Small Intestine 3 (SI 3)

Location: On the outside of the front foot, just above the metacarpal-phalangeal joint (the knuckle where the outer most toe joins the paw).

Uses: It is especially good for neck pain. It can also be used for deafness, sore throat, back pain, and pain in or paralysis of the elbow, forelimb, or digits.

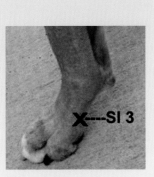

Small Intestine 3 (SI 3) acupressure point.

Stomach 36 (ST 36)

Location: On the rear leg, just to the outside of the tibial crest (the ridge of bone below the knee) and just below the knee joint.

Uses: This is the master point for the abdomen and can be used for any issue in that area. It is also a powerful point to re-energize the body and strengthen the immune system. It can help with abdominal pain, indigestion, vomiting, diarrhea, constipation, dizziness, epilepsy, leg edema or pain, and low energy.

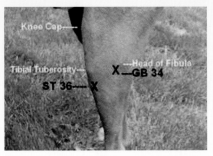

Gallbladder 34 (GB 34)

Location: On the rear leg, just in front of and below the head of the fibula (the lowest bony protrusion on the outside of the knee).

Stomach 36 (ST 36) and Gallbladder 34 (GB 34) acupressure points.

Uses: This is the master point for arthritis anywhere in the body. It can also be used for paralysis, knee problems, vomiting, and liver problems.

ACUPRESSURE POINTS (cont.)

Xiyan ("The Eyes of the Knees")

Location: Consists of two points with one name—below the knee cap and on either side of the patellar tendon.

Uses: These are local points for any knee condition.

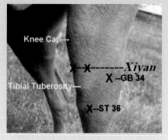

Xiyan acupressure point.

Bladder 60 (BL 60)

Location: On the rear leg. Find it by flexing the ankle so that the foot forms an "L" with the leg. Now gently pinch the web of skin just behind the ankle bone and in front of the Achilles tendon. BL 60 is on the outside of this web.

Uses: Bladder 60 is considered by some to be the "aspirin point" because it can help with pain anywhere in the body, but especially the back. It can also be used for a nose bleed, and is another point that can help with a difficult delivery of pups.

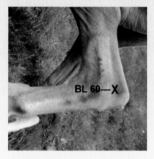

Bladder 60 (BL 60) acupressure point.

Governing Vessel 20 (GV 20)

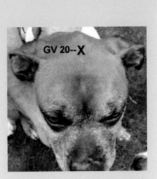

Governing Vessel 20 (GV 20) acupressure point.

Location: On the midline of the top of the head, directly up from the ears. The easiest way to locate the point is to place your index finger on the big bump on the middle of the back of the dog's head. Now trace that ridge forward and, when you get right above the ears, your finger will feel a slight indentation or flattening of the ridge.

Uses: This is a great point to use to calm a pet that is upset. In fact, I use this point with almost every patient I see. As I begin my exam, I stroke this spot to help ease the pet's concerns. GV 20 can also be used to help with head pain, dizziness, and rectal prolapse.

Governing Vessel 26 (GV 26)

Governing Vessel 26 (GV 26) acupressure point.

Location: In the "T" formed below the nose in the filtrum (the crease that runs down the center of the front of the nose and into the upper lip).

Uses: This is a powerful point for resuscitation and can be used for shock, collapse, sunstroke, seizures, and coma.

Acupuncture does not have to be a treatment of last resort for pets. It can be used to avoid certain potentially hazardous surgeries and medications or as a health tune-up. And you can even practice a form of it at home using acupressure.

CHIROPRACTIC CARE

For any organism with a spine, chiropractic care is essential to achieve the highest level of health—yes, chiropractic adjustments are that important. We think of this type of care as a way of helping with spinal problems. And, while chiropractic treatments have been proven invaluable for the treatment of back pain, this modality has so much more to offer.

WHAT IS CHIROPRACTIC?

The word *chiropractic* comes from two Greek words: *Kheir* means "hand" and *praktikos* means "practical" or "operative." Chiropractic, then, means "doing by hand." The term refers to the way chiropractors adjust the spine using their hands, although these days, some forms of chiropractic allow for the use of mechanical devices to manipulate the back.

Chiropractic is the science and art concerned with the diagnosis, treatment, and prevention of mechanical disorders of the spine and the effects of these disorders on the function of the nervous system and the inherent recuperative powers of the body. Chiropractic employs manipulation and adjustment of the spine so that pressure on the spinal nerves and the spinal cord can be relieved, resulting in improved general health. So, chiropractic is not just an aid for sore backs but also a means of keeping the pet truly healthy by assuring proper nervous system function.

CHIROPRACTIC BENEFITS

There are numerous benefits for dogs who receive chiropractic care. Chiropractic therapy can help pets overcome back pain. It can also reduce the recurrence of spinal problems in those who are prone to such conditions. Chiropractic care can aid in the

Chiropractic therapy can help pets overcome back pain.

treatment of back-related lameness. Many varied medical problems that are sometimes the result of spinal nerve interference, such as some cases of incontinence, lick granulomas, and even certain ear infections, have improved with chiropractic adjustments. Even healthy animals perform better when their spines are kept in alignment.

CHIROPRACTIC HISTORY

Various forms of chiropractic have been practiced since ancient times. As early as 2,700 BCE, the Chinese were using bamboo poles for self-adjustment. In 400 BCE, the Greek physician Hippocrates, the father of Western medicine and the source of the medical doctor's Hippocratic oath, stated, "Look well to the spine, for many diseases have their origins in the dislocation of the vertebral column." Egyptian hieroglyphs dating from 200 BCE also document spinal manipulation. In the 1600s, England had bonesetters who worked on the spine. However, it was American healer D.D. Palmer who brought chiropractic into modern times. The adjusting techniques he originated in 1895 began the practice of chiropractic as we know it.

More recently, animal chiropractic was pioneered by Dr. Sharon L. Willoughby. After practicing veterinary medicine for several years, Dr. Willoughby went back to school—this time to earn a Doctor of Chiropractic degree. She blended her expertise in veterinary medicine and chiropractic and, in 1985, developed a 180-hour course for both veterinarians and chiropractors to learn animal chiropractic. Out of this course grew the American Veterinary Chiropractic Association (AVCA). The AVCA tests and certifies the hundreds of animal chiropractors currently practicing in the United States.

SPINAL STRUCTURE AND FUNCTION

To understand the full impact that chiropractic care has on the body, we need to first understand the basics of spinal anatomy and physiology.

The spine has two major components—the spinal cord and the bony spine that surrounds it. The spinal cord is a channel for information between the brain and the organs and tissues of the body. It is made up of millions of long nerve fibers that carry electrical messages—like a living telephone cable.

It's a two-way communication system. Let's say your dog decides to go for a swim. The message is transmitted from the brain to the body, which then jumps into the water. As the body is enveloped by water, all the information regarding the sensations associated with swimming—water temperature, body movement resistance, buoyancy, balance, etc.—is communicated back to the brain. This fragile pathway for bodily communications is totally encased in bone.

AVCA

You can visit the American Veterinary Chiropractic Association (AVCA) on the web at www.animalchiropratic.org.

The Bony Spine

The bony spine is a mechanical marvel. It is quite literally the backbone of the skeleton. It acts as an attachment for many of the body's muscles, allows for the attachment of the limbs, supports the head, transfers the power generated in the hind limbs to the front limbs for locomotion, protects the internal organs of the body, and protects the spinal cord. At the same time, it allows for incredible flexibility. Just watching a dog dart across the yard and perform a jumping pirouette to catch a flying disc gives one an appreciation of the poetry in motion afforded by the spine.

The spine owes its suppleness to the fact that it is made up of a series of small bones called *vertebrae* (pleural of vertebra). There are 27 vertebrae in all, running from a dog's head to his pelvis.

Each vertebra has a unique shape and complicated anatomy, but they all have certain structures in common. We will focus on a very basic understanding of vertebral structure.

Vertebral Structure

The ventral (the part toward the ground when the dog is in a standing position) aspect of a vertebra consists of a solid, roughly cylindrical structure called the *vertebral body*. At the top of the vertebral body, the bone is fashioned into a hollow tube-like structure. The inside of the tube is called the *vertebral canal*, which houses the spinal cord. Jutting upward from this spinal tube, each vertebra has a projection of bone called the *dorsal spinous process*. The dorsal spinous processes of individual vertebrae are the bumps you

The spine owes its suppleness to the fact that it is made up of a series of small bones called vertebrae.

can sometimes feel as you stroke down the midline of your pet's back.

Vertebrae Names and Numbers

Vertebrae are named and numbered based on their location.

- **Cervical Vertebrae**: Starting from the front of the body seven *cervical* vertebrae (abbreviated with a "C") make up the spinal column of the neck. They are numbered from one to seven with C1 (also called the *Atlas*) at the base of the skull, and C7 at the back end of the neck.
- **Thoracic Vertebrae**: There are 13 *thoracic* vertebrae, so named because they serve as attachments for the ribs. Their designations are similar to those of the cervical spine with T1 at the front, attaching to C7, and T13 at the rear of the chain.
- **Lumbar Vertebrae**: The dog has seven *lumbar* vertebrae—L1 through L7—that make up the part of the spine between the ribs and the pelvis.
- **Sacrum**: The back end of L7 is joined to the *sacrum* which is a single bone, formed by the fusion of three vertebrae. The

sacrum serves as the attachment of the pelvic girdle to the spine.

- **Coccygeal Vertebrae**: Bringing up the rear are a variable number of *coccygeal* vertebrae or tail bones.

Joints and Foramina

The vertebrae are joined together by a series of joints. Every vertebral body is joined to the next by an *intervertebral disc* (see below). On each side of the tops of the tubes, the vertebrae are joined together by *zygapophyseal* joints. Every vertebra is joined to the next by these three joints. Each thoracic vertebra is further joined to the next by six extra joint attachments to the ribs, which bridge across adjacent vertebrae. In total, 159 joints affect the spine from C1 to L7. All of these joints must move in a coordinated fashion for proper locomotion of the entire body.

Furthermore, small openings are present on both sides of the spine, between each vertebra, where each bone joins to the next. These openings are called *intervertebral foramina* (pleural for foramen). Spinal nerves pass through these openings—one to either side of the body—carrying information between the body and the spinal cord. Although the spinal cord itself ends between L5 and L6, spinal nerves continue down the vertebral canal and exit through the remaining intervertebral foramina.

Discs act as cushions between vertebrae and allow for the spine's incredible flexibility.

The Intervertebral Discs

The intervertebral discs are major points of attachment between adjacent vertebrae. They also form part of the floor of the vertebral canal, lying on the underside of the spinal cord. Imagine the structure of the discs as a jelly-filled doughnut—a fibrous, outer shell and a soft center filling. Discs act as cushions between vertebrae and allow for the spine's incredible flexibility.

Over time, and under certain conditions, a disc can begin to

Ruptured Disc

It is possible for an intervertebral disc to rupture altogether, allowing the center filling to burst into the vertebral canal and severely damage the spinal cord. A ruptured disc usually causes pain plus complete paralysis of the rear legs. This condition requires immediate surgery.

deteriorate. When this happens, the outer shell weakens and some of the center filling can bulge upward against the spinal cord and the spinal nerves. A bulging disc usually results in intense pain and some loss of bodily function from the affected area of the spine backward, toward the tail. This condition can often be effectively treated with medications, chiropractic care, and/or acupuncture.

The Spinal Cord and Nerves

Communication between the brain and the body, through the spinal cord and nerves, has both conscious and unconscious aspects. The ability to intentionally direct movement is conscious communication—the dog sees where he wants to go and goes there. This ability is lost when a dog sustains a serious neck injury, leaving the animal paralyzed. In this case, the communication lines are effectively severed and, although the dog's brain initiates messages to move, the body does not receive them. This situation also results in the inability of the affected parts of the body to communicate sensations of pain back to the brain.

The vast majority of brain–body communication is unconscious and mediated by the *autonomic nervous system*. This portion of the nervous system is responsible for controlling all the many functions of the body that go on automatically, without conscious control. The autonomic nervous system is involved in the regulation of such things as heart rate, respiratory rate, gastrointestinal motility, blood hormone levels, and blood flow to all the body's organs including the brain.

Spinal nerves carry messages from the spinal cord to the body and from the body to the spinal cord. These nerves are numbered, based on which vertebrae they exit between. So, for example, the pair of spinal nerves that exit the spine between C3 and C4 are called the C4 spinal nerves. The pair that exits between T10 and T11 are called the T11 spinal nerves.

As you might imagine, spinal nerves serve as communication links for nearby structures. For example, the L5 pair at the back of the lumbar spine transmit motor and sensory information for the rear limbs. However, because of the complex interconnectedness of the nervous system, a problem with these nerves could affect a dog's vision. So, it is obvious how essential it is to keep the spinal cord and spinal nerves functioning properly. To understand how to accomplish this, let's look at the practice of chiropractic.

HOW DOES CHIROPRACTIC WORK?

As with other holistic modalities, the chiropractic profession has developed its own concepts and terminology regarding the body, health, and the practice of chiropractic. Because the ideas and vocabulary put forward by chiropractors are foreign to the Western medical way of thinking, there are many misconceptions regarding spinal manipulation. Therefore, it will be helpful for us to explore the words and ideas associated with chiropractic care, to help explain how this modality works.

The Innate Intelligence

Like other holistic practitioners, animal chiropractors believe in a vital force that animates all living creatures. For chiropractors, this vital essence goes by the name *innate intelligence*. "Intelligence" in this sense refers to an ability of the body that we often take for granted. For example, can you imagine calculating the heart rate necessary to maintain a functional blood pressure for a 120-pound (54 kg) person with a given stroke volume who is running at 5 miles (8 km) per hour up a 16-degree slope? The innate intelligence of that person's body makes that calculation with ease.

The innate intelligence is the energetic component of life that allows the body to heal itself and maintain homeostasis. It asserts

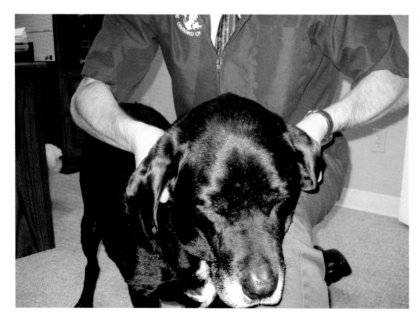

Chiropractic aids healing by relieving the nerve interference caused by joint aberrations in the spine.

Although any breed can suffer from back problems, the Dachshund's shape can make him more prone to intervertebral disc disease.

its influence on the body through the nervous system. It needs a perfectly functioning nervous system to keep the body working smoothly. By relieving the nerve interference caused by joint aberrations in the spine, the animal chiropractor facilitates the innate intelligence and thereby aids healing.

Subluxation

The word *subluxation* is used by chiropractors to denote an abnormally functioning spinal joint. For conventional veterinarians, this word refers to a joint that is almost completely out of joint. This difference in technical jargon has led to a misinterpretation of the science of chiropractic by conventional veterinarians. For the chiropractor, a subluxation is not so much a bone out of place as a joint that is not moving properly.

As mentioned previously, the spinal nerves pass through the intervertebral foramina. These openings are bordered by the zygapophyseal joints, the intervertebral discs, and other structures. Even slight glitches in spinal joint motion—a subluxation—can cause the surrounding tissue to swell and muscles to spasm. This can lead to pressure on the spinal nerves as they exit the spine. A 1986 University of Colorado study demonstrated that the amount of pressure equivalent to the weight of a dime on a spinal nerve was enough to cause it to malfunction in as little as 24 hours.

Subluxations are a common, often painless condition that stresses a dog's spine and interferes with nervous system communication. A subluxation may not appear to cause any problems at first. However, because of the interrelated nature of the spinal column, a problem at one spot eventually leads to problems elsewhere in a gradual chain reaction. Over time, these spinal abnormalities add up and cause real problems for the dog. This process is part of the degenerating health condition our pets face as they age.

Causes of Subluxations

Subluxations have numerous causes. Trauma is the most obvious origin. This includes not only severe trauma such as being hit by a car but more subtle disturbances such as slips, falls, and missteps in the course of everyday life. In fact, birth itself sometimes causes damage to the spine, starting the poor dog off on the wrong foot. Plus, some pets have been bred for traits, such as long backs and short legs, that predispose them to back problems. Confinement and lack of exercise decreases the stretching and strengthening of muscles affecting the spine and can lead to back trouble. Even toenails not kept at the proper length can throw off the biomechanics of the legs, which translates to the spine and causes problems.

Excess weight, which puts abnormal stress on the back, can also cause spinal subluxation, as can the normal aging process, which involves a gradual breakdown of the intervertebral discs, spinal joints, and other supportive tissues. Finally, canine athletes are especially prone to back-jarring incidents. Jumping, racing, and lead jerks can all knock the neck and back out of whack.

Breeds With Back Problems

While subluxations and disc disease can happen to any dog, the body structures of the following breeds make them more prone to back problems (technically called intervertebral disc disease [IVD]):

- Dachshunds
- Shih Tzus
- Pekingese
- Lhaso Apsos
- Cocker Spaniels
- Welsh Corgis
- Toy and Miniature Poodles

Signs of Spinal Problems

Chiropractic spinal problems can manifest in many ways. "Puppy sitting" (sitting with both rear legs shifted to one side) is a subtle but common complaint that often responds to chiropractic. Subluxations may cause neck or back pain and sensitivity to touch. Pacing or other gait abnormalities may be signs of a back issue; so too are weakness or stumbling. It is even possible that abnormal nerve sensations caused by subluxations can cause a dog to chew at areas of his skin, creating lick granulomas. Finally, stiffness, lameness, and a decreased range of motion can all indicate the need for an adjustment.

Of course, all these problems can have other possible causes, so a dog showing these signs must be thoroughly examined—

including X-rays—to rule out nonchiropractic diseases such as fractures or cancer. Adjusting the spine under the wrong conditions could lead to serious injury.

DOES CHIROPRACTIC WORK?

Researchers have proven many beneficial effects of chiropractic.

- A Canadian study showed that chiropractic care was more effective and less expensive than conventional care for back pain in people.
- Human research has shown that athletic performance improved for those receiving regular chiropractic care—even for competitors who were having no obvious symptoms.
- According to another study, chiropractic treatments improved depression in human subjects.
- An additional report demonstrated that chiropractic therapy helped patients in their recovery from vertigo (a condition characterized by dizziness with a sensation of spinning).
- A recent British study reported that chiropractic adjustments benefitted people suffering from asthma.
- Yet another research study showed that chiropractic care had a positive effect on children suffering from ear infections.

TREATING WITH CHIROPRACTIC: WHAT TO EXPECT

Clients are sometimes a little apprehensive about having their dog adjusted because they are not sure what to expect. Based on their own experience with a chiropractor—or lack thereof—these pet owners sometimes have difficulty imagining what the process entails and how their pet will respond. In my experience, it all usually goes quite smoothly.

The Chiropractic Exam

After a rigorous physical exam, the animal chiropractor looks at the animal from a unique point of view. The doctor first watches the animal walk and analyzes his gait and movements. The symmetry of the animal's steps is noted as well as any stiff or jerky movements.

Signs of Spinal Problems

A dog showing signs of spinal problems—including weakness, stumbling, sensitivity to touch, or gait abnormalities—should be thoroughly examined by a vet.

Vinny's Story

Vinny is an extremely cute, black pug puppy who was born with a serious problem. His thoracic spine is severely deformed—on X-ray it looks just as twisted as his corkscrew tail. When I first saw his X-rays, I marveled at the fact that he was able to live with such a malformed chest. His owners brought him to me for chiropractic care. At first, I was gripped by the concern that his owners expected me to straighten him out with chiropractic. Perhaps they were hoping I could just hold his head and pull his tail until his whole spine fell into place.

Luckily, Vinny's owners had realistic expectations. Vinny's little body was formed this way and, even if it were possible to make a drastic change, such heroics would leave him in a worse state. In his case, the ideal of chiropractic care is to maximize the function of the normal areas of his spine, and to improve the mobility of the distorted area.

We have been treating Vinny every few weeks since he was four months old. So far, he seems to be improving with each adjustment. The fact that his owners began chiropractic treatments while Vinny was very young helps improve his development. At some point, we will have made all the improvement possible. Then periodic chiropractic manipulations will help him maintain his mobility.

Chiropractic helped Vinny gain some mobility.

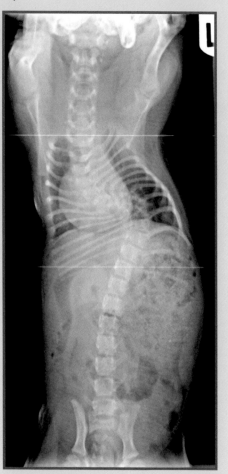

Vinny's x-ray.

Chiropractic Techniques

There are many schools of thought regarding chiropractic, and thus, many techniques. Some chiropractors believe that only the atlas needs to be adjusted and that the rest of the spine will fall in place. Others believe that only the sacral area of the spine needs attention. Some chiropractors use their hands to adjust, while others use a mechanical device to reset the spinal joints.

Whatever the method used, I believe it is important that the chiropractic adjustments be specific. In other words, subluxations should be located and corrected. This philosophy stands in contrast to some chiropractic techniques that involve adjusting every vertebra whether it needs it or not. I would stay away from any animal chiropractor who takes an adjusting tool and snaps it on every vertebra down the spine of every dog. This has the potential of causing harm.

Where's the Pop?

Anyone who has experienced chiropractic care first-hand notices that a popping or cracking noise often accompanies each adjustment. This is not the case in dogs. It is rare to hear anything at all as the dog's spine is adjusted. The cracking sound is simply due to the pressure change in the joint, and does not indicate the success of the adjustment. Dog's spinal joints are different from ours and are usually silent when manipulated.

Next, the doctor goes over the spine with his hands, gently feeling the bones, muscles, and surrounding tissues. Muscle tightness can indicate spasm. Warmth can mean inflammation, while a cool sensation often points to an area of reduced blood circulation. During this assessment, the position of each vertebral dorsal spinous process is also checked for proper alignment. The animal chiropractor makes note of what he finds.

The final part of the chiropractic exam is called *motion palpation*. The doctor works his way up the spine with one hand while supporting the dog's body with the other. The sacrum, pelvis, and every vertebra are gently pushed and the joints are checked for proper mobility

The Chiropractic Adjustment

The chiropractic adjustment is a carefully regulated thrust or force delivered with controlled speed, depth, and magnitude to articulations in the spine. When done properly, the adjustment is a specific force applied in a specific direction to a specific vertebra. The adjustment is made at the same angle as the zygapophyseal joint plane.

Several techniques exist for adjusting animals. Fortunately, none of them involve laying the dog down, belly up, on a chiropractic table and wrenching his neck from side to side. Most commonly, the animal is adjusted while standing. As the doctor performs motion palpation, he combines the information from the chiropractic exam and determines where and how to make the adjustments. When a subluxation is located, a quick, accurate thrust is delivered to correct the problem. It is rare to hear any cracking sounds, as is common during human chiropractic treatments.

Most dogs find the chiropractic process relaxing. Although the animal may flinch during a particular adjustment, by the end of the treatment, his eyes often reveal that he has truly enjoyed the procedure. Usually, right after the final adjustment, the dog will shake his entire body as if shaking off water after a swim. This wave of motion down his body seems to reset his muscles to the new joint mobility.

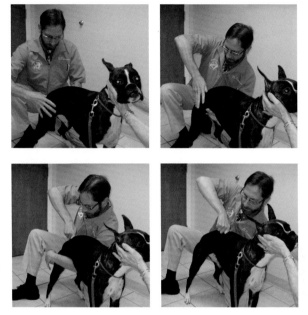

When a subluxation is located, a quick, accurate thrust is delivered to correct the problem.

After the Adjustment

Some patients are sore for a day or two after a chiropractic treatment, because the adjustments are made at areas of the spine where abnormal joint motion has led to inflammation and pain. Sometimes you can't avoid making things appear worse before the body can get back in balance.

It is important to keep the dog settled for a day or two after a chiropractic treatment. Tugging at a leash or running and falling can totally undo the adjustment. At the same time, total confinement would be a mistake too, since the animal needs to move and stretch to help his body readjust.

Frequency

If a pet has a serious back problem, frequent chiropractic treatments are usually required in the beginning, because it takes several reminders for the muscles to hold the new position. Another thing to remember is that once a pet has a back problem, he will forever be prone to flare-ups. For that reason, once the initial insult is brought under control, periodic chiropractic treatments should be continued to keep the back in shape.

For pets who never experience back pain, chiropractic is a great way to keep the nervous system functioning well and the entire

Chiropractic is a great way to keep the nervous system functioning well and the entire pet healthy.

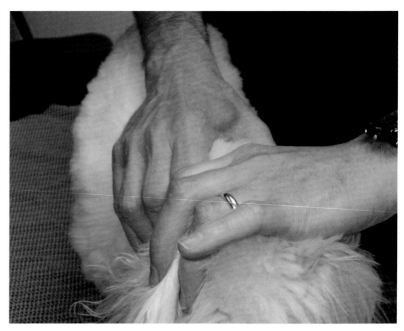

pet healthy. In this situation, adjustments every four to six weeks will usually do the trick. This recommendation can be especially important to help agility dogs and other canine athletes get a competitive edge on the opposition; many nonperformance dogs benefit from regular chiropractic care as well.

FINDING A CERTIFIED ANIMAL CHIROPRACTOR

Be sure to carefully check out the person you trust with your pet's spine. All animal chiropractic certifications are not the same. For example, weekend chiropractic courses are available for veterinarians and chiropractors that teach a quick technique for adjusting the spine. These courses do not provide adequate education about the canine spine, and do not teach veterinarians much about the intricacies of chiropractic.

You may be tempted to bring your dog to your current veterinarian or even your human chiropractor for adjustments, but I would advise against it. While your human chiropractor may do a great job on you and your family, the canine spine is different from the human spine, so without special training she is not the ideal candidate to treat your dog. And, while your veterinarian is an expert in canine anatomy and disease, she lacks specific education in chiropractic and could do damage by attempting an adjustment. I think that the best assurance of proper animal chiropractic training is certification by the AVCA, which assures education and skill in the specialized field of animal chiropractic.

AVCA certification is available for both veterinarians and chiropractors, and involves a minimum of 180 hours of training both in the classroom and on animals, as well as thorough written and practical exams. Doctors seeking certification must also complete a 40-hour internship with an AVCA-certified doctor. To maintain certification, the animal chiropractor is required to complete 30 hours of continuing education every three years. To locate a certified animal chiropractor near you, check out the AVCA website listed in the resources at the back of this book.

HOME SPINAL CARE

Unfortunately, it is not possible for the typical pet owner to learn to adjust his dog's spine. In fact, it would be dangerous for anyone to make such an attempt without extensive training and practice. Even a slight misplaced thrust on a dog's spine could cripple him for life. However, you can apply a simple stretch to your dog to help keep his spine healthy.

The intervertebral discs are especially prone to problems because the blood flow to and through them is somewhat limited. The delivery of nutrients to the disc tissues and the removal of cellular waste require vertebral movement, which is why exercise

Flair's Story

Flair is a beautiful Boxer with a sleek, brindle coat. Her owner, Nancy, sent her away for special training and, when Flair returned, she had a slight hunch to her back. Also, her spine did not move smoothly as she walked. The abnormality was so subtle that most pet owners would never have noticed, but since Flair was destined for the show ring, every detail was important.

At 10 months of age, Flair was brought to me to see if chiropractic could help the problem. I found and corrected several subluxations in her lumbar spine and pelvis. Flair received her first four treatments on a weekly basis to remind the joints how to move. Nancy noticed improvement after Flair's second treatment, and her posture and gait were totally normal after five sessions. Now, Flair returns for regular chiropractic adjustments to keep her spine in shape.

You can stretch out a smaller dog on your lap.

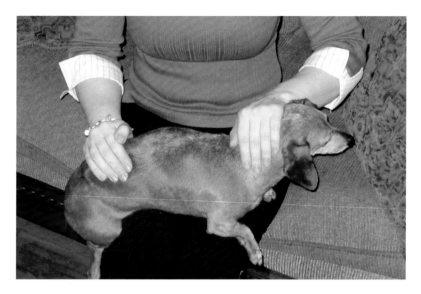

and stretching are so important for a healthy spine.

Dogs are inherently good at stretching. You have probably seen your dog stretch his back by bowing down in front and then stretching his rear legs behind him. In fact, human yoga stretches (*upward facing dog* and *downward facing dog*) are named for this canine exercise. However, despite this natural tendency, a little extra stretching is always helpful.

The Stretch

The idea of this stretch is to create traction in the dog's spine by gently lifting the body from underneath. Several techniques can accomplish this, depending on the size and preference of the pet. Apply the preferred traction technique for about one minute and repeat every three to seven days. This will help keep your dog's discs healthy and his spine flexible and pain-free.

Small to Medium Dogs

For small- to medium-sized dogs:

1. Sit on the edge of a chair with your legs together and your thighs parallel with the floor.
2. Drape the dog over your knees with the front legs hanging over one side and the rear legs over the other.
3. To enhance the stretch you can hold behind the head with one hand and firmly pet down the spine with the other.

Large Dogs

For larger dogs, or those who do not tolerate the first technique:

Use a towel as a sling under the body of the standing dog—be sure to have a broad area of contact, with the towel under both the chest and abdomen.

1. Gently pull up on the ends of the towel, bowing the dog's back upwards.
2. It is not necessary to lift the feet off the ground but rather apply only the amount of traction that the dog can easily tolerate.

Proper alignment and functioning of the spine is crucial for canine health. Chiropractic is the "backbone" of holistic healthcare and can assure your dog's body is working at its highest level from head to toe. It is one more tool to help keep your pet in good physical shape. After all, it's always best to have a "well-adjusted" dog.

To stretch a larger dog's back, use a towel as a sling under the body of the standing dog.

6

MASSAGE THERAPY

Many humans enjoy a good massage, whether it's from a professional or a generous partner. Why not use this relaxing, stress-reducing, health-promoting technique on your canine companion?

WHAT IS MASSAGE?

Massage can be defined as the manipulation, usually by hand, of the soft tissues of the body in order to normalize them. It involves a system of stroking, kneading, percussion, and moving the skin, muscles, and joints. Over 80 forms of massage are used today including Swedish, acupressure, shiatsu, sports, and Rolfing, just to name a few.

Massage can be used simply for the relaxation and rejuvenation of a pet. It can also be applied therapeutically to aid in the recovery of an injury or in preparation for a sporting event. I consider massage for dogs to be "petting with a purpose."

MASSAGE BENEFITS

Massage therapy can benefit the body in many ways. A major outcome of massage is that the gentle strokes increase blood circulation, which aids the flow of nutrients into the tissue. You can demonstrate this effect on yourself by conducting this simple experiment. Grasp your right earlobe with your right thumb and forefinger. Now, firmly squeeze and rub, first your earlobe, then continue the motion to thoroughly cover your entire ear. The whole process can take as little as 15 seconds. Now, feel the heat and tingling in you right ear. Look in a mirror and see its redness compared to your left ear. What an astonishing result from just a 15-second rub!

Massage not only improves blood circulation, it also helps to move lymphatic fluid, which removes waste products and toxins. It can stimulate skin glands and soothe nerves.

Think of pet massage as "petting with a purpose."

Massage relaxes tight muscles and can be used to relieve muscle spasms and release trigger points. It can also break down adhesions, allowing damaged muscles to regain function and improve joint range of motion. After a chiropractic treatment, massaging the muscles along the spine can help them adapt to the new joint set-points caused by the adjustment. This makes it less likely for the muscles to pull the spine back out of place.

Massage can slow the heart rate, induce relaxation, and reduce stress. Stress reduction sounds extravagant when it comes to our canine companions. What could they possibly be stressed about? Plenty! Many dogs are isolated from social interaction all day while their owners are at work. For pack animals, this alone is stressful. The stress hormones released in the body can have far-reaching and devastating effects on a dog's health. Massage is a way of reducing this obstacle to your dog's well-being. Plus, massaging your pet gives him pleasure and strengthens your bond with him.

MASSAGE HISTORY

Massage therapy has been around ever since there have been tight shoulders and hands with opposable thumbs to squeeze them. It is a natural instinct to rub sore muscles, and this inclination has developed over millennia into a healing art and science. The first to document the use of therapeutic massage were the Chinese, in 3000 BCE. Then the Egyptians developed a special foot massage called *reflexology* around 2300 BCE. The father of Western medicine, Hippocrates (460–380 BCE), prescribed "rubbing" for his patients as well. Native Americans also used a form of massage therapy.

With the rise in popularity of holistic care, pet massage therapy has become popular in the past 10 to 15 years. Since more and more people have reaped the benefits of massage therapy for themselves, they have realized the health potential for their pets.

MUSCLE PHYSIOLOGY

To better understand the many benefits of massage, we need to have a basic understanding of the body's musculature and

Early Detection

One less obvious benefit of massage is that, by running your hands all over your pet, you are better able to detect tumors and other signs of disease.

biomechanics. Muscles work in pairs. Every joint has a muscle or group of muscles that contract to flex the joint and an opposing group that extends it. These muscle pairs must work together in a coordinated manner for the normal functioning of the joint. When one group of muscles contracts, the other group must relax. If one muscle in the system does not function properly due to injury, fatigue, or other factors, problems occur.

Tightening of a muscle can occur from trauma, disease, aging changes, or simply from being overworked. Muscle tightening can lead to soreness and a restricted range of motion in the affected joint. Continued use of a tight muscle will lead to muscle spasm. When a particular muscle is tight or in spasm, it cannot function appropriately, which throws off the muscular harmony required for proper joint motion. When things are not functioning up to par, the animal is prone to uncoordinated movements and further injury.

Massage Resources

Check out the Resources section for DVDs and websites on pet massage.

Trigger Points

Over time, muscle tightness and spasm can coalesce into a small, relatively permanent knot of contracted muscle tissue known as a *trigger point*. A trigger point is a firm nodule that can be felt within a taut band of muscle. It is very painful to the touch and often accompanies chronic musculoskeletal disorders. Interestingly, trigger points are often located at acupuncture points.

A key characteristic of trigger points is that they can be located in a discrete area, yet be responsible for radiating pain to nearby musculature. This adjacent soreness is known as *referred pain*. It is impossible to elicit from your dog the fact that when you massage a tight muscle in his shoulder he feels an aching all the way down his leg, but it is important for you to be aware of the possibility. You should also be cognizant of the fact that your pet's shoulder pain could be a result of a trigger point near his elbow.

Muscle injury and microtrauma can eventually cause scarring and adhesions. When tissue is stuck together in this unhealthy way, movement and function are compromised. This is another way that coordination and movement can be disrupted.

TREATING WITH MASSAGE: WHAT TO EXPECT

Pet massage therapists come in many varieties. Some are pet-loving, human massage therapists who have learned how to

A high-impact sport like agility may cause muscle tightness.

adapt their practice to help animals. Others are veterinary technicians who have expanded their knowledge and skill. Still others are nonprofessionals who have learned the art of canine massage.

Most of those practicing animal massage work independently and may see their furry clients in their own homes or may travel to where the pet lives. Some pet massage therapists work out of the offices of holistic veterinarians or animal rehabilitation centers. Whatever the arrangements, you can expect a peaceful treatment for your dog.

The astute therapist will first interview the pet owner to ascertain the purpose for the treatment. She will want to know the extent of any recent injuries as well as the history of any surgeries and medical treatments. She may require a signed release from the animal's veterinarian to be sure that massage is an appropriate treatment. Using this information, she can plan her treatment strategy.

For the treatment itself, the massage therapist sets a serene mood with muted lighting and calm surroundings. Soft music is usually played to enhance relaxation. The dog is allowed to lie comfortably on a blanket or pet bed on the floor and the massage therapist sits or kneels to apply her art.

Slow, gentle, rhythmic strokes introduce the animal to what is in store. As the dog relaxes, the therapist gains his trust and can then begin more therapeutic techniques to go beyond relaxation into helping the pet heal.

The entire process should be a comfortable one for the dog. If the massage therapist moves beyond the animal's pain threshold, she eases off and refocuses on relaxation. It may take a treatment or two for massage to begin helping the pet.

FINDING A MASSAGE THERAPIST

If you plan to have your pet massaged to aid with a medical condition, it is best to leave it in the hands of a professional. Unfortunately, finding a qualified canine massage therapist can be tricky. Anyone can hang out a shingle and start rubbing dogs— possibly the wrong way. Animal massage training courses may involve only a weekend of instruction or even just a few hours. Be sure the person you choose has adequate training.

If the therapist is licensed for human massage, then she should be qualified for canine massage. If she is not licensed, start asking questions and don't be shy. Ask the following:

- What is your experience level?
- Who did you train with, and for how many hours?
- Can you explain the problem my pet is having and come up with a solution?
- Do you acknowledge the importance of a veterinary diagnosis and case evaluation?

Research the answers. Once you decide on a massage therapist, assess the outcome. You should see some results within the first two treatments. If not, then either massage is not appropriate for the problem, or the therapist is not handling the issue suitably.

HOME CARE

Unlike chiropractic and acupuncture, massage is something any pet owner can do at home on their healthy pet. It is a great way to deepen your relationship with your dog and benefit his health. Here are the basics you need to know to become your dog's personal masseuse.

Basic Principles

It is best for the person giving the massage to have a basic understanding of dog muscular anatomy. For the casual owner/massage therapist, it's enough to realize that canine anatomy corresponds to ours. What feels good to you will likely feel good to your pet.

In general, you'll want to use your whole hand to massage the large muscles of the upper legs and back. Use your fingers and apply lighter pressure over small muscles and over thinly muscled areas like the lower legs and feet. Massage is most relaxing when the therapist maintains contact with the dog throughout the massage session. Taking your hands off and putting them back on can feel jarring to a relaxed pet.

Deep, firm strokes are always directed toward the heart. This is done to push the blood through the venous system in the right direction. It is important

You might find a veterinary technician skilled at the art of canine massage.

Massage Precaution

Massage is almost always beneficial, but be aware of the following precautions:

- Do not massage over an open wound, area of inflammation, or incision.
- Do not massage over insect bites or areas of infection.
- Never apply massage to fractured bones or other swellings.
- It is best for the casual massage therapist to avoid massaging any pet who has a fever, swollen lymph nodes, or cancer.

to respect the venous system in this way because veins have valves within them that keep blood flowing toward the heart. If venous blood is forced against the natural flow, the valves can be damaged and circulation problems may follow.

Simple Strokes

If your pet is not having any major medical problems, and you want to help promote his health and bond in a special way, here are some easy techniques you can use.

When preparing for a massage session it is essential to set aside enough time—20 to 45 minutes—to complete the task. Choose a peaceful setting. Get yourself and your dog into a comfortable position together, and set a healing intention in your mind.

Stroking

Stroking involves light, long movements with the fingertips or palms, in the direction of the hair coat, along the length of the muscles. This entails massaging in a direction away from the heart, so keep it light. Stroking is done at a slow speed of one stroke per three to six seconds. It is often used at the start of the massage. Dogs find stroking relaxing, and it prepares them for more active massage later.

Stroking involves light long movements with the palms along the length of the muscles.

Effleurage

Effleurage is a gliding motion using heavier pressure. This is done in a direction toward the heart using even pressure with the whole hand. One hand may be used to smooth out the muscle, or you might grasp a limb with two hands and gently slide up the leg. Effleurage is usually done as a slow relaxing stroke—one per two to three seconds. It may also be done in a rapid motion as a performance warm-up.

Effleurage is done in a direction toward the heart using even pressure.

Petrissage

Petrissage is a kneading and squeezing technique. Deep pressure is applied in rhythmic, circular movements with both hands alternating pressure. Pressure is lightened during the phase of the circle going away from the heart, and more force is used going toward the heart.

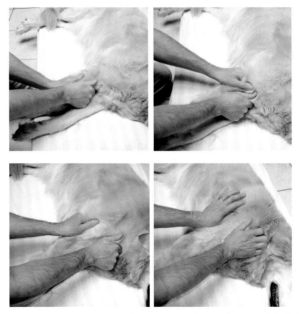

Petrissage is a kneading and squeezing technique done with both hands.

Skin Pinching

Skin pinching is a technique derived from the Chinese massage called *tui na*. As the name implies, lightly and slowly lift the skin between the fingers and thumb. This procedure helps increase circulation over sore joints or muscles. It can be modified into a *pinch and roll* down the spine for aching backs. For this technique, simply grasp a roll of skin at the base of the neck and, without releasing it, walk with your fingers to create a wave of skin that you direct down the center of the spine.

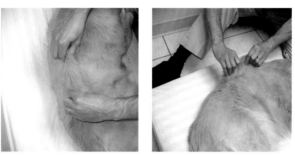

With the skin pinch technique, you lift the skin between the fingers and thub.

With the pinch and roll, a roll of skin is directed down the center of the spine.

Range-of-Motion Exercises

Range-of-motion exercises can be applied to every joint in the body as part of the massage session. Start at the toes of each foot and gently bend each joint individually as far as it will comfortably go in the normal direction of flexion and extension. This exercise should be used with caution on arthritic joints.

With a range of motion exercise, gently bend each toe joint as far as it will comfortably go.

Shake a Leg

Finally, a manipulation I call *shake a leg* is also borrowed from *tui na*. For this massage, the dog must be lying on his side. Grasp a foot and gently shake the leg back and forth in the direction of normal joint motion. Quick, low-amplitude (how widely you are swinging the leg) movement works the lower joints while slow, high amplitude movement works the upper joints. Apply to all four legs, one at a time, for 15 to 30 seconds each.

For "shake a leg," gently shake the leg back and forth in the direction of normal joint motion.

Feedback

While a pet is being massaged, it is crucial that the therapist be keenly aware of how the dog is reacting to the treatment. Signs that things are going well include stretching, dreamy eyes, licking, tail wagging, and drooling. These activities show that the dog is enjoying the process and feeling the effects of endorphins.

Signs that the animal is experiencing pain are dodging, stiffening, biting, and other negative behavior. These signs indicate the therapist should back off and work on another part of the body.

Massage therapy can be a great adjunct to your dog's healthcare regime. It can be applied by a professional for ailing pets or by the pet owner if the animal is healthy.

7

HERBAL MEDICINE

t first glance, the practice of herbal medicine can appear confusing, with its foreign-sounding herb names and the plethora of forms available. To understand herbal medicine and how it can be safely applied to our canine companions, we must become familiar with some basic concepts regarding plant identification, herbal formulations, dosing, and safety.

WHAT IS HERBAL MEDICINE?

This holistic modality goes by many names, including herbalism, medical herbalism, herbology, botanical medicine, and phytotherapy. Herbal medicine involves the use of various parts of specific plants to achieve a healing effect on the body. Herbs produce their curative actions by causing physiological changes within the body or fighting disease-causing germs.

A herb can be defined as a nonwoody plant, a kitchen spice, or any medicinal vegetation. Yes, there is a crossover between culinary and medicinal herbs: the herbs we add to our food do more than enhance its taste. For example, garlic adds flavor to pasta, but can also enhance immune function; cayenne spices up pizza, but can also help relieve arthritis pain.

BENEFITS

Herbs can benefit our pets in many ways. They are helpful for a multitude of conditions for which drugs are currently employed, including fighting infections, easing pain, assisting organ function, and improving hormonal balance, just to name a few. Herbs can even help your dog in ways that drugs cannot, such as improving his immune system function, helping him rid his body of toxins, and strengthening his resistance to environmental stress. At the same time, conventional medications also have a place in your pet's healthcare, and the information provided in this chapter is not meant to replace the proper diagnosis and treatment of any disease by your veterinarian.

Although herbs can often be used in place of drugs—and many drugs have been derived

Herbs can improve your dog's immune system function.

from herbs—herbs are not drugs. Drugs usually consist of a high concentration of a single active ingredient, and they manipulate the body forcefully in a particular direction. Herbs, on the other hand, contain a whole host of ingredients and may have complex effects on the body. Thus, the same herb used to treat diarrhea might also aid a constipated pet.

A major advantage of herbs over pharmaceutical medications is that herbs cause fewer side effects. This is not to say that all herbs are perfectly safe. The trade-off for gentleness of action is that herbs tend to take time (up to 12 weeks) to have their intended effect on the pet.

HERBAL HISTORY

The human practice of using herbs to treat medical conditions is older than dirt. While that may be a slight exaggeration, evidence for the practice has been discovered in caveman coprolites (fossilized feces). Also, remnants of medicinal herbs were found buried with a Neanderthal man in a 60,000-year-old grave in Iraq. Cave paintings in France that date back to between 13,000 and 25,000 BCE show the use of plants for healing. The first listings of herbs and their uses were compiled in China in 3500 BCE. In addition, herbal medicine is discussed in Sumerian texts dating to 3000 BCE.

Let's face it—herbs have been used by indigenous people the world over. Even medical doctors in the United States relied heavily on herbs until the 1930s, at which time we abandoned the more natural approach for the emerging technology of prescription drugs. Still, today, the World Health Organization estimates that 80 percent of the world's population counts on herbs as their primary medicine. Plus, 30 to 40 percent of contemporary German and French physician prescribe herbs.

Modern Pharmacology

Modern pharmacology was born in 1785, when William Withering isolated digitoxin and digoxin (current heart medications) from the leaves of the foxglove plant. Today, scientists continue to isolate the active ingredients in herbs, verifying their mode of action and proving their usefulness. Pharmaceutical companies are currently combing the world's rainforests trying to find plant compounds (*phytochemicals*) that may hold the promise of being the next great miracle cure. Unfortunately, they take this process to the next level by synthetically manufacturing the active ingredients and concentrating them into pills to make drugs. In fact, 25 percent of today's medications are derived from herbs.

Drug

The word *drug* comes from the Middle English word *drogge,* which means "dried root."

The problem that I see with this way of medicating the body is side effects. I think Mother Nature provided us with the remedies we need in the form of herbs, but when the active ingredient is removed from the plant, it is stripped of all the natural chemical synergists that were meant to go with it. I believe that these (yet to be appreciated) chemical compounds work with the active ingredient to enhance its medicinal effects and buffer side effects.

A *side effect* is any outcome that a drug causes other than the intended effect, and all drugs have them. Side effects are funny things. They are like weeds. One person's weed (like the dandelion) is another person's liver cleanser. The drug sildenafil citrate (Viagra) is a good example. It was originally studied as a blood pressure medication. During the clinical trials, some of the gentlemen taking the medicine noticed an unusual and pleasant side effect. It didn't take long for researchers to figure out that there was more money to be made selling a drug to enhance libido than in another boring blood pressure pill. So, now we have a libido drug with a warning about its side effect on blood pressure. How quickly weeds become blossoming flowers.

Chinese herbs are used within the framework of Traditional Chinese Medicine.

Eastern Versus Western Herbology

You may have heard the term *Eastern herbs* and assumed that it refers to the use of special plants that grow only in China. In reality, both Eastern (Chinese) and Western (Euro-American) herbology use many of the same medicinal plants. However, important differences exist between the two schools of thought.

In the West, herbal medicine refers strictly to the use of plants. In China, animal parts and minerals are used in addition to plants. Western herbology tends to use single herbs for healing, while Eastern herbal remedies often contain as many as 12 to 20 medicinal components.

The biggest difference between Eastern and Western herbal practice is that Chinese herbs are used within the framework of Traditional Chinese Medicine (TCM) (see Chapter 4 for more information on TCM). For example, in Western herbology several herbs can be used for an upset stomach (ginger, chamomile, and peppermint, to name a few). The only way to know which herb will work best is through trial and error with each patient. In the Chinese model, different patients with digestive upset may have a different TCM diagnosis (and thus a different medicine) based on the balance of yin and yang, etc. Eastern herbal medicine allows for a more exact fit between patient and remedy.

Zoopharmacognosy

Animals naturally practice herbal medicine. *Zoopharmacognosy* is the study of the process by which animals select and utilize plants, soils, and insects to treat and prevent illness. Observers have noticed that many creatures self-medicate with herbs. Apes have demonstrated a certain herbal sophistication by stripping the leaves of a medicinal plant and then breaking its stem to consume just the juice. Field biologists and others have studied zoopharmacognosy in a wide range of animals, including elephants, gorillas, monkeys, chimpanzees, bison, lambs, pigs, chickens, civets, jackals, tigers, bears, wild dogs, rhinoceros, mole rats, desert gerbils, and even butterflies.

Furthermore, it is possible that we owe our practice of herbal medicine to our friends the animals. Indigenous healers the world over sometimes claim to have determined which plants to use for particular conditions by watching and mimicking the beasts. This assertion is quite likely. So, it is only natural for us to return the favor and utilize herbal remedies for our pets today.

HERB NAMES

While it may be true that "a rose by any other name would smell as sweet," when dealing with medicinal plants it is imperative that our references be more exacting. Common names for herbs can be very deceiving. First, most of the tens of thousands of plants in the world have no common names. Second, many times different herbs share the same common name. For example, cat's claw is a common name that can refer to two related plants: *Uncaria tomentosa* and *Uncaria guianensis*. Although these two plants look similar, they have very different therapeutic actions.

To add to the confusion, a single herb may have many different names. Echinacea *(Echinacea angustifolia)* is also known as purple coneflower, coneflower, rudbeckia, and black sampson. This naming situation can lead to quite a bit of uncertainty when

Herbal Research

Many medicinal herbs have been proven effective through stringent medical studies. Regrettably, most of these studies have been done in foreign countries and not translated for an American medical readership. Even the herbal research done in the United States rarely makes it into the veterinary or human medical journals due to the bias of the editors against natural remedies and for pharmaceuticals.

Animals naturally practice herbal medicine.

selecting an herbal product.

Because of the nonspecific nature of common names, scientific names must be used when discussing herbal remedies. Scientific names refer to plants by their genus and species in Latin. Just as the scientific name for modern-day humans is *Homo sapiens* and that for domestic dogs is *Canis familiaris*, so every plant can be specified by its scientific name. This system allows for precise communication regarding herbal prescribing throughout the world.

HERBAL FORMULATIONS

Another perplexing aspect of herbal medicine is that the remedies come in many forms. Pills and powders, teas, and tinctures—what are we to do when faced with so many choices? The blessing hidden in this conundrum is that such diversity allows for delivery systems to be tailored to each individual pet. If giving a pill or capsule is too difficult, then perhaps a liquid can be coaxed down or a powder mixed with the food. At the same time, if a pet does not like the taste of a particular herb, then a tablet or capsule may be the way to go. Of course, the first step in choosing the best herbal form is having an understanding of what they consist of and how they are made and used.

The active ingredients in herbs—*phytochemicals*—come in many forms including complex polysaccharides, glycosides, lipids, terpenoids, sterols, phenylpropanoids, alkaloids, peptides, and saponins. In different herbs, these medicinal substances are concentrated in different parts of the plant. Plant structures used in herbal medicine include the flower, leaf, stem, twig, root, rhizome (root trunks), seed, bark, and resin (sap). It is important to use the appropriate plant part for each herb to ensure safety and effectiveness.

Fresh Herbs

Herbs can be used fresh out of the ground. Many chefs have gardens close to their kitchens, so herbs such as chives, basil, sage, thyme, parsley, and cilantro can be sprinkled on food as it cooks. Similarly, fresh ginger root can be shredded and added to a dog's food as a digestive aid. Herbs can also be dried, ground into a powder, and mixed into a pet's food.

Herbal Teas

Making an herbal tea (also called an *herbal infusion*) is a way of extracting the plant constituents into water. A tea can be prepared by using one teaspoon of dried plant material, or three teaspoons of the fresh plant, per 8 ounces (236 ml) of boiling water. This is allowed to steep for 10 to 20 minutes and then the plant material is strained off. Once the solution is adequately cooled, it can be mixed with the dog's food or given directly by mouth. Teas can be placed in a closed container and stored in the refrigerator for several days.

The tea-making process is best used for herbs consisting of flowers, leaves, or green stems. If the herbal material to be used is woody in nature, such as roots, bark, or seeds, it must be ground into a powder so the healing constituents can be liberated into the water. When an herbal solution is prepared in this way it is known as a *decoction*.

Herbal Tinctures and Extracts

An *herbal tincture* refers to an alcohol preparation of a dried herb and an *herbal extract* is an alcohol preparation of the fresh herb. A mixture of grain alcohol and water is the ideal solvent for all the important phytochemicals contained in herbs. Tinctures and extracts are more concentrated than teas, so a smaller dose is needed. These herbal preparations may be given directly by mouth; however, some dogs may not tolerate the high alcohol content. An alternative is to dilute the remedy with equal parts hot water to evaporate off the alcohol. The diluted solution can be given when cooled.

Making an herbal tea is a way of extracting the plant constituents into water.

Herbal Glycerin Extracts

Glycerin extracts of fresh herbs are also available and are associated with fewer side effects than tinctures and extracts. Unfortunately, most herbalists agree that this extraction

161

What Formulation Is Best?

Most herbs can be given by any delivery method. With dogs, usually a lot of trial and error is involved in determining what formulation will work best. Some dogs like certain herbs enough that the dried herb can be mixed with food, but another dog (or the same dog with a different herb) might not.

process is not very effective, so the resultant medicine may not be very effective. Recently, herb companies have developed a more complicated extraction process involving alcohol extraction, vacuum evaporation of the alcohol, and addition of glycerin as a preservative. This technique allows for a potent yet well-tolerated liquid product.

Herbal Extract Granules and Concentrated Powders

Some Chinese herbal remedies come in the form of *extract granules* or *concentrated powders*. These are made by dehydrating an herbal decoction, creating a powder that is four to five times more potent than the powdered herb. The extract granules can then be made into a tablet or capsule, or reconstituted in water to make tea.

Purified Herbal Extract

A final herbal preparation is the *purified extract*. For this type of remedy, the active ingredient is harvested from the plant through a series of extraction processes. This assures a nonsynthetic, high-potency remedy. However, the science behind this method assumes that the active ingredient is the only important component of the herb. In general, I think this is an unhealthy approach. But, at the same time, there are cases when a purified extract may be the best choice. For example, when dealing with cancer it might be helpful to use the concentrated form of an anticancer phytochemical so that its potency is not diluted by the other herbal ingredients.

HERBAL POTENCY

One problem with herbal remedies is that plants can be inconsistent in their phytochemical content. The quality of a plant's constituents depends on the quality of the soil it was grown in, water availability, the amount of sunlight, and a variety of other conditions. Even a skilled herbalist cannot always tell just by looking at a plant how potent its herbal effects will be.

Many factors affect the therapeutic activity of the finished herbal product. Herbs must be handled carefully after harvest since the phytochemicals are often sensitive to heat and light. Because the supplement industry is not closely monitored, not all products are equally effective. Look for a label that gives the genus and species of plant, not just the common name. The label should also state the expiration and/or harvest date to assure freshness. Also, be sure the label states that the appropriate part of the plant is being used (leaves, roots, flowers, etc.).

Some herbal companies also analyze their supplements for the amount of "active ingredients" they contain, using a process called *standardization*. In such instances, the key ingredient is seen as a marker. It is assumed that if this chemical is at the right level in the plant, then the other phytochemicals will be there too. This attempt to standardize herbs is helpful. Unfortunately, it is possible for unscrupulous companies to manipulate this system by adding a synthetic form of the active ingredient to inferior herbal material. Although the product looks good when analyzed, it is not likely to have the desired herbal action. Also, some companies claim their product is standardized because they produce it according to a uniform process. The word "standardized" can mean different things, so it is important to read the label carefully.

The bottom line is that, at some point, the consumer must trust the herbal manufacturer. But who to trust? The only way that I know is through research and experience. Find out all you can about the company, realizing that you can't believe everything

Rookie's Story

Rookie was a boisterous German Shepherd Dog who, at the age of nine, was diagnosed with osteosarcoma—an aggressive cancer of the bone. It is sometimes treated by amputating the affected limb, but this strategy rarely buys the patient much extra time. By the time the cancer is noticeable, it has usually already spread. For Rookie, surgery was not even an option because his cancer was in his hip. With no worthwhile conventional treatment available, doctors gave Rookie weeks to live, and he was sent home to die.

Mrs. Guthrie, Rookie's owner, was not willing to give up on her beloved dog. She decided to go holistic. Rookie was started on a natural, low-carbohydrate diet with extra fish oil. He received weekly acupuncture for pain. He was also on conventional medications for pain and anxiety.

The major feature of our integrative approach to Rookie's care was an herbal extract called artemisinin. Artemisinin is a purified extract from the shrub *Artemisia annua*, which has been used in traditional Chinese herbal medicine for millennia for the treatment of many diseases. It is still commonly used today in Southeast Asia to alleviate malaria. Artemisinin's cancer-fighting abilities stem from its capacity to rob cancer cells of iron, causing them to cease growth. I chose this purified herbal extract because of the aggressive nature of Rookie's cancer. We did not have time for the gentle, whole-herb approach.

Although he had cancer, Rookie never lost his spunk. Each week when he came to my office for acupuncture he greeted me with an energetic, almost aggressive, bark. It took months before I realized that he meant no harm but actually enjoyed his treatments. Mrs. Guthrie told me that he got excited at the mention of going to see "Dr. Doug." His excited barking would begin in the car when they were a few blocks from the office.

Rookie lived happily for two more years until cancer finally overtook him.

Artemisinin helped Rookie fight cancer.

you read in the company's marketing material. Try products from various manufacturers and see what works for you. You may need to start out by asking an experienced herbalist for his recommendation for a reputable herb supplier.

HERBAL HOMECARE

Herbal remedies are readily available, relatively inexpensive, and easy for anyone to administer for the aid of many canine conditions. The use of herbs does require a certain amount of patience, as they tend to work more gently and therefore more slowly than the pharmaceuticals we have become accustomed to. With that in mind, the following information will help you in your quest for holistic herbal health for your dog.

Herbal Cautions

Generally, herbs are very safe for pets and have many fewer side effects than drugs. The most common problem with any herbal remedy is gastrointestinal upset. If, after taking a herb, your dog has a loss of appetite, vomiting, or diarrhea, then stop the remedy. When your pet's system returns to normal, restart the herb at half the dose and gradually work up to the recommended level.

Very rarely, a pet may have an allergic reaction to a specific herb, as can happen with any medication. This will usually manifest with the symptoms of hives, itching, and/or a swollen face. If your pet experiences such a reaction, discontinue the herb and find an alternative. Severe hypersensitivity reactions may require emergency veterinary care.

Pets can generally take the same herbs that we do with a few exceptions:

Herbal remedies are readily available, relatively inexpensive, and easy for anyone to administer for the aid of many canine conditions.

Garlic

As we discussed in Chapter 3, garlic can be toxic to dogs in high doses. However, I have never seen any reports of toxicity when given at a reasonable dose of a clove per 50 pounds (22.7 kg). Many times, theoretical cautions for particular herbs are based on certain constituents — but often these concerns do not pan out in the real world, possibly due to the buffering capacity of the plant's other ingredients.

- **Tea tree oil** and **pennyroyal** are very toxic if swallowed by dogs. Even when applied topically, it is possible for a dog to become ill if he licks the area.
- **Hops** are toxic to greyhounds.
- **Comfrey** can cause liver damage in any pet.
- **Garlic** contains phytochemicals that can reportedly cause problems with red blood cells, but I have never seen any reports of toxicity when given at a reasonable dose of a clove per 50 pounds (22.7 kg).

Certain herbs should be used only under the supervision of an informed practitioner if a pet is suffering from specific medical conditions:

- Pets with **kidney disease** should stay away from **dandelion** and **parsley**.
- **Heart patients** need to avoid **motherwort**, **goldenseal**, **Oregon grape**, and **barberry**.
- For pets suffering from any type of **autoimmune disorder**, **echinacea**, **reishi mushrooms**, **maitake mushrooms**, and **astragalus** should be used with caution.
- Dogs with **thyroid disease** should not take **kelp** or **bugleweed**.

Herb–Drug Interactions

Herbs can interact with drugs in several ways, and research on the combined effects of herbs and drugs is in no way complete. We do know that specific herbs can augment the actions of some drugs, necessitating a reduced drug dose. Herbs can also diminish a medication's intended effect. Finally, combining herbs with drugs can create new, unexpected effects. Be sure to consult a knowledgeable veterinarian before using herbs along with pharmaceuticals. Also, when being examined for any problem, let your veterinarian know if you have your dog on any herbs or supplements.

Just to give you an idea of the complexity of herb–drug interactions, here are some examples to keep in mind.

Herbs Can Enhance Drug Effects

Herbs used to treat a certain condition may enhance the effects of drugs used for that condition. Gymnema and bitter melon are herbs used to treat diabetes, and their use may cause a diabetic to need less insulin. Licorice and bayberry can increase the potency of glucocorticoids. White willow bark, the herb from which aspirin was derived, can enhance the effects (and side effects) of nonsteroidal anti-inflammatory drugs (NSAIDs). Convallaria and squill can potentiate digoxin. Hawthorn and ginseng can enhance the effects of any cardiac drug. Finally, valerian can increase the sedation caused by drugs that depress the central nervous system.

Our Feline Friends

Cats have a different detoxification system than dogs do and are more susceptible to side effects from certain herbs and drugs.

Herbs Can Delay Drug Absorption

Other interactions include the fact that high-fiber herbs, such as flaxseed and psyllium, may delay the absorption of any drug. Herbs high in tannins, like grape seed extract and green tea, can inhibit the absorption of certain drugs.

Herbs Can Act As Anticoagulants

Some herbs (gingko, garlic, ginseng, ginger, turmeric, cayenne, reishi mushrooms, and white willow bark) have an anticoagulant effect and should not be used with anticoagulant drugs or in dogs with gastrointestinal ulcers or blood clotting problems.

Herbs Can Interfere With Liver Detox

Last, some herbs, including cat's claw, chamomile, echinacea, elder root, eleuthero, gingko, goldenseal, hops, garlic, licorice, milk thistle, red clover, rosemary, saw palmetto, St. John's wort, valerian, and wild cherry bark, can interfere with a dog's liver detoxification system. They should be used with extreme caution if the pet is on phenobarbital, glucocorticoids, ketoconazole, midazolam, or calcium channel blockers.

This is in no way a complete list of all possible herb–drug interactions, but should give you an appreciation of some

Herbal dosing guidelines for your dog will depend on his weight.

of the possible problems. Although herbs are considered harmless, the combination of phytochemicals and pharmaceuticals can be deadly. If in doubt, do not mix herbs with other medications.

Dosing for Dogs

Some herbal companies specialize in pet remedies. Such products have dosing recommendations on the label. Although it is much easier to find human products, use of these on your dog necessitates calculating the dose yourself. Luckily, this is easily accomplished. If you consider that the human dose is determined for someone weighing 150 pounds (68 kg), then you simply divide your pet's weight by 150 (68 for metric) to get the fraction of the human dose to give your dog. For example, for a 50-pound (22.7 kg) dog the calculation is:

50/150 = 1/3 the human dose (22.7/68 = 1/3 if you are using metric measurements). So, if the directions on a product for humans say to give three tablets three times daily, you would give a 50-pound (22.7 kg) dog one tablet three times daily.

Dosing Guidelines

The chart below outlines general dosing guidelines for dogs based on weight. The frequency for the doses is two to three times per day.

DOSING CHART

Dog Weight	Tea	Dried Herb	Tincture
Under 10 pounds (4.5 kg)	1/8 cup (29.6 ml)	1/8 teaspoon	1–3 drops
10–20 pounds (4.5–9 kg)	¼ cup (59.1 ml)	¼–½ teaspoon	3–5 drops
21–50 pounds (9.5–22.7 kg)	¼–½ cup (59.1–118.2 ml)	½–1 teaspoon	5–10 drops
51–100 pounds (23–45.3 kg)	½–1 cup (118.2–236.5 ml)	1–2 teaspoons	10–20 drops
Over 100 pounds (45.3 kg)	1 cup (236.5 ml)	2–3 teaspoons	20–30 drops

Dosing herbs is less exacting than dosing drugs. All dosing schedules are approximations—some individuals require more than others. The same dog may need one particular dose schedule for a condition at one time and another dose schedule for the same condition at another time. It is usually best to dose to effect. Start off with a low dose and then, after a month or so, evaluate the herb's effect on your dog. If no improvement has occurred, increase the dose. If the pet is improving, continue the initial amount. When the dog is better, taper him off the remedy.

Ten Helpful Herbs to Use at Home

Herbal medicine can easily be applied by any pet owner. To get started, find a reliable source for herbs and begin trying them out on your pet. The information below will give you a place to start. If your dog has any of the problems mentioned, simply give the appropriate herb. Plus, even healthy pets can benefit from tonic herbs like ginseng or from detoxifying herbs like milk thistle.

Try different forms of herbal remedies and rotate off and on various herbs. Get your dog used to taking herbs, so that they will be easy to give when they are really needed. See if he likes the taste of specific herbs sprinkled on his food. Some animals are naturally drawn to the remedies they need.

Chamomile can be used for inflammatory bowel disease, car sickness, and as a digestive aid.

Chamomile

Uses: Anti-inflammatory; antispasmodic; antibacterial; mild sedative; good for inflammatory bowel disease, car sickness, digestion, hot spots.

The flowers of the chamomile plant (*Matricaria recutita*) have anti-inflammatory, antispasmodic, antibacterial, and a mild sedative effect. This herb can be used for inflammatory bowel disease, car sickness, and as a digestive aid. It can be sponged onto inflamed skin as a topical application. For a stronger effect, make a poultice by cooking oatmeal in chamomile tea and apply the mixture to a "hot spot." You then get the anti-inflammatory benefit of both the chamomile and oats.

Cautions: Chamomile can cause skin irritation in pets with a ragweed allergy, and an excessive dose can irritate the gastrointestinal tract.

Use echinacea to help your pet stave off or overcome any infection.

Echinacea

Uses: Enhance immune system; overcome infection.

Ginger can be used to ease carsickness, diarrhea, nausea, and coughing.

Echinacea is a very popular and useful herb for dogs. The scientific names for the appropriate herbal remedies are *Echinacea angustifolia* and *Echinacea purpurea*. The rhizomes and roots are the medicinal plant parts, and echinacea can be used to enhance the immune system. Use echinacea to help your pet stave off or overcome any infection. It can be used alone or with antibiotics, as the situation dictates.

Cautions: There is no known toxicity to this herb (try to find that phrase in any drug insert) but it should be used with caution in pets with any kind of autoimmune disease. Echinacea products are very commonly adulterated—meaning that they contain plant material other than the desired herb—so be sure to purchase your supply from a reputable company.

Ginger

Uses: Digestive tonic; antispasmodic; good for carsickness, diarrhea, nausea, and coughing.

Ginger (*Zingiber officinale*) is one of my favorite herbs. The rhizomes are the medicinal part of this plant. Ginger can be used as a digestive tonic and antispasmodic. It can be used to ease carsickness, diarrhea, nausea, and coughing. To help with the nausea associated with chemotherapy, a dog can be given 25 milligrams of the dried herb per pound of body weight (or 55 milligrams per kg), three times daily.

Ginseng balances the immune system.

Cautions: Large overdoses of ginger have been reported to cause depression of the central nervous system and heart arrhythmias. Because ginger reduces the blood's ability to clot, it should not be used in dogs with blood clotting problems, those with gastrointestinal ulcers, or in conjunction with surgery. Also, ginger has a warming effect on the body and may exacerbate a pet's fever.

Ginseng

Uses: Tonic; balance immune system.

Ginseng (*Panax ginseng*) is another great herb.

As with echinacea, the roots and rhizomes are used. Ginseng is classified as a tonic herb. Sometimes called *adaptogens*, tonic herbs enhance the overall functioning of the body, allowing it to more easily adapt to change. Ginseng also balances the immune system and is synergistic with cardiac medications.

Cautions: It is extremely rare to see toxicity due to its use, but ginseng can possibly cause diarrhea and nervousness. Due to its popularity, it is commonly adulterated.

Licorice

Uses: Anti-inflammatory; good for coughing, dermatitis, gastrointestinal ulcers, inflammatory bowel disease, cancer, infections, and arthritis.

Licorice (*Glycyrrhiza glabra*) is an extremely versatile herb—almost every Chinese herbal formula contains at least some licorice. The roots and rhizomes are the medicinal parts. Licorice has an anti-inflammatory effect, especially on the lungs and gastrointestinal tract. Licorice appears to reduce inflammation at least in part by prolonging the body's utilization of its own cortisol, so reach for this herb instead of giving glucocorticoids like prednisone, prednisolone, and dexamethasone. Problems that can be aided with licorice include coughing, dermatitis, gastrointestinal ulcers, inflammatory bowel disease, cancer, infections, and arthritis.

Cautions: Long-term use of licorice can cause sodium retention, so this herb should be used with caution in pets with heart, liver, or kidney disease.

Problems that can be aided with licorice include coughing, dermatitis, gastrointestinal ulcers, inflammatory bowel disease, cancer, infections, and arthritis.

Marshmallow Plant

Uses: Enhance immune system; suppress coughing; good for bronchitis and respiratory infections; helps treat gastric ulcers, gastritis, enteritis, bladder inflammation, diarrhea, and constipation.

We use the flowers, leaves, and roots of the marshmallow plant (*Althaea officinalis*) for its several helpful effects. Marshmallow helps to enhance immune function, suppress coughing, break up mucous, and moisten mucous membranes, so it can be used for bronchitis and respiratory infections. Its normalizing effect on mucous membranes make it ideal for treating gastric ulcers, gastritis,

Milk thistle is helpful for any liver issue.

enteritis, and bladder inflammation. Marshmallow can also be used for either diarrhea or constipation.

Cautions: Marshmallow has no known side effects, but may delay the absorption of drugs given concurrently.

Milk Thistle

Uses: Protects and restores the liver; antioxidant; body detoxification.

Milk thistle (*Silybum marianum*) is helpful for any liver issue. The fruits, shells, seeds, and leaves are used and have both a protective and a restorative effect on the liver. Milk thistle also has antioxidant properties so it can help protect the body from oxidative damage caused by toxins and aging. Milk thistle increases the compound glutathione in the liver, which helps the body detoxify. In addition to its use in treating liver disease, milk thistle should be given to any animal undergoing chemotherapy—not only because it can protect the liver from the drugs' harmful effects, but it can actually augment the anticancer action of the drugs.

Cautions: There is no known toxicity from milk thistle.

Oregon Grape

Uses: Anti-inflammatory; antibiotic; digestive tonic; good for fighting infection and sluggish digestion.

In place of the popular herb goldenseal—which should be avoided due to the fact that it has been overharvested—I recommend the use of Oregon grape (*Mahonia aquifolium*). The roots of this plant have anti-inflammatory, antibiotic, and digestive tonic effects. Oregon grape can be used to help a pet fight off any type of infection and can also be used for sluggish digestion.

Cautions: Oregon grape should be used with caution in dogs with liver disease.

Saint John's Wort

Uses: Calming effect; nerve tonic; good for hyperactivity, separation anxiety, nerve injuries.

The leaves and flowers of Saint John's wort (*Hypericum perforatum*) are used for their calming effect and also as a nerve tonic. This is the herb for hyperactive dogs and those with separation anxiety. It can also be used to help with any type of nerve injury.

Cautions: Saint John's wort should not be used in conjunction with other antianxiety medications; prolonged use has been associated with skin sensitivity to sunlight.

Saw Palmetto

Uses: Decrease inflammation; good for enlarged prostate gland; appetite stimulant.

Saw palmetto (*Serenoa repens*) berries can be used to decrease inflammation and to reduce the effects of male hormones. This herb is ideal for dogs with benign prostatic hyperplasia (an enlarged prostate gland). Saw palmetto may also be used to stimulate a pet's appetite.

Cautions: There is no known toxicity to this herb.

WHAT TO EXPECT

Herbs tend to take longer to have their effect than drugs do. You must be patient and consistent. Often, subtle signs of improvement are the first indication that you are on the right track. For example, the first signs of progress for a dog with red, itchy, flaky patches of skin may be lessening of skin odor. The longer the condition has been affecting your dog, the longer it will take for his body to respond.

FINDING A VETERINARY HERBALIST

Herbal medicine can be easily applied by any dog owner for mild conditions or, with the help of a knowledgeable veterinarian, for more severe conditions. As with other alternative methods, human practitioners may not be aware of the unique aspects of prescribing herbs for pets. Several certification courses are available for veterinarians using both Western and Chinese herbal medicine, and the field of veterinary herbalism is growing quickly. For more information on herbs for pets, and to locate a veterinarian with training in this area of expertise, check the resources at the back of this book.

C h a p t e r

HOMEOPATHY

H omeopathy is an extremely unique alternative therapy. It is also the most misunderstood and least accepted of all holistic modalities. As you will see, this method of treatment is based on principles that seem to totally contradict the Western view of disease and therapeutics. Yet, all of its basic underpinnings have been derived from rigorous, scientific experimentation and meticulous observation. In spite of homeopathy's strange concepts and mysterious mode of action, this therapy can produce profound, even unbelievable, results.

WHAT IS HOMEOPATHY?

The word homeopathy is derived from the Greek roots *homoios* meaning "similar" and *pathos* meaning "suffering." The derivation points to the basic treatment principle of homeopathy: the *law of similars* or "like cures like." Simply stated, it means the problems a substance causes can be cured by that substance. We will explore this proposal in greater detail as we proceed. A good question to start with is, "Who ever came up with this idea in the first place?"

BENEFITS

Homeopathy has many benefits, including:

- Homeopathic remedies are inexpensive
- Remedies are easily accessible without a prescription
- Homeopathy is free of side effects (unless grossly misapplied)
- Homeopathy provides permanent cures for serious conditions
- Many homeopathic remedies can be of help in first-aid situations

HOMEOPATHY HISTORY

The suggestion that a medicine that causes certain symptoms could be used to cure a

This store showcases a display of homeopathic remedies.

patient suffering from those symptoms is actually very old and widespread. It was used as a treatment principle by ancient Egyptians, Chinese, Incas, Aztecs, and Native Americans.

In the West, the idea of "like cures like" was first discussed in the Hippocratic writings (460–370 BCE). However, the Greek physician Galen (129–200 CE) formally instituted the law of contraries as the basis of practice. This common-sense approach proposed such things as treating a fever with cooling medications and treating a dry condition with moisture. Galen was such a successful and influential figure that his theories became dogma and went unchallenged until the mid-16th century. In the meantime, the law of similars was relegated to the realm of folk medicine.

Paracelsus

The Swiss-born physician, Theophrastus Bombastus von Hohenheim (1493–1541), popularly known as Paracelsus, actually coined the phrase *similia similibus curantur*— "like cures like"—among other treatment theories. Although Paracelsus was an innovative physician and prolific writer, due to his radical doctrines, abrasive personality, and proclivity to wander from place to place, his ideas were never accepted. He was considered to be a quack by his contemporaries, and that reputation held for centuries to come.

Samuel Hahnemann

Homeopathy was formally developed into an exacting science by the German physician, Samuel Hahnemann (1755–1843), who may have been influenced by Paracelsus (although he would never admit to it). Hahnemann was a genius during a time when the practice of medicine was crude and brutal. He was surrounded by physicians who bled patients to the point of shock, gave large doses of toxic substances (such as mercury), and gave purgatives to induce violent diarrhea to "clear the body" of disease. These medical practitioners had studied at prestigious institutions and were considered well-educated. Their methods were considered state-of-the-art at that time in history.

It was obvious to Hahnemann that the medical community was misguided and did more harm than good. He decided to drop out of the practice of medicine and utilize his exceptional linguistic talent by translating medical texts. This activity exposed him to the ancient homeopathic principle.

During this time, there was a dispute among Hahnemann's peers as to why cinchona bark was a useful herb for curing malaria. One physician thought that it was due to various properties of that remedy. Hahnemann argued that there were other herbs with similar properties that had no effect whatsoever on malaria. He came to believe that there was a unique property of cinchona bark that matched the qualities of malaria.

With the law of similars on his mind, he decided to experiment on himself. He began taking doses of cinchona bark and noting the changes in his body. Over time, he developed the very symptoms that malaria patients suffered. This test confirmed to Hahnemann the value of the homeopathic principle, and he immediately put his new methods to work on patients.

Buoyed by his success, Hahnemann loudly criticized the medical practitioners who continued the accepted but atrocious methods of his time. He coined the word *allopathy*, meaning "other suffering," to denote any medical practice that does not utilize the law of similars. This hostility, combined with the fact that new ideas are not easily accepted, led to staunch opposition to homeopathy by the established medical community—an opposition that continues to this day.

Homeopathy was formally developed into an exacting science by the German physician, Samuel Hahnemann.

Homeopathy Spreads

In spite of this tension, the practice of homeopathy quickly spread across Europe and even into India. It made it to the United States in the 1820s. In fact, homeopaths established the first national medical association, the American Institute of Homeopathy (AIH), in 1844. The allopaths quickly answered by forming the American Medical Association (AMA) in 1846. From correspondence between the founding members of the AMA, it is clear that they had as their main objective the discrediting of homeopathy. In spite of AMA harassment—such as

The use of homeopathy for pets is becoming more popular.

not allowing doctors to speak to homeopaths—by 1900, 22 homeopathic medical schools and over 100 homeopathic hospitals were established. At that time, one-fourth of all American physicians were homeopaths.

Due to medical technological advances, the development of antibiotics, and the power of the AMA, the practice of homeopathy declined drastically in the United States in the early twentieth century. However, in the last 40 years, as Americans have grown weary of Western medicine's expense, side-effects, and limitations, homeopathy has made a comeback.

In countries free of the influence of the AMA, homeopathy has always been popular. Even today, 39 percent of French physicians and 20 percent of German physicians prescribe homeopathic medications. Forty-five percent of Dutch physicians consider them to be effective, and 42 percent of British physicians refer patients to homeopaths.

Homeopathy in Pets

The use of homeopathy in pets in the U.S. has been championed by Richard Pitcairn, DVM. He graduated from veterinary school in 1965, from the University of California at Davis, California. After a few years in practice, he went back into academics and research, earning an additional degree in Veterinary Microbiology, and teaching at the Washington State University Veterinary School. Dr. Pitcairn became intrigued by homeopathy and began training programs for veterinarians in 1986. In 1995, the Academy of Veterinary Homeopathy was founded as a nonprofit, professional organization for veterinarians interested in this modality.

SEVEN BASIC PRINCIPLES OF HOMEOPATHY

As previously mentioned, homeopathy is based on scientifically derived principles. Hahnemann discovered and developed these concepts through years of application and observation. The final product of this work is a complete system of healing that is as technically precise as it is controversial. Homeopathy can best be understood by familiarizing oneself with seven basic principles.

#1: The Vital Force

The first basic principle is the philosophy of *vitalism*—it's the foundation of homeopathy. Yes, once again we come across the idea that there is something special about living things—life force energy. Hahnemann called this invisible power the "vital force." He saw the vital force as an energy pattern that governs and animates the physical body. It is this unseen template that is responsible for maintaining the harmony and homeostasis of every living being. If the vital force is in order, then the body is healthy. If the vital force is affected by a disturbance, then the body will soon be negatively affected as well.

The idea of unseen forces is nothing new to science. Both gravity and magnetism have never been directly seen. Their existence is inferred by their effects. Just so, the organizing principle of life can be assumed by the fact that individuals maintain their identities even though their bodies change. Think about it—a ten-year-old dog literally has a totally different body than he did when he was one year old. Every cell in his body has been replaced and every molecule in his DNA has been swapped. The essence of his being, his vital force, is the only constant.

#2: Symptoms Are Not the Disease

The second important concept is that symptoms are not the disease. We assume that it is "bad" for a dog to vomit or have a thick, green nasal discharge. However, if the dog ate something toxic or is being attacked by a gastrointestinal pathogen, then vomiting may be a way for his body to avert disaster. And the flow of a nasal discharge, which is full of white blood cells and antibodies, helps the body rid itself of disease-causing organisms.

Symptoms are the body's response to stress and thus are part of the body's defense mechanism. When we use medications to abolish symptoms, we interfere with the body's means of regaining health. According to the principles of homeopathy, symptoms are not to be controlled, managed, or eliminated. Such a treatment strategy drives the disease deeper into the energy system.

Academy of Veterinary Homeopathy

You can visit the Academy of Veterinary Homeopathy (AVH) on the web at www.theavh.org.

Homeopaths use symptoms as a guide for choosing the right homeopathic remedy. Each patient is carefully evaluated for the key features that represent his response to the particular disease. The symptoms provide a picture that signals which remedy is appropriate. In fact, the word *symptom* is derived from a Greek

Vitalism, the idea of life force energy, is the foundation of homeopathy.

word meaning *signal*.

A veterinary homeopath evaluates all symptoms a pet experiences. This detailed assessment includes not only physical symptoms, such as limping, vomiting, and skin rash, but also mental/emotional issues such as phobias, behavioral habits, and personality dispositions. Homeopaths look closely at the qualities of the symptoms. They ask such questions as, "What color was the vomitus?" and "Is the itching relieved by warm or cold applications?"

Finally, all the symptoms the pet has experienced throughout his lifetime, as well as his current condition, are used to help find the right homeopathic remedy. For homeopaths, only one disease is responsible for all of the problems an individual experiences. This single abnormal energy pattern often expresses itself in various ways throughout life. The disease responsible for all the symptoms can be cured with the matching homeopathic remedy.

#3: The True Nature of Disease

The third important homeopathic principle regards the true nature of disease. According to homeopathy, all disease starts as a disturbance of the vital force. Thus, disease manifests energetically before there is a physical trace of it. In conventional medical terms, we call this a *functional* disturbance. A period of time exists when an animal starts to become ill but has not reached the point of detectable organ damage. From a conventional perspective, no disease is measurable at this point, but the disturbance in the vital force is obvious to the owner. The pet is not suffering from a named, Western disease, but he is surely not healthy.

Because the root cause of disease is an energy disturbance, it can only be effectively treated on the energetic level. Symptoms can be treated with conventional medications and surgery, but only homeopathic remedies address the underlying cause of disease and eradicate it from the body.

#4: The Law of Similars

The fourth basic concept of homeopathy is that the law of similars is the most effective way to treat disease. Since symptoms are the body's response to disease, then strengthening this response will help the body balance the disturbance. So, a remedy that causes specific symptoms in a healthy person can be used to cure a person suffering from a disease that causes those same specific symptoms.

Symptom

The word *symptom* is derived from a Greek word meaning *signal*.

After Hahnemann came to understand the law of similars by experimenting on himself and treating others, students flocked to him to learn this new healing technique. He used his students to investigate new homeopathic medicines. Volunteers would take a substance and keep detailed notes on any changes they experienced. The notes from various people about each remedy were compiled to determine each substance's unique symptom profile and thus their medicinal properties. Hahnemann called these human experiments *provings*. Hundreds of materials have been so tested, including herbs, toxins, minerals, foods, and bacteria.

#5: Remedy Specificity

The fifth homeopathic concept has to do with the specific nature of the homeopathic remedy. For homeopathic success, the remedy must match the patient's entire, unique symptom picture. Each individual may manifest the same disease differently.

For example, a dog infected with canine parvovirus is likely to have a loss of appetite, vomiting, and diarrhea. But, the dog's diarrhea may be bloody, tarry, brown, or even yellow. He may vomit constantly or only after drinking water. He may vomit clear fluid, yellow fluid, or he might not vomit at all. Each of these nuances of disease points to a different homeopathic remedy. So, no

Burned Your Finger?

Here is a simple homeopathic treatment that anyone can try on themselves. The next time you burn your finger on the stove, instead of running cold water over it, hold your finger in water that is as warm as you can tolerate. "Like cures like," and you will find that, although the warm water treatment is not very soothing, your burn will blister less and heal faster than expected. I have personally experienced this effect, and I assure you it works

one homeopathic remedy exists for canine parvovirus; each patient must be viewed individually to determine the appropriate remedy. Conventional medicine treats diseases, while homeopathy treats patients.

#6: Remedy Dilution and Potentization

The sixth concept has to do with how homeopathic remedies are made. Hahnemann soon noticed that since the remedies he was giving mimicked the symptoms the patient was suffering from, the remedy would often cause the patient's symptoms to get worse before the patient got better. This outcome came to be known as an *aggravation.*

In order to alleviate the disease without increasing the patient's suffering, Hahnemann began to dilute the remedies. He found that the diluted remedies did not lose their ability to affect the patient's vital force. To the contrary, when Hahnemann agitated the remedies vigorously as he diluted them—a procedure known as *succession*—the remedies gained energetic potency. The combination of dilution and succession of the homeopathic remedy is responsible for its *potentization.*

The most common dilution is 1:100, which Hahnemann called a "C" dilution (C standing for *centesimal* or 100). Each remedy started with a solution of established chemical strength. Hahnemann would take one part of this *mother tincture* and dilute it with 99 parts water to create a "1C" potency. He would then take one part of this dilution and add to it 99 parts water to continue the potentization process. With each dilution, he shook the mixture vigorously 100 times. A remedy that has undergone this dilution method 30 times is known as a 30C potency of the remedy.

Other systems for diluting the remedies have also been devised. For example, remedies that are diluted one part tincture to nine parts water are called "X" potencies. A 24X remedy has been diluted 1:10, 24 times.

Usually, the potentized water is poured onto sugar pellets to form homeopathic remedy granules. These granules come in various sizes. The granules do not need to be swallowed, but simply need to make contact with the mucous membranes of the mouth, to dissolve and initiate their action.

Less Is More?

It is easy to see why conventional medical practitioners have a hard time swallowing homeopathy. It seems ridiculous to think that the more dilute the remedy, the stronger it becomes. Everyone knows that the more you take, the more powerful are the effects of any medicine.

And the problem for homeopathy's credibility gets worse. Eventually, in any dilution process you reach the point where no molecules of the original substance are detectable in the mixture. It is a chemical fact that any homeopathic potency over 24X or 12C has not one molecule of the mother tincture in it. How can homeopaths claim their remedies do anything if they do not exist?

From the homeopathic point of view, the potentization process transfers the energy of the medicinal substance to the remedy. The more material the remedy contains, the less energy there is and vice versa. The forceful agitation of the solution with each dilution seems to be key to the energy transfer. Remedies that are diluted without proper succession do not gain potency.

Dosing Differences

A significant difference between homeopathic dosing and that of conventional drug dosing is that, in homeopathy, the potency of the remedy is important, not the number of pills given. So whether a dog is given two 30C granules or six 30C granules, the effect on his energy system is the same. However, giving two granules three times daily has a much different effect than six granules once daily. Also, giving two 30C granules would cause a totally different outcome than giving one 60C granule.

For homeopathic success, the remedy must match the patient's entire, unique symptom picture.

Potentized Remedies Are Not Always Homeopathic

We tend to think of potentized remedies as being homeopathic, but an important point must be made. By definition, homeopathy refers to the law of similars, so the thing that makes a remedy homeopathic is not how it is made but rather how it is used. A remedy is homeopathic when it is used as an individual remedy for a disease that matches the remedy's unique symptom pattern. Potentized pills containing multiple remedies as a catch-all treatment are not homeopathic.

#7: Treatment Outcomes

According to homeopathy, there are only three possible outcomes from any medical therapy. The first, *suppression,* occurs when the symptoms of disease are artificially removed through medication or surgery. Since symptoms are the body's way of dispersing the disease, any interference with this process can drive the disease deeper. So, when cortisone is given to alleviate a dog's rash, the pet may feel better on the surface, but the underlying disturbance of the vital force may be made worse. Even a simple surgery to remove a wart can suppress the primary disease. When a disease is suppressed, then more serious problems will develop in the future.

A second possible outcome of medical treatment is *palliation.* Palliation occurs when the symptomatic treatment temporarily covers the symptoms but is not strong enough to suppress the disease. This is what happens when a medication causes a rash to go away, only to have it return shortly after the treatment is discontinued. Palliation allows the underlying energy imbalance to progress while the patient is more comfortable. Continued palliation of symptoms often eventually leads to suppression of the disease.

The third potential result of a given therapy is *cure.* Cure has a very different meaning in homeopathy than it does in conventional medicine. For instance, cancer therapies are often said to be "curative" if the patient is alive a few years after chemotherapy, even if the person is continuously sick and dies shortly after the deadline. For the homeopath, cure means that the disease has been totally abolished from the patient's energy field. No trace of that problem will rear its ugly head again.

Surgery is almost always suppressive since it strongly affects symptoms. Conventional medications can be either suppressive or palliative. Homeopathy, being the only therapy that works on the vital force, it is the only treatment that can truly cure a patient. However, if misapplied, homeopathy can palliate or suppress disease, too.

THE SCIENCE BEHIND HOMEOPATHY

By now you can realize the strangeness of homeopathy. The mode of action has yet to be fully explained from the conventional standpoint. Of course, it is not unusual for humans to utilize something before we totally understand the process. Sailors ate fruits to cure and prevent scurvy hundreds of years before vitamin C was discovered. We do not fully comprehend the modes of action of many drugs we currently use. We can't even explain how light can be both a wave and a particle—but that does not stop us from flipping the light switch. Having acknowledged the difficulties with understanding homeopathy, it's important to note that some scientific concepts and medical research validate this modality.

Information in Water

One of the criticisms directed against homeopathic remedies is that they are no different from water. However, evidence suggests that water can store information. Research has shown that, although no two snowflakes are exactly alike, when an ice crystal is thawed and then refrozen under identical conditions, the exact

Since symptoms are the body's way of dispersing the disease, any interference with this process can drive the disease deeper.

Sam's Story

Sam was a six-year-old Labrador Retriever who was rushed to my office on emergency one Sunday afternoon. He had collapsed from heat stroke after playing too long in the hot July sun. His owner carried him in, and I could see right away that he was in serious trouble. His bright red tongue hung out of his panting mouth, and he had a life-threateningly high temperature of 107.8°F (42°C). His pupils were very dilated, and he was in a mental delirium. The dog also flinched with spasmodic motions whenever he was touched. I was concerned that, if he lived, he would have permanent brain damage.

I immediately started IV fluids to support his cardiovascular system and to cool his core. With heat stroke, it is important not to chill the body too fast so a cold water bath was out of the question. In the midst of the emergency, I remembered my homeopathic training. The two main remedies for heat stroke are Aconitum and Belladonna. Both treat hot animals, but Aconitum is associated with fear and restlessness, while the Belladonna patient has dilated pupils, delirium, and spasms. Sam was a Belladonna patient.

I grabbed my homeopathic kit and dosed Sam with 30C Belladonna every five minutes. After the fourth dose, Sam became more comfortable, his panting subsided, and his pupils returned to a more normal size. He also stopped having spasms. I stopped the remedy, waited, and watched.

About forty-five minutes later, I noticed that Sam was starting to slowly relapse with a return of the panting and twitching. I dosed him once again with the 30C Belladonna and within minutes he once again improved—this time for good.

I kept him overnight for observation, but it was just a formality. Sam was cured and went home looking and acting just as normal as he had been before his exuberant exercise incident. That was the fasted recovery from serious heat stroke I had ever witnessed, and I have never doubted the power of homeopathy since.

crystalline structure will reform. Also, magnetic resonance imaging (MRI) analysis of high-potency homeopathic remedies shows a difference between them and pure water even though they are chemically identical.

Hormesis

There is an effect in chemistry known as the Arndt-Schultz law, also known as *hormesis*. It describes biphasic drug action—meaning a drug that has two phases of action. We think of drugs as having a linear effect on the body. If you give one pill, you have a certain response. If you double the dose, you get twice the effect, and so on. Well, it turns out that at very minute, homeopathic doses of a given medication, you can actually get a response that is exactly opposite to the expected drug reaction.

For example, atropine is a drug that usually causes the body to shut down secretions such as salivation and tearing. Nevertheless, at homeopathic dilutions, atropine increases secretions. Also, iodine, bromine, mercuric chloride, and arsenous acid—chemicals used to kill yeast—given at homeopathic doses actually stimulate the growth of yeast.

Toxicology Studies

Homeopathic toxicology studies have been done. This research involves giving such poisons as arsenic, bismuth, cadmium, mercuric chloride, and lead to rats. Before and after the poisoning, one group of rats is treated with a 15C or greater potency of the given toxin, while the other group is given no therapy. (Remember, any potency over 12C is chemically identical to water.) The results show that the homeopathically treated group of rats excreted more of the toxin and suffered 40 percent fewer deaths than the untreated group. Pretty good results considering there was "nothing" in the remedy given to the treated group.

Clinical Trials

One double-blind, placebo-controlled clinical trial looked at the use of homeopathy for treating human asthma. Eighty-two percent of the homeopathically treated group improved versus 38 percent of the placebo group. A similar trial studied the homeopathic treatment of Nicaraguan children with diarrhea. The treated group showed significant improvement and recovered 20 percent faster than the untreated group. Interestingly, the homeopaths used 18

While homeopathy can seem strange to the uninformed, there are scientific concepts working behind it.

Meta-Analysis

A meta-analysis is a scientific investigation that evaluates comparable research and compiles their data. Such an analysis of 100 homeopathic toxin studies found 40 of them to be of high quality. Of those 40 studies, 27 showed a significantly positive result of using homeopathics.

Meta-analysis of 107 clinical trials where homeopathy was used to treat such problems as infections, hay fever, and pain found 22 high-quality studies. Of those 22 studies, 15 were favorable toward homeopathy. (Incidentally, lest you get the impression that homeopathic research is sloppy, conventional clinical trials have a similar percent of flawed studies.)

different remedies, individually selected based on the patients' symptom pictures.

TREATING WITH HOMEOPATHY: WHAT TO EXPECT

Homeopathic remedies are inexpensive and readily available at most health food stores.

However, knowing which remedy to use in a given situation takes a lot of training and practice. In addition, it is somewhat difficult to prescribe for chronic disease states.

Homeopathic repertories have been compiled for humans. These dense texts contain a listing of symptoms and, after each symptom, a list of remedies that have been known to cause that symptom is given. The remedies for a given symptom are rated on a three-point scale as to the likelihood that it will cause that symptom.

From the list of symptoms, the homeopath chooses the most helpful. He goes to the homeopathic repertory, looks up each symptom, and lists the appropriate remedies from each. Now, by comparing lists of remedies that are highly associated with each symptom, the homeopath can usually find just a few that can cause all that individual's symptoms. (Computer programs are now available to simplify this process.) The doctor then chooses the best of these remedies to give the patient.

It is not easy to find the right remedy for people. This difficulty is complicated many times over when prescribing for animals. For one thing, many of the important homeopathic symptoms are mental and cannot be directly reported by the canine patient. Some mental attitudes can be inferred by the dog's behavior, but people often misinterpret their pet's motives. The language barrier also makes it difficult for the homeopath to elicit important details. If a dog is limping, we can assume he is experiencing pain. But is the pain throbbing, stabbing, or burning? Each of these variables points to different remedies.

The Exam

The veterinary homeopath "takes the case" by examining the pet and questioning its owner, eliciting many details of the pet's behavior and symptoms. Often the most unusual symptoms are the most important to differentiate one remedy from another. For instance, knowing that a dog has diarrhea is not very helpful since hundreds of remedies could match that symptom. Knowing that an animal has a fear of little white dogs is very unusual and more specific for finding the right remedy.

Potency and Frequency

Homeopathic remedies come in a multitude of potencies. Different potencies are used according to the condition of the individual patient, but the most commonly used potency is 30C. Also, the frequency of administration of the remedy is determined by the pet's disease state. In general, for chronic, ongoing problems, the remedy is given less frequently—maybe every few weeks—while for acute conditions the remedy may need to be given every few minutes.

Knowing which remedy to use in a given situation takes a lot of training and practice.

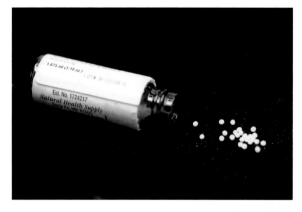

Homeopathic remedies come in a multitude of potencies.

Observing After the Remedy

One remedy is given at a time, and the patient is carefully observed.

No Response

If no response occurs, then most likely the wrong remedy has been selected. No harm, no foul. In this case, the homeopath has learned useful information about the nature of the disease and, because there is no chemical medicine in the remedy, there is no danger of side-effects.

Symptoms Worsen

If, after the remedy is given, the symptoms get worse, it could be an aggravation, which is a good sign because it means that the right remedy has been selected. Worsening of symptoms can also indicate that the wrong remedy was used and the disease process is progressing. It takes keen observational skills to differentiate between these two reactions. An aggravation is characterized by a short duration of symptom worsening while the overall condition of the pet improves. With progression of disease, both the symptoms and the general health state of the dog deteriorates.

Symptoms Get Better

If symptoms get better after the remedy is given, then it could be that the right remedy and right potency were used and the disease is responding. However, it is also possible that the symptoms have improved because the disease has been palliated or even suppressed. If the same symptoms continue to return after repeated dosing, then most likely the remedy is palliating the disease. If the symptoms disappear, but the dog's overall condition worsens or more serious symptoms appear, then the remedy suppressed the disease. If the symptoms improve and remain gone, and the pet's total situation improves, then the remedy is on the way to curing the patient.

Other Symptoms Arise

If, some time after the remedy was given, new, less serious symptoms arise, then the remedy has cleared a layer of disease and

a previous layer is now apparent. At this point, the homeopath takes the new symptoms into consideration, selects a new remedy, and the entire process is repeated.

Homeopathy Is Not a Complementary Therapy

Homeopathy is holistic, but it is not a complementary therapy. Because the homeopath needs to evaluate the patient's response to the remedy he gave, it is usually contraindicated to use conventional medications, or even other holistic modalities, at the same time as homeopathy. These other treatments can interfere with the action of the remedy as well as cloud the homeopath's ability to judge whether changes in the case are due to the homeopathic remedy or the other modality.

Veterinary Homeopaths

As you can see, it is very difficult to use homeopathy for chronic conditions. It is best to consult a trained veterinarian for this type of problem. Lay practitioners do not have the training and animal expertise to competently treat pets. Homeopathic certification courses are graduating excellent veterinarian homeopaths every year. To find one, go to the resources in the back of this book.

The following points will help you choose a homeopath for your dog:

- It is best to choose a veterinarian.
- Be sure the vet has adequate training—the best credential is AVH certification.
- Some veterinary homeopaths work over the phone, which is okay if you have no alternative, but it is best to use one who can physically check your pet.
- You need to have a veterinary homeopath who you feel confident in and comfortable with.

HOMEOPATHIC HOME-CARE

Whereas treating chronic diseases is complicated, homeopathy is a safe and effective means of treating many kinds of acute problems. There is no possibility of negative effects from giving a few doses of the wrong remedy. The worst that will happen is nothing. The 30C homeopathic potency is the easiest to find and use. You may find it handy to have a kit of remedies on hand for life's unforeseen troubles.

THe Homeopathic Perspective on Vaccines

From a homeopathic perspective, vaccines are very harmful. The damage caused by this practice goes far beyond the obvious concerns about the effects of overvaccinating on the immune system. Homeopaths have coined the word *vaccinosis* to label any adverse condition brought on by vaccinations. According to homeopaths, vaccines cause a severe disturbance of the vital force. Energetic troubles and the resultant physical symptoms that originate from vaccination may not be apparent for years. Symptoms that homeopaths associate with vaccines include epilepsy, arthritis, allergies, tumors, and warts. Vaccines can also be a block to the action of homeopathic remedies and can even undo the positive effects of homeopathic treatment. Homeopaths believe that vaccines should be avoided at all costs.

The following information about remedies and situations can help the typical dog owner apply homeopathy to their pets. *This material is not meant to take the place of appropriate veterinary care. If your pet has a serious condition, then you need to get him to your veterinarian as soon as possible.* Of course you could pop your dog a few doses of the appropriate homeopathic remedy while you are on your way.

Abscesses

For abscesses, two main remedies are used. To choose the best one, take into consideration both the nature of the problem as well as that of the pet.

- *Hepar sulphuris 30C* is used if the abscess came on suddenly, is painful, and not draining. It is especially used when there is a foreign body to be expelled from the wound. The dog who needs this remedy usually acts as if chilled and has an irritable or even nasty disposition.
- *Silicea* (sometimes called *Silica*) *30C* is for slowly swelling or chronic abscesses that are draining and nonpainful. The pet requiring Silicea is usually timid.

Choose the remedy that best matches your dog's situation.

Bleeding

For bleeding, the two most common remedies are:

- Use *Phosphorus 30C* if the blood is bright red.
- Use *Hamamelis 30C* if the blood is dark and oozing.

Cat Bites

Cat bites can cause much more injury than they appear to on the surface. I know a veterinarian who was sent to the hospital for a few days of IV antibiotics because of a cat bite to her finger. The usual remedy for a cat bite is *Lachesis 30C,* which is derived from the venom of the deadly bushmaster snake. (Don't worry, the homeopathic remedy no longer contains any snake venom.)

Injuries

Arnica 30C comes from the herb leopard's bane and is one of the most useful homeopathic remedies. It is generally used for traumatic pain. Understand that this remedy does not just cover the pain but rather helps the dog rapidly regain normal function. Pain relief is a byproduct of healing. Arnica can be give any time a pet is injured. Examples include:

- a dog who has been hit by a car (give while he is being rushed to the emergency room)
- trauma that causes deep muscle bruising (it's especially helpful for this type of injury).
- recovery from surgery

For other types of injuries, different homeopathic remedies are more appropriate:

- *Symphytum 30C* for bone injuries and fractures

When administering a remedy, pour a few of the granules onto a folded piece of paper and dump them into the dog's mouth.

- *Rhus toxicodendron 30C* for joint damage
- *Ruta graveolens 30C* for injured tendons and ligaments
- *Bellis perennis 30C* for trauma to internal organs
- *Ledum 30C* for puncture wounds
- *Calendula 30C* for wounds with loss of tissue

Insect Bites and Stings

For insect bites and stings, four common possibilities are available:

- Use *Apis mellifica 30C* if the area is swollen and the pet seems comforted by cold applications.
- Use *Ledum 30C* if the wound is not very swollen and the pet likes cold compresses.
- Use *Cantharis 30C* if the wound is hot and blistered.
- Use *Urtica urens 30C* if the dog prefers warm compresses applied to the sting.

Nerve Injuries

Hypericum 30C, made from the herb Saint John's wort, is useful for nerve injuries. It is especially indicated for injuries to a dog's feet, toes, or toenails. It can also be used for dental pain and is a good remedy to use after a pet has had an extraction.

Ruptured Disc

If your dog ruptures a disc in his back and is suddenly paralyzed seek immediate veterinary care. In the meantime, there

The homeopathic remedy for a cat bite is Lachesis 30C.

are two possible homeopathic remedies:

- Use *Nux Vomica 30C* if the dog is acting as if chilled and has become irritable when he is normally friendly.
- Use *Hypericum 30C* for any dog who does not fit the description above.

Vaccinosis

The main remedy for vaccinosis is *Thuja occidentalis 30C*. Because warts are considered to be caused by vaccinosis, this would be a good remedy for any pet with multiple warts. I also commonly give Thuja to dogs at the time of vaccination to mitigate the negative energetic effects of the injections.

Homeopathy is an amazing holistic therapy that can be used for conditions that cannot be identified by conventional medical means. When properly applied, homeopathy can help the body heal itself.

Other Remedies

You can also try the following homeopathic remedies. Use:

- **Hecla lava 30C** for jaw tumors or tooth root infections
- **Nux Vomica 30C** for constipation in newborns, gastric dilatation, and volvulus (GDV), or for an umbilical hernia
- **Secale cornutum 30C** for labor difficulties
- **Silicea 30C** for chronic anal gland problems

Homeopathic Remedy Tips

- Be aware that the names of homeopathic remedies are often abbreviated. For example, *Arnica montana* is shortened to Arn. and *Nux vomica* is Nux-v.
- It is required that the remedy label have a list of indications and an expiration date. Don't let the label confuse you. The most common indications for use are listed, but many more problems can be treated by a given remedy than can possibly fit on the label. Also, if handled properly, homeopathic remedies appear to stay active for decades, so the expiration date is not important.
- Homeopathic remedies are not damaged by exposure to air, but they can be deactivated somewhat easily by unexpected means, such as:
  - vaporous materials (such as camphor), which can diminish their potency
  - electromagnetic fields (they should not be placed near microwave ovens or other electrical devices)
  - direct sunlight and high heat
- Remedies should not be directly handled since a person's skin may harbor materials that can deactivate the granules. When administering a remedy, pour a few of the granules onto a folded piece of paper and dump them into the dog's mouth.
- Do not put the remedy in the pet's food or water bowls as this will neutralize them.
- It is best to give a homeopathic remedy an hour before or after any food or water intake.

Chapter 9

OTHER HOLISTIC
Therapies

In the previous chapters, I addressed some of the most popular holistic therapies in great detail. We looked closely at acupuncture, chiropractic care, massage therapy, herbal medicine, and homeopathy, not only because of their popularity, but also because they are tried-and-true alternative approaches to health. For mild conditions, some of these treatments can be applied by an untrained pet-lover. However, dog owners can and should seek trained professionals to administer these treatments in complicated cases.

This chapter is dedicated to lesser-known holistic modalities. These therapies can be very helpful for the health maintenance of any canine, although the efficacy of some of them has not been scientifically proven. The brief summaries presented here are meant to familiarize the typical dog owner with some basic information and to help him understand the relevance of such treatments.

APPLIED KINESIOLOGY

Applied kinesiology (AK) is sometimes called simply kinesiology or *muscle testing* (although there are differences in the meanings of these three terms). The word *kinesiology* literally means "the study of muscles and their movement." Kinesiology is a specialized area of medical study in which the causes and consequences of physical activity are examined. However, it has little to do with AK. The inventor of AK added *applied* to distinguish this therapy from the formal discipline of kinesiology. By definition, applied kinesiology is used as a diagnostic tool by a licensed professional in conjunction with other medical tests. It is not so much a holistic modality as it is a technique that is sometimes used by holistic practitioners.

History

AK originated with the work of Dr. George Goodheart in the 1960s. As a chiropractor, Dr. Goodheart began to study treatment methods to improve muscle strength. In the process, he discovered factors that could negatively affect muscle function. He found that

When using AK on dogs, surrogate testing is required.

the strength of specific indicator muscle groups could consistently point out what supplements an individual would benefit from. When the patient held a supplement that he needed, his muscles became strong and when he held a supplement his body did not need, his muscles became weak. The process of testing the strength of a group of indicator muscles is known as a muscle test.

How It Works

Applied kinesiology tests an all-or-nothing muscle response to a given stimulus. A positive stimulus induces a strong muscular response while a negative stimulus causes the muscle group to weaken. The process is simple. The patient holds an arm straight out from his body with his elbow locked. The practitioner holds the patient's arm at the wrist, gives a statement, and then presses downward. If the shoulder joint holds, then the statement is "true," if the shoulder gives way, the statement is "false."

Interestingly, the patient's body responds correctly whether or not he consciously knows the answer. In fact, the patient does not even have to hear the question. The process of AK taps into the subconscious mind of the patient. The wisdom of the body is reflected in the function of its muscles.

Surrogate Testing

This all sounds great, but how do we test an animal? We can't very easily ask Fido to hold out his paw as we push down. This is where *surrogate testing* comes into play. To apply AK to dogs, we need to introduce a person into the equation. This surrogate touches the pet with one hand while his opposite arm is used for muscle testing. The combination of the bioelectric fields of the pet and the surrogate, along with the intention of the practitioner to test the animal, allows for access to the animal's inner physiology.

Many techniques are used for muscle testing. Some are good while others are not reliable. There are also various ranges of skill of and training for practitioners. Some holistic veterinarians really seem to be able to make this system work for them and their patients.

Benefits

AK can allow the holistic practitioner to noninvasively access important physiological information from a patient. It helps answer such questions as, "What is the underlying cause of this condition?" or "What remedy would best help this patient?" AK can be very helpful in getting answers from canine patients who have few ways of communicating their feelings.

AROMATHERAPY

Aromatherapy literally means "treatment using scents." This designation is a bit of a misnomer since the scent of the oil accounts for only part of its therapeutic effect. Aromatherapy involves the use of essential oils for healing. Essential oils are volatile liquid plant materials that play a key role in the biochemistry of the plant. These oils are located between the cells of the plant and act as messengers and regulators. Essential oils protect the plant from parasites and disease, and assist the plant in adapting to its environment.

History

Essential oils have been used in healing for thousands of years. The Chinese burned plant-derived materials as incense to balance the body as long as 6,000 years ago. The Egyptians used essential oils for healing and also for embalming. They even developed a crude distillation device to extract the oils from plants. Greeks and Romans continued the aromatherapy tradition in the West.

The word *aromatherapy* was actually coined by the French chemist René-Maurice Gattefossé in the 1920s. While working in his laboratory, he suffered a third-degree burn to his hand and forearm. He instinctively thrust his arm into the nearest liquid, which happened to be a container of pure lavender oil. His injury healed so quickly that he began researching and writing about the medicinal use of essential oils.

Aromatherapy involves the use of essential oils for healing.

Today, in the United States, aromatherapy is used mostly in conjunction with massage therapy or infused into the air for relaxation. In France, where the modern science of aromatherapy originated, the use of essential oils is incorporated into mainstream medicine.

In that country, some oils are regulated as prescription medications for their antiviral, antifungal, and antibacterial properties. Doctors determine which oil to use by culturing the disease organism and testing the ability of different oils to kill the germ. This technique is called an *aromatogram* and is similar to the antibiotic sensitivity tests commonly used in conventional medicine.

Dilution Warning

Cinnamon, clove, lemongrass, oregano, and thyme oils should never be applied topically without being diluted due to their caustic natures.

How It Works

Essential oils possess a healing effect due to their many constituents. Between 200 and 800 different chemicals are present in any given oil. Just a few of the common compounds include *esters*, which have antifungal and sedating properties; *ketones*, which ease congestion; *alcohols*, which are antiviral and antibacterial; and *sesquiterpenes*, which are anti-inflammatory and can cross the blood–brain barrier. Essential oils have a relatively small, simple, and lipid-soluble molecular structure that allows them to pass easily through the skin when massaged topically, which is the most common mode of treatment.

The scented oils can also be diffused into the air as a way of allowing assimilation of their healing qualities through the sinuses. Only a few specific oils can be taken orally. The mode of treatment depends on the condition being addressed as well as the oil being used. Some oils are toxic if ingested and some can cause skin irritation when applied topically.

Lavender is a helpful essential oil for car sickness.

Dilution

It is best to dilute any essential oil before applying it to a dog's skin. This expands the oil and makes aromatherapy more economical; it also lessens the chance for skin irritation. The best way to dilute an oil is to mix 30 drops of the essential oil into one ounce of cold-pressed almond oil. To apply topically, massage several drops of the diluted oil into the dog's ear flaps.

Quality

Pure essential oils used for aromatherapy are called *therapeutic grade*, but this designation is based on industry consensus and is not always reliable. There is a vast difference in the quality of oils between companies. Research the oil producer carefully to choose the best product. Two of the most important factors that determine the quality of essential oils are how the plants are grown and how the oils are extracted. It is ideal that the oil-producing plants be grown organically to limit contaminants. The oils should be extracted by low-pressure, steam distillation to limit damage to the oil components. Also, be sure any oils used have not been adulterated by the addition of synthetic chemicals.

Be aware that perfume oils, fragrance oils, or fragrances are vastly different from essential oils. They contain synthetic chemicals and can do more harm than good. Because the term aromatherapy is loosely used on labels, it is important to read the ingredient list carefully when selecting an oil for aromatherapy use.

Common Essential Oils	
Oil	**Use**
Citronella	Insect repellent
Cumin	Immune stimulant
Frankincense	Calming effect; tumors
Lavender	Car sickness
Lemongrass	Joint injuries
Peppermint	Digestive aid
Sandalwood	Bronchitis
Thyme	Asthma; colitis
Ylang Ylang	Balances blood pressure

Benefits

Aromatherapy can be quite useful for common canine conditions. A recent study published in the *Journal of the American Veterinary Medical Association* showed that lavender oil is helpful for easing car sickness in dogs. Lemongrass can be massaged directly onto injured joints twice daily to speed healing. Frankincense can be infused or applied topically for its calming effect for stressed, anxious, or overexcited dogs. It can also be used topically once or twice daily on a wart, cyst, or any tumor to help the body break it down. A good book on aromatherapy will give you more suggestions for the use of essential oils.

AYURVEDIC MEDICINE

The name *Ayurveda* comes from two words from the ancient Sanskrit language. *Ayus* means "life," and *veda* means "knowledge." So, Ayurveda means the science of living. It is a holistic medical system that has been practiced in India since approximately 6,000 BCE.

History

The physicians of ancient India proposed a complicated system of factors that interact to influence health. Their medical terms and

concepts are extremely foreign to our current understanding, but not too dissimilar to those of Traditional Chinese Medicine (TCM). In Ayurvedic medicine, health is seen in terms of balance between the individual and the natural world.

Doshas

An interesting aspect of Ayurvedic medicine is the idea of the existence of three physical/psychological constitutional types called *doshas* and their relationship with health and disease.

- **Kapha**: The first dosha we'll discuss is called *Kapha*, a word that means "phlegm." It refers to an individual who has a solid body type and tends to gain weight easily. They are slow to get going but have loads of stamina. Kapha types are slow to learn, but once they grasp a concept, they never forget it. They are patient, even tempered, and have a caring nature. Kaphas do not like humidity and dampness but can tolerate heat and cold conditions well. When out of balance, this type tends to have symptoms involving fluid and mucous that may lead to swelling. Dog breeds such as the Newfoundland and the Great Pyrenees tend to manifest the Kapha type.
- **Pitta**: The second dosha is called *Pitta* which means "bile." It refers to an individual who is of a medium build and balanced body type. Pittas have a big appetite and digest their food quickly. They prefer cold food and drink, and they tend to be alert and focused. This type is confident and courageous but also anger easily. Pittas do not tolerate heat well. When out of balance, they have symptoms involving acid and bile, leading to inflammation. Dog breeds such as the Rottweiler and the Pit Bull Terrier often are Pitta types.
- **Vata**: Finally, the dosha called *Vata* means "wind." This

refers to an individual who is thin and can eat anything and everything without gaining weight. They tend to have a dry skin and hair coat. Vatas have irregular appetites— sometimes they are ravenous and other times they have no appetite. Their energy levels fluctuate, and they may have a burst of activity that requires a rest to recover. Their moods change easily too. The Vata type is enthusiastic and, although they learn things easily, they do not have good long-term memories. Stress can make them feel fearful and insecure. Vatas do not like cold weather, food, or drink. When out of balance, they tend to have gas and nervous energy resulting in pain. Vata-type dog breeds include Greyhounds and Afghan Hounds.

You may recognize aspects of your dog in these descriptions. According to Ayurvedic medical thought, every individual manifests facets of all three doshas, but one or another tends to dominate. When treating a patient with Ayurvedic herbs, the dosha is considered as well as the disease. Each individual may manifest the same disease slightly differently, thus requiring a different treatment.

How It Works

Ayurvedic medicine is truly holistic in that it addresses the health of the body, mind, and spirit. It deals with the promotion of health and longevity as well as the treatment of disease. The Ayurvedic approach to health involves lifestyle, diet, massage, exercise, meditation, and the use of herbs. For dogs, Ayurvedic herbs are the most commonly utilized feature of this healthcare system. The practitioner does not necessarily need to be an expert in this ancient medicine to prescribe Ayurvedic herbs for pet disease conditions.

Benefits

Ayurvedic medicine is a gentle but powerful holistic modality. It addresses health issues from a different perspective than Western medicine. Ayurvedic herbs can address such issues as arthritis, allergic skin disorders, kidney dysfunction, liver failure, heart disease, hypothyroidism, diabetes, and gastrointestinal disturbances. This ancient modality has withstood the test of time.

Rescue Remedy

One very popular flower essence mixture called Rescue Remedy was created by Dr. Bach himself. This formula is a blend of five flowers—rock rose, clematis, impatiens, cherry plum, and Star of Bethlehem—and was made to use in the case of any mental, emotional, or physical crisis.

BACH FLOWER REMEDIES

Bach Flower Remedies are a way to tap into "flower power"—the healing ability of flowers. The Bach flower remedies represent a "subtle" method of healing. Similar to homeopathy, these remedies work on the energy field of the individual rather than on the physical level. Sometimes called *flower essences*, their potency is not related to the smell of the flowers but rather the blossom's energetic/vibrational qualities.

History

Edward Bach (1886–1936) was a successful British homeopathic physician who excelled in bacteriology, immunology, and pathology. His clinical experience led him to conclude that illness and suffering has its roots in emotional/spiritual derangements. He believed that an individual's "higher self," or soul, continuously seeks to influence the life of every individual through the expression of thirty-eight "virtues." Disease is caused by the patient losing touch with his higher self, either due to having been mistreated or by his own misunderstanding of life situations. This condition, according to Bach, causes each of the virtues to transform into a specific negative emotion. Starting in 1930, at the age of 43, Dr. Bach gave up his lucrative medical practice and devoted the last six years of his life to search for a simple, natural form of treatment for the emotional links to illness.

Bach intuitively discovered that certain flowers had energetic properties that could reinforce soul virtues. He developed a form of diagnosis based not on physical symptoms but on determining the exact emotional disharmony of the patient. Each of his thirty-eight flower essences vibrationally counteract specific negative emotions and reestablish an individual's contact with his higher self. Rather than fighting the negative emotions as symptoms, these remedies inundate them with higher vibrations of energy that raise the vibrations of the patient and open his channels for the uninhibited expression of his soul. This treatment strategy melts the negative emotional states away like "snow in the sunshine," as Bach put it. According to Bach, "There is no true healing unless there is a change in outlook, peace of mind, and inner happiness."

The method in which the flowers are harvested is important.

Harvesting the Flowers

Dr. Bach developed a simple but very stringent method for harvesting flowers and extracting their energetic essence. The flowers must be harvested from the wild on a warm summer day in full sunshine. The bloom, which is where the energies of the plant are concentrated, is picked at the point of full maturity, just before it falls to the ground. The flowers are then immediately processed in one of two ways.

With the "sun method," enough flowers are put in a glass bowl of spring water to cover the surface, and the bowl is placed in the sun. Through the power of the sun, the energetic essence of the flowers is transferred to the water, charging the liquid with subtle vibrations. After two to four hours, the flowers are removed from the charged water and an equal portion of brandy is added as a preservative. This stock solution can be further diluted in water for treatment purposes.

Because not all plants bloom at a time of the year when plenty of sunshine is available, Bach also processed some flowers using the "cooking method." This technique involves boiling the flowers in spring water, then filtering the solution several times. Preservation and use of the stock solution are similar to the sun method.

How It Works

Use of the Bach Flower Remedies is straightforward. No special training is required, as the remedies produce no side effects unless a pet is intolerant of the brandy preservative. Even this concern can be diminished by diluting the stock remedy in water before giving it to the pet.

Each remedy has its associated virtue as well as negative emotion (any book on Bach Flower Remedies can be consulted for detailed information). The patient is simply evaluated for the lack of specific virtues or the display of particular negative emotions. The proper remedy is then selected and administered.

Bach Flower Remedies can be used to help with any emotional issue a pet may be dealing with such as fear, aggression, and anxiety. As many as five remedies can be mixed together and used simultaneously. The remedy is usually given orally by diluting it in water

Bach Flower Remedies can be used to help with any emotional issue a pet may be dealing with such as fear, aggression, and anxiety.

Bach Flower Remedies

Here is a listing of the thirty-eight Bach Flower Remedies and an abbreviated description of the negative emotion associated with each.

Agrimony: Anxiety hidden behind a mask of cheerfulness

Aspen: Fear of the unknown

Beech: Hypercritical

Centaury: Weak-willed

Cerato: Self-doubt

Cherry plum: Destructive impulses

Chestnut bud: Failure to learn from experience

Chicory: Self-centeredness

Clematis: Easily distracted

Crab apple: Low self-esteem

Elm: Overwhelmed by duties

Gentian: Despondent

Gorse: Discouragement

Heather: Self-absorbed

Holly: Jealous, suspicious

Honeysuckle: Emotional attachment to the past

Hornbeam: Weariness

Impatiens: Impatience

Larch: Self-doubt

Mimulus: Shyness

Mustard: Depression of unknown cause

Oak: Over-striving beyond one's limits

Olive: Overworked

Pine: Inability to accept oneself

Red chestnut: Worry for well-being of others

Rock rose: Deep fear

Rock water: Self-denial

Scleranthus: Indecision

Star of Bethlehem: Shock or trauma

Sweet chestnut: Anguish

Vervain: Overbearing, intolerant

Vine: Domineering

Walnut: Need for life transition

Water violet: Aloof

White chestnut: Obsessive

Wild oat: Indecision about life direction

Wild rose: Resignation

Willow: Resentful and bitter

and using a dropper to put it directly into the mouth. A few drops can also be added to drinking water or food.

Because Bach Flower Remedies work on the energy system, they do not need to be swallowed to have their effect. Other ways to introduce the remedies into the energy field of the pet include massaging a few drops into the ear pinna or making a spray and lightly misting the animal.

Most emotional problems require frequent dosing with flower remedies. Pets usually need to be treated three times a day for several weeks. This gentle therapy can gradually rebalance a pet's emotional energy, solving even longstanding, difficult behavior issues. Of course, if possible, the cause of the pet's difficulty should be addressed. Also, proper dog behavior training is always helpful for behavioral issues. It is often wise to consult a canine behaviorist for serious problems, like aggression.

Benefits

Bach flower remedies are free of side effects and work gently to balance the difficult emotional issues that some dogs face. This holistic modality requires no special education to apply. The remedies are relatively inexpensive and can be found at most health food stores or on the Internet.

CRANIOSACRAL THERAPY

Craniosacral therapy entails an intuitive use of light touch to locate and liberate restrictions in the soft tissues associated with the central nervous system.

History

This modality originated from the osteopathic tradition developed by Andrew Taylor Still, in the 1870s. Dr. Still realized that the function and health of the body depended on the structure of the musculoskeletal system. He developed a system of treatment using manipulation of the bones and soft tissues of the body to restore balance and harmony.

William Sutherland graduated from Still's school in the late 1890s and began focusing on the movement of the bones of the skull. We don't think of the bones of the skull moving in relation to each other, but there are joints between them. Dr. Sutherland developed a theory of what he called the "primary respiratory mechanism." This system works not to move air or blood—but rather to pump cerebrospinal fluid (the liquid that surrounds the brain and spinal cord). His experiments led him to realize that the movement of the cranial bones facilitates a pumping of this fluid from the skull to the sacrum and back again.

How It Works

Structural abnormalities cause the pumping system to malfunction, leading to a disharmony that can eventually result in disease. Craniosacral techniques can detect and correct subtle restrictions in the cerebrospinal pumping system. Using gentle traction and/or pressure on the skull and different areas of the spinal column, the craniosacral practitioner slowly eases the body back into balance. Only in the past few years has this therapy become popular for pets.

Benefits

Craniosacral therapy can help treat a wide variety of problems, including seizures, motor dysfunction, and chronic pain.

ENERGY HEALING

Energy healing is a term I'm using here to designate the many forms of "laying on of hands" therapies. This holistic modality has been around for thousands of years and was even used by Jesus and the early Christians. There is something healing about the combination of touch and intention. Although energy healing goes by many names, the basic principle is the same.

How It Works

Energy healing is based on the idea that there exists a universal energy field that encompasses all of creation. This is not unlike the unified field that Einstein tried desperately to describe mathematically. Each individual's life force is part of this energy field, but the field extends beyond every being, throughout the universe. Inanimate objects as well as living creatures are infused with it. Vast expanses of empty space are alive with it. This benevolent force is the mysterious glue that holds the universe together. It is through this energy that natural law is played out. Some would call it an aspect of the Divine.

Human intention seems to be the key to utilizing this Divine energy. Similar to the idea of prayer, energy healers direct the universal energy to the ailing person or animal. Each type of energy healing has its own system for calling forth the healing power. With many forms, the practitioner opens herself as a channel of healing. She visualizes the energy flowing down from above, through her body, and into the patient. The energy then goes to where it is needed, bringing balance and harmony.

With other forms of energy healing, the healer generates energy within herself to direct to the patient's body systems as needed. Another way to think of the process is that the healer is simply acknowledging the spark of the Divine that is within the patient.

Bringing a conscious awareness to this ember is like fanning it into a healing flame that enlivens the body and enhances its ability to flourish.

There are many forms of energy healing, or "laying on of hands" therapies.

Everyone has an innate ability to tap into this stream of energy and help others. At the same time, there seem to be those with a special gift for this kind of healing, just as some athletes are better than others. Those with special talent need to practice their gift to bring it to its full potential. Likewise, those who are less gifted can improve their abilities with practice.

The main obstacle to energy healing is the inability to focus. Often, our minds are a constant stream of thoughts that distract us. Energy healing generally requires the practitioner to get herself out of the way. All thoughts of why the patient is sick, how serious the problem is, and how the healing should take place must be banished for the energy to flow and grow. A regular meditation practice is helpful for aiding any healer to overcome the distraction barrier.

Benefits

Energy healing is gentle and very relaxing for our canine companions. With instruction and practice, anyone can do energy healing on their pet to facilitate recovery from any condition and to improve the human–animal bond.

Types of Energy Healing

Healing Touch

Healing Touch is a gentle energy practice that was developed by a nurse, Janet Mentgen, who taught the first official Healing Touch class in 1989. She developed her techniques by combining the healing philosophies and methods of the many energy healers she researched.

Healing Touch works with the subtle energy systems of the body. The practitioner places her hands on or near the body of the patient in various positions with the intent to redirect aberrant energy patterns. By restoring balance to the body's energy structure, healing is facilitated.

Because of the medical connections of its founder, Healing Touch has been integrated into conventional medical care. It is taught in nursing programs, medical schools, and other settings internationally to medical professionals and nonprofessionals alike. It is used in hospitals, nursing homes, and hospices. This form of healing can also be of help to ailing dogs.

Qi-gong

Qi-gong or *Chi Kung* (pronounced "chee gong") is the oldest documented form of energy medicine. Like acupuncture and herbs, it is an aspect of TCM. The term Qi-gong comes from the combination of two Chinese words: *Qi*, which, as we saw before, means "life force energy" and *Gong*, which means "the skill of working with or cultivating." So Qi-gong means "the skill of working with life force energy."

The practice of Qi-gong involves a combination of meditation, breath work, body movement, and visualization in an attempt to become aware of, and guide the flow of, Qi in the body. Currently, more than 3,000 different styles of Qi-gong are practiced around the world; these therapies can all be divided into two basic forms.

Internal Qi-gong is the art of building the strength and optimizing the flow of energy within the practitioner's own body. One type of internal Qi-gong, known as *Tai Chi*, is practiced by large groups of Chinese people every morning in public parks throughout that country.

With discipline, dedication, and desire, the practitioner can achieve a level of proficiency at which he can emanate Qi from his body. This ability (called *external Qi-gong*) allows the practitioner to direct this

Pets can benefit from the energy exchange in these types of therapies.

energy to another for healing.

Medical Qi-gong involves external Qi-gong applied by the practitioner to the patient as well as internal Qi-gong exercises for the patient to use to enhance his own health. Medical Qi-gong is based on the theories of TCM. It involves directing Qi energy into the patient's meridians and organ systems to dispel pathogens and bring the body into harmony. Pets too can benefit from this energy exchange.

Reiki

Reiki is a very popular energy medicine that originated more recently in Japan. The name *Reiki* is derived from two Japanese words: *rei* means "universal wisdom or God's wisdom" and *ki* is the Japanese word for Qi or "vital energy." So, the name means "Divinely guided vital energy." Reiki is a deeply spiritual philosophy but has no connection to Buddhism or any other religion. There is no dogma, and there are no mandatory beliefs.

The Reiki energy healing technique originated from the work of a Japanese Buddhist named Dr. Mikao Usui (1865–1926). The process came to him after an extended period of meditation, and he began teaching it to others in 1922. Reiki was brought to Hawaii by a woman named Hawayo Takata, after her visit to Japan in the late 1930s. The process of instruction and the healing techniques used have evolved over time, as Reiki has been handed down from teacher to student. Many variations are now being taught.

Reiki training involves instruction in the concepts of energy healing and the practice of special techniques. Reiki uses specific symbols and hand positions to invite the flow of energy. The student is also given *attunements* by the instructor. The attunements consist of one-on-one ritual blessings that are said to enhance the learner's healing ability. Various levels of instruction indicate the level of training and attunement of the practitioner.

The Reiki practitioner considers himself to be a channel of universal energy that is directed to the recipient. This philosophical view has it that disease is often a result of a person having an energy level that is below optimum. Reiki acts as a transfusion of energy that boosts the patient's body to a level at which it can heal itself. The universal energy is guided by its own innate wisdom. Unlike the case with Qi-gong, the Reiki practitioner need not direct the energy or even know what kind of condition is being treated.

Even apparently healthy individuals can profit from an increase in life-force energy.

TELLINGTON TOUCH

Tellington Touch, or *TTouch*, is the name given for light touching techniques developed by Linda Tellington-Jones.

History

Linda Tellington-Jones began developing this unique form of body work for animals in the late 1970s. Her methods evolved into physical training exercises, body manipulations, and light touching techniques. She began with work on horses, but the practices soon were adapted for use on dogs and other animals.

How It Works

When performed, these procedures look like massage strokes but, unlike massage, TTouch does not involve manipulating the animal's musculature. On the contrary, TTouch is meant to stimulate the nervous system by manipulating only the skin. This light sensory input has the effect of bringing the animal's awareness to the treated areas of the body.

The basic TTouch stroke is very precise. The palm and thumb of the treatment hand are gently rested on the animal's body. The opposite hand is placed on the animal's body near the treatment hand to complete the circuit. The fingertips of the treatment hand are used to push the skin in a circular path for one and one-fourth rotation. The hand is then slid to an adjacent area and the process is continued.

TTouch was developed on horses and was eventually adapted for other animals.

Variations on this movement are based on those parts on the fingers on the treatment hand that are in contact with the skin, the speed of the stroke, the spread of the fingers, and the pressure used. The different strokes are named after animals such as the *Clouded Leopard* and the *Bear* to aid the student in remembering the techniques. Each stroke is also designed to achieve slightly different objectives such as relaxation, relief of fear and anxiety, and influencing positive behavioral changes.

In addition to the circular stroke, TTouch

Energy Healers

Many more forms and philosophies of hands-on, energy healing exist. Countless gifted healers around the world have developed their own systems, which they teach to those who are drawn to them. Gifted students often take what they have learned and adapt it to their liking, and the process continues. Most energy healers are inspired, sincere, and trustworthy. Some have given up profitable, conventional jobs to follow their dream of helping others. Nevertheless, the potential for abuse exists, as it is easy to be fooled by a convincing act. When seeking an energy healer, be sure to check him out thoroughly.

encompasses a number of other skin lifting and touching techniques. The ears can be gently manipulated from the base to the tip. This technique takes advantage of the many acupuncture points in the ears that affect the entire body. Fast manipulation can help an animal recover from shock, while a slower technique facilitates relaxation and calming. The lips and gums can also be worked with to help settle aggression.

Trained TTouch therapists are available to help pets. Books, videos, and classes also are available for anyone interested in this incredible body-work program.

Benefits

The techniques are easy to learn and apply to ailing pets. TTouch can help calm hyper pets, reduce aggression, and ease pain and stiffness. Furthermore, it is a great way for any dog owner to strengthen the human–animal bond.

We have now explored many modalities of holistic medicine, each one varying greatly in style and technique, but all sharing the central holistic philosophy of treating the entire individual—mind, body, and spirit.

FILLING THE HOLE
In Holistic Medicine

Throughout this book, we've been exploring holistic care for your dog. In the first chapter, we saw that holistic medicine is so named because it addresses the whole animal—body, mind, and spirit. When I first encountered this intriguing way of looking at healthcare I was struck by a glaring anomaly. If we are talking about a system that looks at the being as a *whole* (spelled with a "w"), then why is it spelled *holistic* (with an "h")?

It wasn't until I had been using holistic modalities for quite some time that I finally found the answer to this puzzling problem. It turns out that this spelling of holistic was coined by a group of unconventional medical doctors who formed the American Holistic Medical Association in 1978. They chose this spelling to emphasize the *holiness* of the *healing* process. In fact, the words *whole*, *heal*, *health*, and *holy* are derived from the same Old English root word, *hal*. So being healthy means being whole, and to be whole is to be holy.

As you may have noticed while reading about the holistic therapies presented in this book, there wasn't much mention of spirit as it relates to healing. There was a lot of talk about the physical, some discussion of the mind, and a healthy discourse on of vital energy but, until Chapter 9, we saw very little mention of spirit. It appears that I have left a hole in the true understanding of holistic medicine. In this chapter, I am going to remove the stethoscope from around my neck and step outside—way outside—the realm of the typical veterinary practitioner as we explore the spiritual connection we share with our pets.

SECULAR SPIRITUALITY

From the start of our foray into spirituality, I want to clarify that I am not referring to religion. Religions consist of belief systems, rituals, practices, and behaviors that help to bring the faithful closer to the Ultimate Reality or the Divine. Religions give meaning to life for many people, and throughout the world, a wide variety of

We share a spiritual connection with our pets.

religions exist. Although there are many ideas about what's the best path to God, the goal for all religions is similar. This common objective is within the realm of spirituality. And one common strand that runs through most religions is the value of *compassion*. We will return to this theme throughout this chapter.

It is difficult to talk about spirituality without using religious jargon. I will attempt to discuss terms that people of all faiths can accept. I have found that every religion has somewhat different definitions of certain words, so I will define the spiritual terms I am using as we go, to reduce confusion over vocabulary.

Spirit

Our discussion of the spiritual nature of healing necessitates that we first define what exactly is meant by the term *spirit*. The word spirit comes from the Latin word *spiritus,* which means "breath." Early religious thinkers realized that the breath is invisible. It mysteriously comes into the body at birth and just as inexplicably leaves at the time of death. In ancient times, the spirit was seen as a nonphysical force that enlivens the body. In some ways, this aspect of spirit can be equated with the idea of life force energy embraced by the Vitalists.

On the other hand, the word spirit encompasses much more than just the vital force. Spirit has the quality of otherworldliness. It is eternal. It has a power that cannot be measured in physical terms. Think of the word *inspiration*. It is derived from the word spirit and can mean the taking in of breath. Inspiration can also denote an enthusiastic insight that possesses a person, seemingly out of nowhere.

Let me designate the word *soul* to mean an individualized expression of spirit—a spark of the Divine. It is the true self that underlies the layers of ego and outwardly displayed personality. The soul is our consciousness itself. It directs our thoughts and bodies. An individual has a body. An individual has a mind and thoughts. Although we commonly speak of a person *having* a soul, it is probably more accurate to say they *are* a soul. The soul is the thinker of the thoughts. It survives the body after death and goes on to whatever lies beyond.

What does it mean to have a soul? Underneath all the fur, do pets have souls as well? After they die, will we see them again in heaven? What does all this have to do with healing anyway?

SOUL MATES

It is impossible to prove that we have souls. Let's just go on the assumption that we do. So, if we think we have souls, then what are the qualities that cause us to believe this conjecture? Most people would answer that the qualities of the soul are those traits that make us human. In other words, the qualities that set us apart from the rest of the animals on this planet. From the start, many people have the attitude that we have souls and animals do not.

So, what are these exclusively human qualities? To answer this, many focus on emotions. Feelings and emotions are totally subjective. The outside observer cannot quantify what a person or animal is feeling. How bad does a person feel when he is yelled at? What does a dog feel when he is reprimanded? We have absolutely no way of knowing. It is true that the body's biochemistry, such as stress hormones, can be gauged, but those measurements do not directly correlate to a person's or animal's actual experience. After all, who can measure the feeling of love? Since inner experiences such as feelings and emotions are beyond physical assessment, I conclude that they therefore meet the criteria for soul qualities.

The next question is, "Do dogs experience emotions?" It is intuitively obvious to the vast majority of pet owners that our companions experience a wide range of emotions. However, many people still believe, as I was taught in veterinary school, that animals are simply stimulus–response machines capable of nothing more than instinctual reactions. Just because dogs often respond predictably to operant conditioning, it does not necessarily follow that their minds are not capable of deeper levels of thought. Hungry humans also salivate at the thought of food and can be manipulated by Pavlovian training techniques. Although dogs are not little people in fur coats walking around on all fours, they do experience emotions similar to ours.

Emotions in Motion

Feelings are conscious mental experiences that evolved as survival mechanisms. They are what ultimately dictate all of human and animal behavior. We all seek to avoid unpleasant feelings and to move toward activities that cause pleasant feelings. So, unpleasant feelings act as an internal punishment and pleasant feelings are an internal reward. The feeling of pain guides one to shift weight off an injured foot, thus limiting further damage. The feeling of hunger causes one to seek food. The feeling of loneliness leads one to look for companionship (there is safety in numbers). The feeling of love causes a mother to care for her offspring.

Some might say that dogs care for their young strictly out of instinct, but how can they be so sure? When you see a female dog care for her puppies, or risk her own life to protect them, it sure seems that there exists a loving bond. If a human mother cares for her child out of love, why is the same behavior viewed as instinct in animals?

You might remember Dr. Candice Pert's research on neuropeptides, which we discussed in Chapter 4. Well, Dr. Pert discovered these "molecules of emotion" and their receptors in animals as well as in people. If animals have the same emotional messengers that we do, then they must have the same emotional feelings. Is it possible that dogs are capable of showing compassion? Sometimes, deeds speak louder than words.

Animal Altruism

Do dogs experience emotions? Many pet owners believe so.

Stories of hero dogs abound in the news. One such drama played out the evening of October 12, 2006, near Buffalo, New York. An 81-year-old couple, Eve and Norman Fertig, had ventured out to their backyard wildlife sanctuary to treat sick birds. A freak snowstorm hit, and the couple found themselves trapped by fallen trees and deep snow. They soon realized that they were in serious trouble since neither had on a heavy coat or gloves. Getting back to the house looked impossible, and the temperatures were dropping as night fell.

Undaunted by the task at hand, the couple's 160-pound (72.5 kg) German shepherd-wolf mix, Shana, bounded into action. She dug a one-foot (30 cm) wide tunnel under a large, downed tree and through the snow for 20 feet (6 m), back to the house, a process that took several hours. She returned and began to bark at the couple to encourage them to crawl to safety. When the pair hesitated, Shana grabbed Eve's jacket. The dog pulled the 86-pound (39-kg) woman onto her back and drug her slowly back through the tunnel to the house, with Norman holding on behind.

The threesome struggled through the back door of the house, and the exhausted seniors fell to the floor. By now it was two o'clock in the morning, and the power was out. Not to worry—Shana stayed close to the Fertigs, keeping them warm until they were found the next morning. Shana herself had been rescued from an abusive situation by the Fertigs seven years earlier when she was only two weeks old. I think she must have felt a tinge of pride to have returned the favor with such a gutsy act.

This story is just one example of a dog resorting to extreme measures to save her human companions. Some animals will risk their own lives by swimming into rushing water or by running into burning buildings to rescue their human family members. Certainly you have seen the news clips.

Is It Just Instinct?

Many scientifically minded people would write these dogs' daring deeds off as instinct. After all, it is ridiculous to think of animals as being brave. Canines are pack animals that will lay their lives on the line for a fellow group member out of a natural impulse. And dogs do treat the humans they live with like pack members.

However, if we attribute the valiant actions of Shana and her canine cohorts to simple animal instinct, then to what do we credit the actions of human heroes? When speaking of people, we call it courage. Of course, when asked, most of those people will say that they just did what came naturally. They did not think about it, they just acted. That sounds like instinct to me.

Perhaps courage is an instinct of compassion. After all, it does seem innate to want to help another who is in peril. If such caring comes naturally, is this not evidence of an underlying presence of goodness within individuals? This altruistic tendency certainly testifies to the presence of a soul. If so, then it appears that our beloved dogs qualify as soul mates.

The Pet Connection

There is an intangible quality to the animals we love. A person often forms a bond with a particular dog—a relationship that defies reason. Fifty percent of pet owners report that their dog anticipates the arrival home of one or more family members. The animals often become aroused and wait near a window or door—activities that are termed *anticipatory behaviors*. One scientist set out to objectively explore this claim.

Dr. Rupert Sheldrake has done hundreds of trials to test the theory that certain dogs can somehow read their owner's minds from a distance. Shedrake would install cameras in the dog-owner's home to monitor the canine, and send the person off to run errands. The owner would then be paged to come home at completely random times, and return driving an unfamiliar vehicle. This procedure ruled out such skeptical explanations as the idea that the dog is simply responding to the time of day, or his ability to smell or hear his owner's vehicle.

Sheldrake found statistically significant anticipatory behavior in some dogs. A dog's extrasensory ability seemed to be greatest in those with an especially close relationship with their owners. These findings show that an invisible link can exist between certain dogs and their owners. This nonphysical association is further proof of a deep soul connection that sometimes exists.

Soul Survivor

Dogs treat their humans as pack members.

Many of us feel a special bond with our pets. For numerous families, dogs are like children. We naturally want to believe that this relationship will go on, even after death. Perhaps the idea of reuniting with a beloved pet in heaven is just wishful thinking.

On the other hand, I think we have established that dogs possess soul qualities and are capable of compassion. But do dogs have the same moral mission that people do? Can we judge their actions by our standards? Should a dog who steals another's bone be arrested and tried by a jury of his peers? (Okay, maybe it is possible to take this whole soul thing too far.)

Yet, just because an animal's spiritual attributes are not the same as those of a person, does not diminish the inherent value of our pets. Dogs do have a spiritual

Pet Two Poodles and Call Me in the Morning

It is interesting to note the healing effects of pets. Numerous studies over the past 25 years prove that pets provide health benefits to people. Petting a dog can lower your blood pressure. Heart attack patients with pets live longer than those without animals. Nursing homes that allow pets in the living quarters have reported lower death rates and a drop in the need for medications. Pet owners in general have fewer doctors' visits and they live longer than those who do not have pets. To what can we attribute this amazing pet power?

The fact that animals afford such benefits doesn't seem to make much sense when you look at it logically. Pets are a drain on a person's resources. It costs money to feed and provide medical treatment for them. Caring for pets and cleaning up after them takes time as well — a commodity that is in high demand these days. Pets in bed are also a documented source of insomnia for animal lovers. It makes no sense whatsoever that we bother to share our lives with animals at all.

Despite the down side of pet ownership, more and more people are drawn to this lifestyle. In fact, in the United States, there are currently more households with pets than there are with children. We seem to have lost our minds . . . but found our hearts.

essence that I believe qualifies them for a romp in the afterlife. Evangelist Billy Graham agrees with me on this one. He said, "God will prepare everything for our perfect happiness in heaven, and if it takes my dog being there, I believe he'll be there."

DIVINE INTERVENTION

Pets fill a hole in the lives of those who love animals. With their instinct to comfort, heal, and rescue us, they demonstrate qualities that even humans often lack. I believe that pets have such an effect because they help us maintain contact with the natural world, which our modern lifestyles have all but forsaken.

Nature is infused with the Divine. It is impossible for most people to study biology without developing a sense of awe for the beauty of the balance that is maintained within intricate, natural systems. Each one of the billions of cells in the body has a life of its own, and yet they all cooperate to function as a whole. Animals, plants, microorganisms, and inert materials have developed amazingly complicated, synergistic relationships in every ecosystem in the world. Even the celestial bodies have an orderly rhythm that mystifies the human mind. All of creation is alive with a palpable, heavenly heartbeat.

One scientist who was struck by the beauty of nature and our relationship with creation was none other than Albert Einstein, who wrote:

All Things Are Considered

What is man without the beasts? If all the beasts were gone, men would die from loneliness of spirit. For whatever happens to the beasts happens to man. All things are connected.

—Native American Chief Seattle

A human being is a part of the whole, called by us "Universe," a part limited in time and space. He experiences himself, his thoughts and feelings as something separated from the rest—a kind of optical delusion of his consciousness. This delusion is a kind of prison for us . . . . . Our task must be to free ourselves from this prison by widening our circle of compassion to embrace all living creatures and the whole of nature in its beauty.

With a lick of the tongue and a wag of the tail, a dog can reunite us with the mysteries of the universe. Dogs may or may not have souls. Indeed, they are not little people—thank goodness for that, for dogs are so much more. However, there is certainly no denying that they possess an intangible quality—a spark of the Divine—that is available to those who choose to connect.

Tapping the Divine that lies within all of creation is a means of achieving balance and healing. This is the meaning of holistic health. When we share our lives with a special canine companion, we enter a healing relationship—one that is mutually beneficial. Holistic health is made possible by such a relationship. Connecting with your dog on a spiritual level is one way of connecting with the Divine.

MAKING THE CONNECTION

In this chapter, I have attempted to fill the hole in our understanding of holistic medicine by addressing its spiritual side. It is all well and good to look at spirituality and our relationships with our dogs from the intellectual standpoint. Hopefully, you have found some of the stories and quotes in this chapter inspirational as well as informational. At the same time, it is not possible to truly understand the spiritual aspects of life by reading about them. The only way to *know* the spirit is to *experience* it.

I would like to invite you to make a special connection with your pet and the Divine. This requires taking time to separate from the daily grind—15 to 30 minutes should do. I am proposing that you spend some time in quiet, prayerful meditation with your dog. This is a deeply moving process that can benefit both the person and the pet.

Choose a time when both yourself and your canine companion are relaxed and will be uninterrupted for awhile. Turn off the phone and find a quiet place, either inside or better yet, out in

Every Single Creature

Apprehend God in all things, For God is in all things.

Every single creature is full of God

And is a book about God.

Every creature is a word of God.

—Meister Eckhart, fourteenth century Christian theologian

nature. Now, get in a comfortable sitting position with legs uncrossed and feet flat on the floor or ground. Help your dog relax either in your lap or next to you. Have one or both hands on your pet or touch him with some part of your body. Feel the tangible connection. The following script can be read slowly and prerecorded to be played back as a guided reverie, or followed as best as possible by memory.

Pets fill a hole in our lives.

Begin by allowing the problems and concerns of daily life to fall away . . . take about five minutes to simply breathe deeply and slowly . . . feel the breath flowing effortlessly in and out . . . it is almost as if the breath is breathing you . . . breath in relaxation . . . with each exhalation, allow all of the tension in your body to flow out . . . (pause) imagine that God is breathing into you the breath of life. . . (pause) this same breath of life is also flowing within your companion. . . (pause) envision the amazing underlying life force, the spirit that is stirring, pulsing, vibrating within both you and your dog. . . (pause) we are all the result of the same divine plan. . . (pause) feel the presence of your dog there with you. . . (pause) feel the warmth of his body. . . (pause) feel the soft fur. . . (pause) become aware of your dog's breathing. . . (pause) feel his chest rise and fall. . . (pause) really connect with this other living being . . . (pause) bring to mind some special event the two of you have shared. . . (pause) remember that feeling of closeness you experienced. . . (pause) become aware of your own heart and feel the compassion you have for this animal companion. . . (pause) sense the warmth of your love expanding inside your chest. . . reaching out and embracing this other being. . . (pause) as the love continues to expand you find you both are floating in a giant sea of love. . . (pause) allow yourself to fully experience the oneness you share with this creature and with all of creation. . . (pause) melt into this feeling of oneness. . . (pause) now abide for awhile in this silent oneness. . . (pause) if you find that your mind has wandered off, gently bring it back to this feeling of oneness. . . (pause)

When you feel ready, slowly return to the present moment and your body. . . bringing with you that peaceful feeling of oneness.

I hope that you have the opportunity to practice this exercise and spend some quiet time with your dog. Such contemplation, on a regular basis, can improve your health as well as your bond with your pet. Over time, this meditation can positively affect the health of your dog, too. Affirming the healing spirit of compassion draws it forth into your lives.

JOURNEY'S END

We have traveled quite a distance together through mysterious territory. Now, we have reached the end of our journey of discovery about holistic care for your dog. You have acquired an understanding of holistic modalities and you have learned some natural healthcare techniques. I would like to leave you with ideas to help you integrate this new knowledge into the lifestyle of your special friend. I like to think of these as the five Ps of dog care.

Prevention

The first P is for *prevention*. An ounce of prevention is worth a pound of cure. In other words, it is much easier to develop a healthy lifestyle with your pet and keep him healthy than to let things get out of hand and repeatedly fight disease. One dis-ease prevention tip to keep in mind is to review Chapter 3 and start your pet on a natural diet that comes as close to mimicking Mother Nature as possible. At the same time, limit vaccines, medications, and chemicals to a prudent level, as discussed in Chapter 2. Use more natural alternatives to medications when you can.

Proactive

The second P is for being *proactive*. Your canine companion's health is in your hands. At the first sign of a problem, seek a solution. Take your pet to your veterinarian and find out what is going on. If examination and testing are normal, continue to pursue an answer. Research the issue, perhaps using some of the resources in this book. You know your pet better than anyone else, and you can tell when something is amiss. A holistic veterinarian may be able to help you discover the imbalance and set your pet back on the right course. When a serious health challenge occurs for your pet, be sure to educate yourself about the condition and all of the treatment options (including the holistic modalities mentioned in Chapters 4 through 9).

Partnering

The third P is for *partnering* with your veterinarian. Many conventional veterinarians are somewhat holistic by virtue of their attitudes. Most of us have chosen this profession, and made

Nature

I believe in God, only I spell it N-A-T-U-R-E.

—Frank Lloyd Wright, architect

it through the rigorous training, because of our love for animals. Compassion is an important component of holistic health. I think it is vital for all dog owners to find a veterinarian with whom they feel comfortable and confident. A partnership must exist between doctor and client so that the caregiver's input is valued. Such a veterinarian will most likely be one who practices with heart and soul. The resultant compassionate care leads to true holistic health.

Pet Connection

The fourth P is for your *pet connection*. Our furry friends are a source of love, fun, companionship, healing, and even spiritual well-being. Enjoy and foster your unique bond. Be aware that your canine companion can pick up on your thoughts and feelings. The most important element in the healing process is often the attitude with which the animal is addressed. If a person is extremely upset about his dog's diagnosis, often the animal will sense that negative emotion, which can reduce his ability to heal. Likewise, a strong belief in a certain doctor or therapy can augment a dog's recovery. A special power is generated from potent feelings that can be transmitted from the human to his canine companion.

Power

The fifth P is for *power*. I encourage you to embrace the power you have to affect your dog's health. You are now equipped to make truly informed decisions about your beloved dog's healthcare. You also have treatments you can apply for his improved well-being. Remember that although the Western, mechanistic view of healthcare stands in contradiction to holistic ideals, these two philosophies of handling disease need not be seen as adversarial ways of life. Each conventional medical technique and every holistic modality has its place. Animals are benefited most by an approach to healthcare that is integrative rather than exclusive. You have the power to choose what is best for your special friend.

Take some time to make a special connection with your pet.

There is more to health and healing than meets the eye. Holistic care for dogs is the wave of the future. You are invited to ride that wave for the benefit of your canine companion.

HOLISTIC MEDICINE— GENERAL

BOOKS

Becker, Marty, MD. *The Healing Power of Pets: Harnessing the Amazing Ability of Pets to Make and Keep People Happy and Healthy*. New York: Hyperion, 2002.

Dossey, Larry, MD. *Healing Words: The Power of Prayer and the Practice of Medicine*. New York: HarperCollins Publishers, 1993.

Jacobson, James and Kristine Chandler Madera. *How to Meditate With Your Dog: An Introduction to Meditation for Dog Lovers*. Maui: Maui Media, LLC, 2005.

Knueven, Douglas E., DVM. *Stand by Me: A Holistic Handbook for Animals, Their People, ant the Lives They Share Together*. Virginia Beach: A.R.E. Press, 2003.

Lipton, Bruce, Ph.D. *The Biology of Belief: Unleashing the Power of Consciousness, Matter and Miracles*. Santa Rosa: Mountain of Love/ Elite Books, 2005.

McMillan, Franklin D., DVM and Kathryn Lance. *Unlocking the Animal Mind: How Your Pets Feelings Hold the Key to His Health and Happiness*. Rodale, 2004.

Pitcairn, Richard H., DVM, PhD and Susan Hubble Pitcairn. *Dr. Pitcairn's Complete Guide to Natural Health for Dogs and Cats*. Rodale, 1995.

Radin, Dean. *Entangled Minds: Extrasensory Experiences in a Quantum Reality*. New York: Paraview Pocket Books, 2006.

Sheldrake, Rupert. *Dogs That Know When Their Owners Are Coming Home: And Other Unexplained Powers of Animals*. New York: Three Rivers Press, 1999.

ORGANIZATIONS

American Holistic Veterinary Medical Association (AHVMA)
2218 Old Emmorton Rd
Bel Air, MD 21015
Telephone: 410-569-079
Fax: 410-569-2346
E-mail: Office@AHVMA.org
www.ahvma.org
Find a holistic veterinarian at www. holisticvetlist.com

ACUPUNCTURE

BOOKS

Becker, Robert O., MD and Gary Selden. *The Body Electric: Electromagnetism and the Foundation of Life.* New York: Quill, 1985.

Kaptchuk, Ted J., OMD. *The Web that has no Weaver: Understanding Chinese Medicine.* Lincolnwood: Congdon and Weed, Inc., 1983.

Pert, Candace B., PhD. *Molecules of Emotion: The Science Behind Mind-Body Medicine.* New York: Touchstone, 1997.

Schwartz, Cheryl, DVM. *Four Paws Five Directions: A Guide to Chinese Medicine for Cats and Dogs.* Berkeley: Celestial Arts Publishing, 1996.

ORGANIZATIONS

American Academy of Veterinary Acupuncture (AAVA)
100 Roscommon Dr, Suite 320
Middletown, CT 06457
Telephone: 860-632-9911
E-mail: office@aava.org
www.aava.org
Find a veterinary acupuncturist at www. aava.org/pub/directory_links_public.html

International Veterinary Acupuncture Society (IVAS)
P.O. Box 271395
Ft. Collins, CO 80527-1395 Telephone: 970-266-0666
Fax: 970-266-0777
E-mail: office@ivas.org
www.ivas.org

Find a veterinary acupuncturist at www. ivas.org/member_search.cfm

CHIROPRACTIC CARE AND MASSAGE

ORGANIZATIONS

American Veterinary Chiropractic Association (AVCA)
442154 E 140 Rd.
Bluejacket, OK 74333
Telephone: 918-784-2231
Fax: 918-784-2675
E-mail: avcainfo@junct.com
www.animalchiropractic.org
Find an animal chiropractor at www.avcadoctors.com

The Healing Oasis Wellness Center
2555 Wisconsin St.
Sturtevant, WI 53177-1825
Telephone: 262-886-1100
www.thehealingoasis.com/html/school.html
Massage program open to all licensed veterinary professionals, licensed massage therapists, and physical therapists.

DVD/VIDEO

Vaughn, Lynn, LMT, and Deborah Jones, LMT. *Bodywork for Dogs: Intuitive Touch Through Massage, Acupressure and Awareness.* Pound Ridge: Animals Healing, Inc., 2006.

WEBSITES

Touch Research Institute
www6.miami.edu/touch-research
Institute dedicated to studying the effects of touch therapy.

CONVENTIONAL MEDICINE INTEGRATION

ORGANIZATIONS

American Animal Hospital Association (AAHA)
P.O. Box 150899
Denver, Colorado, USA 80215-0899
Telephone: 800-252-2242
Fax: 303-986-1700
E-mail: info@aahanet.org
www.aahanet.org

American Veterinary Medical Association (AVMA)

1931 North Meacham Rd, Suite 100
Schaumburg, IL 60173-4360
Phone: 847.925.8070
Fax: 847.925.1329
E-mail: avmainfo@avma.org
www.avma.org

WEBSITES

www.aahanet.org/About_aaha/About_Guidelines_Canine06.html
Current vaccination guidelines.

DIET AND NUTRITION

BOOKS

Brown, Steve and Beth Taylor. *See Spot Live Longer: How to Help Your Dog Live a Longer and Healthier Life*. Eugene: Creekobear Press, 2005.

MacDonald, Carina Beth. *Raw Dog Food: Make It Easy for You and Your Dog*. Wenatchee: Dogwise Publishing, 2004.

Schultze, Kymythy R., CCN, AHI. *Natural Nutrition for Dogs and Cats: The Ultimate Diet*. Carsbad: Hay House, Inc., 1998.

Strombeck, Donald, DVM, PhD. *Home-Prepared Dog and Cat Diets: The Healthful Alternative*. Ames: Iowa State University Press, 1999.

Wysong, R. L., DVM. *The Truth About Pet Foods*. Midland: Inquiry Press, 2002.

WEBSITES

A Place for Paws
www.aplaceforpaws.com
Offers a complete line of biologically appropriate raw foods.

Balance IT
www.BalanceIt.com
Board certified veterinary nutritionists formulate diets for your pets.

Bravo!
www.bravorawdiet.com
Raw diet for cats and dogs.

Nature's Variety
www.naturesvariety.com
Natural, nutritionally dense, bio-available diets and treats.

Wysong
www.wysong.net
The educational resources, premium and natural foods, and organic health products.

RESOURCES

HERBAL MEDICINE

BOOKS

Kidd, Randy, DVM, PhD. *Herbal Dog Care.* Pownal: Storey Books, 2000.

Wulff-Tilford, Mary L and Gregory L. Tilford. *All You Ever Wanted to Know About Herbs for Pets.* Irvine: BowTie Press, 1999.

ORGANIZATIONS

Veterinary Botanical Medicine Association (VBMA)
1785 Poplar Dr.
Kennesaw GA 30144
E-mail: Office@vbma.org
www.vbma.org
Find a veterinary herbalist at www.vbma.org/search.cfm

HOMEOPATHY

BOOKS

Cummings, Stephen, MD and Dana Ullman, MPH. *Everybody's Guide to Homeopathic Medicines: Taking Care of Yourself and Your Family with Safe and Effective Remedies.* Los Angeles: Jaremy P. Tarcher, Inc., 1991.

Day, Christopher. *The Homeopathic Treatment of Small Animals: Principles and Practice.* Essex: C W Daniel Company Limited, 1990.

Dooley, Timothy R., ND, MD. *Homeopathy Beyond Flat Earth Medicine: An Essential Guide for the Homeopathic Patient.* San Diego: Timing Publications, 1995.

Macleod, George, MRCVS, DVSM. *Dogs: Homeopathic Remedies.* Essex: C W Daniel Company Limited, 1989.

Vithoulkas, George. *The Science of Homeopathy.* New York: Grove Press, 1980.

ORGANIZATIONS

Academy of Veterinary Homeopathy (AVH)
P.O. Box 9280
Wilmington, Delaware 19809
Telephone/Fax: 866-652-1590

E-mail: office@theavh.org
www.theavh.org
Find a veterinary homeopath at www.theavh.org/referral/index.php

OTHER HOLISTIC THERAPIES

BOOKS

Miles, Pamela. *Reiki: A Comprehensive Guide.* New York:Tarcher/Penguin, 2006.

Scheffer, Mechthild. *Bach Flower Therapy: Theory and Practice.* Rochester: Healing Arts Press, 1988.

Tellington-Jones, Linda and Sybil Taylor. *The Tellington TTouch : A Revolutionary Natural Method to Train and Care for Your Favorite Animal.* Middlesex: Penguin Books, 1993.

ORGANIZATIONS

Craniosacral Therapy Association
Monomark House
27 Old Gloucester Street
London, WC1N 3XX, UK
Telephone: 07000 784 735
E-mail: office@craniosacral.co.uk
www.craniosacral.co.uk

The Dr Edward Bach Centre
Mount Vernon, Bakers Lane
Brightwell-cum-Sotwell, Oxon, OX10 0PZ,
UK
Telephone: +44 (0) 1491 834678
Fax: +44 (0) 1491 825022
www.bachcentre.com

International Association of Reiki Professionals
P.O. Box 6182
Nashua, NH 03063-6182
Telephone: 603-881-8838
Fax: 603-882-9088
E-mail: info@iarp.org
www.iarp.org

National Association for Holistic Aromatherapy
3327 W. Indian Trail Road PMB 144
Spokane, WA 99208
PH: (509)325-3419
FAX: (509) 325-3479
www.naha.org

Qigong Institute
561 Berkeley Avenue
Menlo Park, CA 94025
www.qigonginstitute.org

Tellington TTouch Training
P.O. Box 3793
Santa Fe, NM 87501
Phone: 866-488-6824
E-mail: info@TTouch.com
www.lindatellington-jones.com

veterinary medicine (CAVM), 6
complementary medicine, 6, 191
confirmation bias, 27–28
constitutional considerations, 23–24
conventional medicine, 6–7. *See also* Western medicine
coprophagia, 92
coronavirus, canine, 35–36
craniosacral therapy, 207–208, 233
cure, 184

D

demodectic mange, 57, 93
dental health, 46–47
determinism, 12–13, 14–15
Devine intervention, 221–222
DHA (docosahexaenoic acid) deficiency, 68–70, 90
diagnostic testing, 62–63. *See also* applied kinesiology
diatomaceous earth, 53
dietary deficiencies, 68–70
dietary supplements, 84–93
    brand selection, 85–86
    chondroitin, 46, 92
    digestive enzymes, 91
    fish oil, 46, 69, 87–91
    glucosamine, 46, 92
    multivitamins and minerals, 86–87
    probiotics, 43, 44, 92–93
    synthetic vs. whole, 84–85
diets. *See* commercial foods; natural canine diets; nutrition
digestive enzymes, 91
dilated cardiomyopathy, 68
discospondylitis, 20
discs, intervetebral, 131–132, 194–195
dis-ease, 11, 18–19
disease, nature of, homeopathic view, 180–181
disease prevention, 21–22
distemper, canine, 33
DNA research, 14–16
docosahexaenoic acid (DHA) deficiency, 68–70
doshas, 202
drug interactions, herbs and, 166–168

E

ear cleaning, 50–51, **51**
ear mites, 50–51
Eastern herbology, 158
Eastern medicine, 7
echinacea, 169–170, **169**
EFAs (essential fatty acids), 87–91
effleurage, 151, **151**
Einstein, Albert, 14, 221–222
electrical field of body, 108–110
electrical instruments for acupuncture, **113**, 114

emotions in dogs, 217–218
endorphins, 106–107
energy healing modalities, 208–212
environment, and gene expression, 15–16
epigenetics, 15–16
essential fatty acids (EFAs), 87–91
essential oils, aromatherapy, 199, 200–201
euthanasia, 47–49
extract granules, herbal, 162
extracts, herbal, 161

F

fatty acids, 87–91
feeding. *See* commercial foods; natural canine diets; nutrition
female dogs, neutering of, 61
fish oil, 46, 69, 87–91
fleas, 51–54
flower essences. *See* Bach flower remedies
food analysis, 67
food trials, 67
fruits, in diet, 78

G

garlic, 54, 166
gate theory of acupuncture, 106
Gattefossé, René-Maurice, 199
gene expression, 15–16
genetic determinism, 14–15
ginger, 170
ginseng, 170–171, **170**
glucocorticoids, 45
glucosamine, 46, 92
glycerin extracts, herbal, 161–162
Goodheart, George, 197–198
grain contaminants, 73
grains in diets, 72–74, 79

H

Hahnemann, Samuel, 176–177
healing capacity of body, 21
healing crisis, 24–25
Healing Touch, 209–210
heart disease, herbal medicines and, 166
heartworms, 54–55
heat stroke, homeopathy for, 186
herbal homecare, 165–173
    cautions, 165–168
    dosing for dogs, 168–169
    drug interactions, 166–168
    herbs for, 169–173
herbalists, 173
herbal medicine, 155–173
    benefits of, 155–156
    description, 155
    formulations, 160–162
    herb names, 159–160
    history of, 156–159

homecare with. *See* herbal homecare
    for inflammation, 46
    potency, 162–164
    research in, 159
    resources, 231
    what to expect, 173
herbs
    for flea control, 53
    for homecare, 169–173
    names of, 159–160
    processing of, 162–164
holism, 9–10, 12–16
holistic medicine. *See also specific treatment modalities, e.g.,* acupuncture
    basic concepts. *See* holistic medicine, basic concepts
    common terms, 5–8
    defined, 7
    derivation of term, 215
    individualized treatments in, 24
    integration into pet care, 224–225
    popularity of, 6
    pseudoscience criticism of, 26–28
    resources, 226
    safety and, 28–29
    Western medicine compared to, 8–12
holistic medicine, basic concepts, 18–26
    dis-ease, 11, 18–19
    disease prevention, 21–22
    healing as peeling, 25–26
    the healing crisis, 24–25
    individuality of patients, 23–24
    reliance on body's healing capacity, 21
    symptoms as warning signals, 22–23
    wellness as dynamic balance, 19–21
homecare
    with herbs. *See* herbal homecare
    homeopathic remedies, 191–195
    massage techniques, 149–153, **150–153**
    spinal care, 141–143
home-cooked diet, 80
homeopathic nosodes, 34
homeopathic repertories, 188
homeopaths, 191
homeopathy, 25, 38, 175–195
    benefits of, 175
    description, 7, 175
    history of, 175–178
    home care remedies, 191–195
    principles of, 178–185

PHOTO CREDITS

DEDICATION/ACKNOWLEDGEMENTS

This book is dedicated to my wife, Judy Knueven, who has given me both the inspiration and the encouragement to journey down the road less traveled.

I would like to acknowledge all of my teachers including my parents, family, friends, instructors, clients, patients, my own pets, and God Above and Within. Thank you all for your part in making me who I am and for making this book possible.

ABOUT THE AUTHOR

Dr. Doug Knueven received his veterinary degree from Ohio State University in 1987 and has been practicing veterinary medicine in Beaver County, Pennsylvania ever since. Dr. Knueven owns and operates Beaver Animal Clinic, a full service animal hospital, and shares clinical duties with two associates.

Besides his 18 years of experience lecturing to kennel clubs, Dr. Knueven is a popular speaker at veterinary conferences. In the past 10 years he has lectured on holistic topics at numerous conventional and holistic veterinary conferences across the United States.

Dr. Knueven is a pioneer in holistic pet care in the Pittsburgh region. He has earned certification in veterinary acupuncture, veterinary Chinese herbal medicine and animal chiropractic. He also has advanced training in veterinary clinical nutrition, massage therapy, and homeopathy.

In the past few years Dr. Knueven published six articles in *Clean Run* magazine. For four years he by-lined a weekly pet health column in *The Beaver County Times* and *The Allegheny Times*. Dr. Knueven is the author of *Stand by Me, A Holistic Handbook for Animals, Their People, and the Lives They Share Together* (ARE Press, April 2003).

Nylabone® Cares.

Millions of dogs of all ages, breeds, and sizes have enjoyed our world-famous chew bones—but we're not just bones! Nylabone®, the leader in responsible animal care for over 50 years, devotes the same care and attention to our many other award-winning, high-quality innovative products. Your dog will love them — and so will you!

Toys   Treats   Chews   Crates   Grooming